Trowel and Error

Also by Alan Titchmarsh

FICTION

Mr MacGregor
The Last Lighthouse Keeper
Animal Instincts
Only Dad

NON-FICTION

Alan Titchmarsh's Favourite Gardens
Gardeners' World Complete Book of Gardening
How to be a Gardener Book One: Back to Basics (Book One)
Ground Force Weekend Workbook

ALAN TITCHMARSH

Trowel and Error

Notes from a Life on Earth

Hodder & Stoughton

Copyright © 2002 by Alan Titchmarsh

First published in Great Britain in 2002 by Hodder and Stoughton
A division of Hodder Headline

A CIP catalogue record for this title
is available from the British Library

ISBN 0 340 76542 9

Typeset in Minion by Palimpsest Book Production Limited,
Polmont, Stirlingshire

Printed and bound in Great Britain by
Clays Ltd, St Ives plc

Hodder and Stoughton
A division of Hodder Headline
338 Euston Road
London NW1 3BH

For Alison
with love
and thanks for everything

Contents

FOREWORD

'And is there a dark side?' asked the researcher from *Parkinson*. She was a pleasant girl with a broad Scots accent, and she asked the question at the end of our pre-show chat, almost as a nurse asks, 'And have we had a bath today?' Shame to disappoint her. I battled to find one. I mean, if you have a dark side, it gives depth to your personality. I really ought to have one; it would offset those accusations of being 'relentlessly cheerful', as though it were some sort of personal failing. Presumably its all right to be 'relentlessly miserable', but I get weary of folk who make a living out of angst – their own and other people's. Too many people confuse irritability with intellectuality. Me? I suffer fools reasonably gladly, but then I know how they feel.

My dark side? Well, I'm bit gloomy now and then, but it's usually because I haven't been eating enough roughage, or because it's been raining for days – nothing that can't be cured by a couple of Weetabix and a sunny afternoon in the garden. Hardly black depressions. And anyway my mother never had much time for complainers, subscribing to the school of thought which believes that a trouble shared is a trouble dragged out till bedtime. As a result I've never had much sympathy with Hamlet; he should have married the girl, had kids and got himself a garden. That way Ophelia's knowledge of botany could have been put to good use, and Denmark, not Britain, would have been the horticultural centre of the Universe.

But then I'd have been born in the wrong place.

BACKWORD
a conversation with a conscience

It was witty enough, I suppose, and to the point, but it sounds a fraction too flippant and self-assured to be completely . . . well, honest.

Well, I'm a private sort of person.

But I see you on television every week.

Oh, I know I have cameras in my garden for *Gardeners' World* but I refuse to have them in the house or open my doors to *Hello!* or *OK!*

Are you trying to keep us in the dark then?

No, it's not that. After all, I admit to having a wife, Alison, and two daughters, Polly and Camilla, who are now in their early twenties, but I don't parade them like props and we don't do the rounds of premières and parties that are the staple fare of the gossip columns.

Why?

Because I reckon that just because you live part of your life on the screen it doesn't mean that that's the only place where it exists and that people should know everything about you. They might not want to. And anyway, why would I want the inside of my house plastered over ten double-page spreads? To swank? To show burglars where the silver is? There's a more practical reason, too: I haven't got enough glamorous clothes.

So why write about your life if you're private? Isn't it better just to write novels and gardening books rather than an autobiography?

Ah, except that this is more a touch of the memoirs – not an autobiography. I've asked them not to put that on the title page.

Why?

Well, only worthy people – older people – write autobiographies.

Like pop stars?

Yes. No. Well, quite a lot happens when you're a pop star.

Most of them are still in their teens.

Yes, but they've lived.

And you haven't?

Well, yes.

So you think you've got something to say?

I hope so.

About what?

About growing up in the Fifties and Sixties. About feelings. About how odd it is that someone who thought they were not particularly good at anything has actually managed to find a niche and make a reasonable fist of things.

Sounds a bit smug to me.

You couldn't be more wrong.

So you're not smug?

Nope.

What then?

Surprised.

Am I supposed to believe that?

Suit yourself.

Will I learn much that I don't know?

I think so. Though I'm a bit wary of bitching. You know what the papers are like. They'll just pick out any sharp bits and quote them out of context so that I'll sound bitter and twisted.

And you're not?

Nah. It's not worth it.

But you do bitch then?

Well, I do relax with my friends and let slip the odd indiscretion.

Any danger of that here?

Occasionally.

So is it worth reading this book then, or am I just going to be bored rigid reading about how you became a gardener?

That rather depends.

On what?

Your reasons for reading it.

Not much of a recommendation, is it?

Well, look. I'll try and be readable and mildly amusing. It might fill an hour or two, it might make you smile, shed a tear, have a laugh, and at least you might come away thinking, well, he's not a bad lad, this Titchmarsh.

Is that all you want? A reader who likes you?

No. Not really. Though it's preferable to the reverse.

What then?

Why does anyone write anything? To share things. To try to understand things. To remember pleasantly, and to entertain.

I suppose that's fair enough. Go on then.

Thank you.

'Alan Titchmarsh is a man who has made
his way in life by trowel and error.'

Sir David Frost

1

The Outsider

'My clearest memories of childhood are all outdoors. I am squinting at the sun, or hearing my feet squelch inside my boots, or breathing deeply through my nose and feeling my nostrils fill with ice. Maybe I was destined to lead an outdoor life.'

Samuel Jonas, *Rustic Rambles*, 1885

My small fingers traced the outline of the round, smooth boulder. It was heavier than I was, and covered in a silky brown coating that made it slippery to the touch. It was in about a foot of water, in the River Wharfe at Ilkley in Yorkshire. Age? About seven or eight. I stood facing upstream, feeling the cold water swirling past my legs; spidery legs that stuck out from a pair of shorts. Thin legs, dusted with golden hairs. The curled toes of my freezing feet hung on to the stony riverbed in the hope that I'd avoid losing my grip and I flicked the thick and ever-present fringe of hair out of my eyes, peering past the glittering reflections on the surface of the water to the amber depths around the boulder.

It was here somewhere. A catfish. A big one – streamlined and sly, whiskered and wary of the approach of a small pair of hands intent on catching it – its tail twitching to keep it in line with the current. I pounced. Too late – a splash of water and that was it. The catfish was gone, perfectly camouflaged in the beer-brown pool, and I'd nothing to show for my trouble but wet, rolled-up sleeves and soggy-bottomed shorts. I picked my way gingerly to the grassy bank and lay down on my stomach among sweet-smelling foxtail and rye. I looked at the jam-jar containing three bullheads – slower, duller and easier to catch. They were gasping for air, and nudging at the Robertson's Golly to find a way out. I would let them go. In a bit.

Childhood summer holidays seemed always to be like this – lived out in the open – and they must be the reason that I've grown up the way I have, a direct result of both nature and nurture, the perfect hybrid. The world indoors has never held any attraction for me, except in the worst of weathers. I rise early – always have – anxious not to miss out on anything. If the sun is shining and I have to stay indoors, I become irritable and eager to escape. A childhood in Wharfedale is to blame. But I'm not complaining.

On the north side of the valley were the woods, carpeted with bluebells and wild garlic in spring; knee deep in rusty oak leaves and black mud in winter. To the south were the moors, looming over the town, purple with heather in late summer, orange with bracken in winter, or else almost black under heavy rain clouds. At the bottom of the dale, the silvery river snaked its way between playing fields and houses, separating the two wilder parts of the town. With no television to watch for the first few years of my life, that was the choice in fair weather, and often in foul: woods, moors or river.

The moors with their unforgettable fruity tang of bracken and heather, bilberry and crowberry, provided the scenery for imagined Westerns where, without a horse but with a rhythm of hoof-beats, I would gallop along paths of silver sand and then shin up massive lumps of millstone grit to survey the scene below. Genteel Ilkley became Arizona, Rocky Valley on Ilkley Moor a cowboy canyon. Occasionally these imaginings would be played out with a friend, but more frequently I travelled solo, or with our dog, a corgi-cairn-and-border-terrier-fluffball called Cindy. She would shoot through the bracken so that only the quivering fronds could offer a clue as to where she was heading, and I would breast my way through the greenery in pursuit, running madly downhill and often falling headlong on top of her in fits of mad laughter.

Middleton woods provided the richest source of birdlife, to be identified in Ladybird books and ticked off on a checklist covered in brown paper and entitled in spidery letters, 'British Birds – Notes'. Thrushes and lapwings were commonplace; curlews and magpies a rare treat. I even found an injured hawfinch once, a shy bird with foxy plumage and a beak that could crack nuts. It seemed uninterested in my penny toffee bar and unwilling to open its beak. 'Hawfinches do not like toffee.' Another lesson learned, and noted down for future reference.

But the river was the heart of my universe. It changed its mood with the seasons – deep and thunderous, the colour of Oxo and seventy feet across when in full spate after winter or spring rains, but drying out in summer to a benign stream that could be traversed without wetting the bottom of your shorts if you pulled them up a bit.

In the pools at its edge you could find minnows, and under and around its rocks crayfish lurked, along with the portly slow-movers we called bullheads, and that elusive catfish. Real fishermen caught brown trout; I had to make do with leaning over the stone parapet of the Old Bridge, watching as these sleek and foot-long beauties nosed their way upstream. I wondered why the fisherman who was several yards away casting his fly on the deep pool downstream did not come up here and place his fly right over their noses.

I made my own rod every summer from a long willow wand

cut from the trees that dipped their pendulous branches in the water. To the long bent stem, stripped of its narrow leaves, I would fasten a cotton reel, the thread guided through small screw eyes and a bent pin tied to its end. I never caught anything, in spite of the fact that my worms were fat and juicy. It wasn't long before I realised why; but fly fishing was something I waited another forty years to try.

Beside the Old Bridge was a little nursery, and as I leaned over the wall I would dream of what it would be like to grow plants there. The perfect existence – a small nursery, a potting shed and a couple of small greenhouses – with the birds and the sound of the river for company. But the nursery had its own permanent warning about the fickle behaviour of the river: behind the rows of lupins and delphiniums, neatly set out in raised beds of deep, dark soil, and the rock plants grown in discarded plastic cups and arranged on makeshift tables, the potting shed door was decorated with painted lines that showed the depth of the flood water in successive years. It did not happen every winter, but when it did I felt sorry for the man who grew the plants, and longed to help him put the place back in order. In summer I'd see him – a burly bloke with fair, curly hair, wearing khaki shorts, white vest and heavy boots – working the soil and watering the plants. In winter he was less in evidence and the iron gate was bolted, more often than not, with a 'Closed' sign nailed to a post inside. The nursery is still there. And so is the door with its watermarks. And I still dream.

At school we were told the story of Walter de Romilly who lived further upstream at Barden Tower. He had set out with his dog one morning, hundreds of years ago, and crossed the river at the spot known as 'The Strid', just a stride wide, but deep and thunderous between enormous rocks. That fateful morning as Walter leaped the river his dog held back on the lead and the boy disappeared under the water, never to be seen again. His mother, we were told, died of a broken heart.

It was a story that was difficult to believe in summer, when the dawdling river trickled by, but all too easy to understand on those grey, rain-lashed days when the river had no time for play and the rocks were submerged by the raging, man-high torrent.

After half an hour or so of summer's afternoon fishing, my bullheads would be tipped out of the jar and back into the water, and I'd pull on my black, elasticated pumps, pick up my jam-jar and fishing rod and head for home, still dreaming of the one that got away, and what a brown trout would feel like in your fingers.

The walk home took me past the allotments where my mother's father grew his vegetables, then past the gasworks where we went every Friday for a sack of coke for the central heating boiler (first in the street to have it, though when your dad's a plumber it doesn't really count). Rounding the corner of Nelson Road, past the Ledgard's bus garage with its shiny blue and chrome coaches, and the tall red brick wall where we played cricket, I'd meet the lads in the street who had been to the pictures. Waste of a Saturday, I reckoned. Who'd want to spend the daylight hours cooped up in the darkened mausoleum of the Essoldo or the Grove Cinema when you could be out catching fish, watching birds or running with a mad dog? And to be up and about when the rest of the world slept, especially on a bright and sunny morning, was the best feeling in the world. But then early morning, as my dad always said, is the best time of the day.

So it's always struck me as odd that I arrived late.

2

The Aged Relatives

'It is with relatives as it is with wives, one always wishes one had somebody else's.'

Kay Parker, *Sons and Leavers*, 1932

I was born at nine o'clock in the evening on Monday, 2 May 1949, to Alan and Bessie Titchmarsh (née Hardisty). I was their first child and I arrived during a heatwave, as my mother regularly reminds me, as though it were an excuse for my later behaviour. It was a tough delivery and my mother 'nearly burst a blood vessel', but both of us recovered and now there is not much to show for her exertions, except that the top of my head is pointed rather than flat. It's something that I've continually tried to disguise with my thick brown hair which, in spite of widespread disbelief among my grey-haired contemporaries, I have never dyed. St Winifred's Maternity Home sat on the very edge of the moor, and the window of my mother's room looked out across the heather and bracken towards White Wells – the old bathing house on the side of Ilkley Moor.

St Winifred's is still there. It's a large, detached stone house of stolid, uncompromising proportions, and it's no longer a maternity home. Having been part of Ilkley College for a few years, it's now been turned into flats, but a generation or two of Ilkley children can always boast that the fresh air of Ilkley Moor was the first to fill their lungs. I saw scaffolding encasing it on a visit a year or two ago, and read the advertisement for 'Luxury Apartments'. I enquired about them – fanciful of maybe owning the room where I was born – but they had all been long since let, in spite of the fact that not one of them was yet completed. My sister told me that the estate agent's advert in the *Ilkley Gazette* had boasted that the building was the place where I was born. Maybe they'll put a blue plaque on it. Maybe not.

Both Mum and Dad were Ilkley natives. My father's father, Fred, was a journeyman gardener whose family hailed from St Ives in Huntingdonshire. He died before I was born and was always known in conversation as Granda. Dad's mum was Florrie – Florence Alice Padgett – from a large family of girls in Beverley, North Yorkshire.

I grew up with a generous supply of great-aunts on my father's side: Auntie Edith, the eldest, whom I cannot remember, then Auntie Lizzie and Auntie Ethel who, like Dad's mum, had a prickly kiss. Auntie Clara was kindly and walked with a stick, Auntie Nellie had rosy cheeks and laughed a lot, Auntie Maggie was married to Uncle Archie who rode a cream motor scooter and Auntie Annie was in the Salvation Army. There were nine sisters in total, I think, all of them small, busy and bird-like. Their only brother, Uncle Will, had died in action during the First World War.

Dad was the youngest of three children and had a brother, James (Jim) and a sister, Alice. Jim married and had two sons; Auntie Alice remained single, continued to live with my widowed grandmother in a tiny two-up, two-down plus an attic in Dean Street with its cobbled back lane, and saved up threepenny bits for pocket money for her nephews and niece. She worked in service for a lady called Mrs Heap, who always sounded to me as though she must live in a dreadful state of untidiness. From time to time Auntie Alice took to bed with attacks of what were known in the family as 'idleitis'. This was blamed on the fact that she had once, when young, been involved with the Oxford Group Movement – something to do with 'moral rearmament' – and never quite got over it. She seemed to spend the rest of her life waiting for reinforcements.

But she was a kind, if nervy, soul with curly hair and feline features who, in later years, sat by the gas fire until her legs became red and mottled, and whose hands shook rather a lot when she was eating meals or drinking tea. Her social life seemed to be confined to beetle drives, whist drives and the occasional foray into bingo with her chain-smoking friend Phyllis Lupton, but mostly she just sat by the fire in floral crimplene dresses that were a touch too tight for comfort.

Grandma, in her time, had been a 'nippy' – a waitress – at the Bluebird Café, all shiny chrome and black vitriolite panels on Ilkley's smartest street, The Grove. In spite of her small stature – she was barely five feet tall – it was rumoured that she could carry half a dozen plates up each arm, and was a dab hand at 'silver service'. I was always a little bit frightened of her. Like many small women she had a forcefulness that could take a small child's breath away. But then I might have been influenced by my mum, whose relationship with Grandma Titchmarsh was always uneasy. My dad said little about it, but then he probably thought a lot.

Mum's mum, Catherine Naylor, came from Bradford, and her dad, George Herbert Hardisty, from Skipton. Herbert was a 'ganger' – a sort of foreman – on the council's highways department. He smoked a pipe filled with rich-smelling Condor tobacco and was bald with a walrus moustache. He seemed always to be wearing dark trousers, a dark waistcoat with a watch chain, and a white collarless shirt. A flat cap (or black trilby on Sundays) covered the bald head when he was out. By the time I came along he was retired and had time to be a small child's perfect grandad, kindly, gentle and with a few tricks up his sleeve. While Grandad was short and stocky, Grandma was angular and slender featured with swollen rheumatic knuckles. She was, of our two grandmas, the one who spoiled my sister and me the most.

In the back kitchen of the Hardisty household in Ash Grove – the other side of the Leeds Road from Dean Street and where we would visit them two or three times a week – were produced toasted currant teacakes, spread with butter that melted and ran in rivulets down our chins. Grandma had an amber sugarbowl, and Grandad would keep his empty tobacco tins and matchboxes for us, making long trains out of them and pushing them over the edge of the brown chenille-covered table to land with a clatter on the stone-flagged floor. He could make a squeaking noise with his hands – we called it 'cupty-cupty' – and, to the despair of my mother, he would drink his tea from his saucer, having poured it there from his cup to cool it down before slurping it up under the drooping grey whiskers of his moustache. Then he'd wink at us, fill his pipe and sit by the open fire to smoke it.

Sometimes, in moments of sentimentality, he would sing 'My Old Dutch' to Grandma, who would turn away and mutter 'Shut up, Herbert', wiping a tear from her eye with the corner of her pinny.

Wallflowers, sweet williams and tulips grew in the front garden of the neat stone-built terrace house, and in the back yard lived Smudger, a smooth-haired fox-terrier. There she would lie in the sun, and I can still smell the fragrance of gently cooking dog on York stone slabs, and see her white, moulted hairs caking the mossy earth in the gaps between the paving.

Life at Ash Grove seemed to revolve around the kitchen and its massive black range with cosy fire and chrome-handled ovens.

The front room, with its twin glass domes of stuffed exotic birds on the mantelpiece, was cold, gloomy and seldom used.

My mother was one of two sets of twins. Of the first set, Barbara and Charles, only Barbara (Bee) survived. Charles died on St Patrick's Day when he was just six weeks old. His mother said it was because he should have been born first, not second. 'Barbara and Charles,' said my grandmother, 'were born the wrong way round.' My mother, Bessie, and her brother, George Herbert (Bert), were born exactly four years later.

Mum and Dad went to school together, having first been introduced in their prams while their mums were out walking. There was an age gap of just two months. My mother must hold some kind of scholastic record. She started school, with her brother Bert, at the age of two, the twins having followed their sister Bee to school. The teacher said they could stay but they would not be on the register. A year later she relented and their names were added, so full-time schooling began for Mum at the age of three. It ended when she was fourteen and went to work drawing wool in Lister's mill in Addingham, a couple of miles up the Wharfe valley.

Dad, rejecting his father's trade, became an apprentice plumber with a local firm when he left school. When war broke out, plumbing became a 'deferred occupation' and he did not join up immediately – Hitler might have curtailed certain activities on the part of the British population but he was powerless to interfere with their sanitary arrangements. Plumbers were still necessary. During the latter part of the war Dad joined the Royal Electrical and Mechanical Engineers and with typical military misapplication of craftsmanship he then spent a couple of years in India fitting new treads to worn-out tyres.

Dad wasn't especially enamoured of India. 'Never seen such a filthy 'ole', was about the extent of his appreciation. The troops slept upstairs in his particular billet, while the natives bedded down below. 'At night,' he said, 'they went jungly.'

I mused for hours on what 'going jungly' meant. My mum said that the natives did war-dances and things. Seemed appropriate to me. There was a war on, when all was said and done. Perhaps they were just trying to help.

After a healthy number of assorted relationships between their school days and during the war, Alan and Bessie found themselves in the same group of friends once war had ended. On 4 November 1946 they all went to a dance at the King's Hall in Ilkley, the girls in their floral frocks and peep-toe shoes, the men in their baggy suits. Halfway through the evening Mum recalls looking up at the balcony that ran round the Winter Gardens. 'I looked up and saw your dad. I waved. He waved back. The he came down and we started dancing. We courted for six months, then we were engaged for six months and we got married on 3 December 1947.'

'Was it love?' I asked.

'Well, it must have been something, mustn't it?'

I think we'll take that for a 'yes'. This is Yorkshire, after all.

Mum and Dad married two years after hostilities ceased. They went to live with Florrie, my father's mother – two-up, two-down, an attic and an outside lavatory – while Auntie Alice moved in with Mrs Heap. It wasn't a particularly comfortable state of affairs, Florrie being an interfering, if well-meaning, busybody, and my mother being just a touch volatile, and needled at being constantly compared with Uncle Jim's wife, Jenny. 'Jenny does it this way, why don't you?'

Still, somehow they all muddled through for a couple of years until four months after I was born when Mum and Dad bought their own house in Nelson Road, a ten-minute walk from Dean

Street – near enough for Grandma Titchmarsh to irritate my mother by turning up every afternoon at tea time to enquire what we were having. 'Mmm. That looks nice!' she'd say, leaning over our shoulders and scrutinising the contents of our plates. Mum felt obliged to offer her some. At first.

Auntie Alice eventually moved back to live with Grandma Titchmarsh and for the next thirty years or more they aggravated one another daily. Auntie Alice would watch Russ Conway on the television and say, 'I wish I could play like him,' to which Grandma would snap back, 'Well, you could have done if you'd practised.' The thought of my Auntie Alice playing 'Sidesaddle' and winking at the television camera is something I still can't come to terms with.

By the time my sister arrived, four and a half years later, my parents had become a bit more adventurous in the naming stakes. She was christened Kathryn Victoria. I've always felt slightly resentful that Kath has more regal-sounding names than mine.

Before my birth my mother cherished a fondness for the name Rodney, but the doctor advised against it. 'For God's sake, don't call him Rodney!' And so, with sentiment worthy of Mills and Boon, when her newborn infant was placed in her arms and she was asked what name I was to have, she said that I was to be called after my father: Alan. It was later decided that I should carry my grandfather's name as well: Frederick. Quite noble, really. Until, at the font, Florrie told Mum quite curtly that her late husband's name lacked the 'Erick'. It was 'Fred', plain and simple.

So here I am – Alan Fred. Both perfectly acceptable names for a gardener, so that's all right.

3

Nelson Road

'I love children. Why I was only remarking to Mr Whittaker yesterday that in the right place I think they can be quite decorative. They get grubby, yes, but at a distance (and distance, it seems to me, is always preferable with children) one is apt not to notice.'

Joan Morris, *The Pleasure of Propriety*, 1832

Nelson Road was a typical northern street of stone-built terraced houses with purple slate roofs, and it was surrounded by other streets bearing similarly patriotic names – Nile Road, Trafalgar Road, Wellington Road and Victory Road – though a few streets away the more honestly descriptive Brewery Road added an air of relaxed normality. Number 34 was, like all the others, on three storeys. My mother and father moved in during the autumn of 1949, having bought the freehold, on a mortgage, for £400. They had their own place at last, and my mother could heave a sigh of relief at being at least an arm's length from her mother-in-law.

The front door of Number 34 was reached by crossing a tiny patch of lawn, bordered with lily-of-the-valley and enclosed by a privet hedge and a gate with a clinking sneck. The door led directly into 'the front room', used as a sitting room, and two further doors led off it, the left-hand one opening on to the cellar and coal 'ole steps, and the right-hand one leading into the back kitchen. A door in the kitchen revealed the stairs which led up to the landing with double bedroom at the front (Mum and Dad), single bedroom at the back (me until my sister arrived) and loo. The top floor, with its dormer window, was an attic which, on my sister's arrival, was converted into a bedroom for me (at the front with the dormer) and a bathroom at the back (with a skylight).

My father might have been a plumber by trade but at home he was also a builder and carpenter of necessity. He painted the outside of the house and pointed the stonework, glazed windows, divided up the attic and installed the bathroom, put in central heating and flushed the old-fashioned panelled doors with smooth hardboard, replacing the dated brass knobs with chrome and plastic handles set at a 45-degree angle. He replaced stone-flagged floors with modern floorboards and turned what was a down-at-heel terraced house into a home that became a part of us. My mother did what so many mothers did in the Fifties and Sixties – she brought us up full time, an operation which included decorating, curtain making, accounting, shopping, cooking, sewing, knitting, dressmaking and every other aspect of housekeeping.

There were one or two mothers in the street who worked, in shops or factories, but in our hearts we knew that it wasn't right. A mum was meant to be at home when you wanted her. We felt sorry for kids whose parents were both out all day.

Behind the house was a tiny yard, where bikes leaned against the wall under old pram covers and sacks. Then came 'the back' – a rough lane – and then our back garden, perhaps thirty feet long and fifteen feet wide with an old sycamore at the end and cabbages and Brussels sprouts down either side. By the garden gate stood a stone-built outhouse, the midden. It contained nothing except spiders and woodlice.

'Don't ever go in there,' warned my mum. 'I don't want you catching something nasty.'

So we never did, but then it was the most uninviting building I ever saw, with a flat concrete roof and peeling maroon-painted stable doors that seemed to be falling off their hinges. In all the sixteen years we lived there I never stepped over its threshold. Stupid really.

If the River Wharfe was the hub of my childhood universe, then the back lane was at the heart of my childhood social life. It was here that we rode 'bogeys' – wooden carts made from spare timber and old pram wheels, and steered with a loop of rope. My dad would make them for me, and I'd replace the wheels when they fell off due to overwork. I'd build elaborate canopies for them from wartime blackout material to turn them into stage coaches, and start them off at the top end of Nelson Road, hurtling happily down the one-in-six gradient and either turning right into the bus-garage wall at the bottom, or left into Mennell's builders' yard that surrounded the saleroom.

Dacre, Son and Hartley's saleroom played a large part in our lives. We seldom had anything new in the way of furniture, but my sister and I became accustomed to returning home from school and discovering a different three-piece suite or set of dining chairs from the ones we had left behind in the morning. We went through the Parker Knoll and Ercol phases, as well as what I now recognise as being a set of six oak Arts and Crafts dining chairs that the V & A would kill for. They all came and went, and my mother enjoyed the variety that spiced our lives.

'I think it must be the gypsy in me,' she'd say. Anyone less like a gypsy than my mother I cannot imagine.

Our bikes came from the saleroom, too. My first was a plum-coloured Hercules, and I learned to ride it down the back lane with my dad holding on to the saddle. Until the time that he didn't and I turned around to speak to him at the bottom of the lane and saw that he was still at the top. I never fell off again. Well, not until I hit something.

Sales were usually held once a fortnight, but the rest of the time the kids in the street had great fun playing with the stuff that was unsaleable and had been chucked out. We'd smash tiles with stones, melt down broken lead statues in tin cans over bonfires, and partake of other childhood activities that would now be branded as wanton violence and mindless cruelty.

We came across an old man burying a cocker spaniel on the other side of the saleroom wall, and went to tell the older lads in the street. They gave it a week, and then went along armed with spades and dug it up to see if it had gone to heaven. It hadn't. We were all disappointed and tried to think of a reason.

'Maybe it takes dogs longer to get there than people,' suggested Dokey Gell.

'Maybe animals don't go,' offered Mickey Hudson.

The question was not resolved satisfactorily and the dog was covered up again and forgotten.

In moments of supreme creativity we'd put on plays on the patch of concrete down the back street that was known as 'Barker's Square'. Mr and Mrs Barker were an older, childless couple with a back kitchen that always smelled of nutmeg. Mrs Barker wore black, single-buttoned 'character shoes' every day, and on Sundays you could see Mr Barker directing traffic while wearing navy blue uniform and white gloves; he was a special constable, which I always thought rather glamorous. He kept two tortoises – Tommy and Thomas – of even greater age than the Barkers themselves.

The concrete square – the only made-up part of the back lane – was where Mr Barker parked his motor bike and sidecar, but he'd move it for our plays. They weren't plays really; more like entertainments. The girls would dance ballet to records played on an old wind-up gramophone, and I'd announce what they were doing, trying to remember not to say 'paz de dukes'. Then we'd sing advert jingles in the interval: 'Have you tried Robinson's Lemon Barley, lemon fresh, barley smooth? If you haven't tried Robinson's Lemon Barley, well . . . you should!' Toe-curlingly embarrassing to recall.

Indulgent parents would sit down on the row of half a dozen chairs and watch a show that took, at most, two and a half minutes.

'Very good. Yes, very good.' Then they'd smile and walk back to their respective kitchens to put the kettle on and get on with things.

The rest of the time we played the usual games, cricket and football against the bus-garage wall at the bottom of the street. We seldom had to stop for cars. Oh, and kick-can – a bit like hide and seek, but when you dashed out from cover on being found, you had to kick an old tin can before the person who had located you managed to put their boot in.

But I was, as my dad observed fairly early on, always a bit of a loner. It's not that I'm antisocial, it's just that I'm also happy on my own, with my own thoughts and my own all-too-vivid imagination. Even now, although I enjoy the company of a close family and an unusually large number of good friends, I still need time to myself. Time to think. Time to write. Time to be quiet.

Not that life at home was quiet.

Gardening is what I have done for as long as I can remember. I have a photograph of myself and Grandad Hardisty on his allotment. He is leading me, a podgy-legged one-year-old in baggy bloomers, between rows of sweet peas, among which dangle the shiny lids of Cadbury's cocoa tins, put there to frighten off the sparrows. His allotment, on the banks of the river, had a small and lopsided shed filled with tools, spilled seeds and bags of pungent fertiliser. Blackberries scrambled over brass bedsteads, and a sunken tank of sootwater provided the wherewithal to discourage greenfly, caterpillars and anything else that might want to eat his cabbages and cauliflowers, all of which seemed to be covered in a thin black film of soot. Grandma must have had to scrub each brassica for hours to remove the deposit.

In spite of the fact that my father's father, and his grandfather, had both been gardeners, Dad took up the spade on the allotment only reluctantly, when my mother's father found it too much. His own father had made him pull up weeds as a boy and he had never found any joy in the garden. It was Mum who fanned the flame in me. But that came later.

At the time of my sister's arrival, my father went down with pneumonia, as a result of which I was farmed out to my Auntie Bee in Otley. In later life I came to look upon Auntie Bee with great fondness. She was a good artist, though she never had the opportunity to use her talent. Only in old family autograph books can her artwork be admired – pencil sketches and pen-and-ink drawings of Mickey Mouse and other characters drawn out of her imagination. She was a love, a gentle creature with a good sense of humour, totally overshadowed by her assertive greengrocer husband.

When I was four and a half, Otley, though only eight miles from Ilkley, seemed hours away, my cousins David and Arnold struck me as strangely different, my Uncle Herbert Burnett was gruff and grumpy and often didn't wear his teeth, and Auntie Bee, not surprisingly, was impatient. 'Be quiet, the pair of you', are the only words I remember her saying during that time. She also admonished my cousin at the dinner table for speaking with his mouth full, but her instruction did not come out quite as she intended. 'David! Don't talk with your mouth open!' He spent ages trying to work out the alternative.

A black-and-white photograph of David and myself standing side by side in a garden wearing carpet slippers, cardigans and morose expressions seems to sum up my feelings of that brief but unhappy episode.

I suppose I must have been aware of the reasons for my removal, but it did nothing to cheer me up. I returned home after however long it was – probably only a couple of weeks – to discover my mother in the back bedroom of her own mother's house with a baby at her breast. I levered myself up on the bed to watch my sister feed and enquired, 'Is that what those things are for?'

4

Tales of the Unexpected

'I quite like my sister. When I'm not with her.'
Barry Utterworth, *Samson Smith*, 1963

The arrival of my sister came as something of a shock. I suppose I must have been told she was on her way, but it was only when she started muscling in that I realised the implications of the presence of a woman other than my mother in my life. From the word 'go' we got on like a house on fire. Oh, there were days when we could cheerfully hate one another, and when it all ended in tears, but they were, to be honest, few and far between. The four-and-a-half-year difference in our ages didn't seem to matter at all, probably because I was a slow developer and my sister anything but. It sort of levelled us out.

There were times when it embarrassed us to confess to other brother-and-sister partnerships who were at each other's throats like cat and dog that we quite enjoyed each other's company. We played together, ate together and generally got on, though she would leave me alone when I wanted to play with my electric train, and I would leave her to change the clothes and brush the hair of her dolls. The fact that the head came off Prudence – the Victorian china doll with a leather body – was, I would like to make clear, not my fault. She was very old and more fragile than she looked.

None of our toys was what you'd call high technology, but then a play station is a vicarious sort of entertainment. Safe, yes (if you don't count microwaves and radioactivity); but expensive, and not exactly character forming.

Where once there was waste ground or scrubland that could be transformed by imagination into any part of the world, from tropical jungle to Australian outback, there are adventure playgrounds. You can see them on the side of playing fields, with their rubber floors and chipped bark cushioning under the swings. They are carefully constructed to remove any danger. Parents feel much more secure as a result. Shame really. We seem to have crafted a childhood influenced more by the threat of litigation than by the need to grow up and be able to take a few knocks.

It does make me appreciate my own parents' willingness to let us grow up more naturally: 'Look right, look left, look right again, and then if all is clear, quick march, don't run. Oh, and don't talk to strangers.' That was all we were armed with when let out for the day.

There's more traffic about today, so your quick march might be quicker still, but I suspect that life's quotient of 'strangers' is probably about the same. We're just made more aware of them by an increasingly alarmist press.

It was years before I realised that the road sweeper clad in khaki overalls about whom we were warned, 'Don't take any sweets from him because he's got a nasty disease,' was probably a child molester. As it was, we just crossed over the road whenever we saw him and never caught anything.

Not that I recommend some of the things we got up to. Apart from melting lead from saleroom throw-outs, fire was a real fascination. But we were careful. Experimentation showed us what it could do, and how hot it became. So the day that I, playing the 'good' cowboy, was tied to an old wooden chair (at my own suggestion) with a fire lit beneath it while I tried to escape from my mates, 'the baddies', was, in effect, a carefully controlled situation. I'd made sure that I could stand up and walk with the chair on my back so I escaped with no more than a pair of melted soles and singed denim. Wise? No. Fun? You bet!

We climbed trees. We tumbled over. In the course of growing up I split open my eyebrow, my lip, gashed my knee twice and always had a few scabs to pick at. One day I fell ten feet from the top of a flight of steps in the saleroom yard flat on to my stomach and wondered, having been winded, if I'd ever be able to draw breath again.

Fortunately we were not mollycoddled. Quite the reverse. Trying to get a day off school, my sister and I discovered, required hard work and application. Nothing less than dramatic and continuous vomiting would stop you from being bundled out of the front door of a morning. I wouldn't say my mother was a hard woman, but a slight headache or a bit of tooth- or earache was no reason to stop you from getting on with life. She was caring, but not in the Florence Nightingale league.

That was bad enough, but she also trained my dad in her image. I fell over down by the allotments once, hurting my knee on an ash and cinder path. I burst into tears and clutched at my damaged limb.

'Come on! Get up! We'll be late for dinner.'

You know those times when you seem to be speaking a different language from your parents? This was one of them. To be fair, I suppose I wasn't terribly coherent, burbling away and pointing at my left knee.

In the end, he hoiked me up on to his shoulders, muttering about me being a cry-baby and looking at his watch, fearing both the state of the Sunday roast and my mother's patience in view of our impending late arrival.

It was only when we got home and he dumped me down on the kitchen floor that I managed to roll down my knee-length sock and examine the inch-long gash at the side of my leg that he showed any remorse. He went pale and quiet, and my mother went for the TCP.

I've still got the scar. And a bit of cinder forever embedded in my knee. No offence, Dad. It's a kind of battle scar now.

The most amazing thing of all is that until I was well into my teens I never once heard my dad swear. He must have done at work, but at home, no. Never. Until one day in summer when I was upstairs helping my mum decorate my attic bedroom. It was a lovely pale green paper with ducks flying across the marshes. I haven't seen it in the shops for ages, now.

Anyway, there we were, on the top floor of the house at about four in the afternoon and we heard a shout from downstairs. It was my dad, but his voice was indistinct.

Mum was at the top of the ladder and I was handing a newly pasted strip of paper up to her.

'Go and see what he wants while I hang this bit, will you?'

So down the stairs I went, rounding the corner at the bottom of the last flight to see my father standing on the back doorstep in his working clothes of navy blue overalls, tweed jacket and flat cap. On his face was a look of complete dejection. On his cap, his jacket, his overalls and his cheeks was a smattering of brown, smelly gunge.

He looked at me and I looked at him.

'Go upstairs,' he said, 'and tell your mother I've been showered in shit.'

There followed, that evening, the story of how he came to be standing at the top of a ladder unblocking a waste pipe into which six lavatories of the local hotel discharged, as did his further expletives at the hotel waiter who had decided to flush the lavatory at the far end of the line, having been for his afternoon clear-out.

My father, marooned at the top of his ladder, could do nothing except wait for the colourful torrent to subside. His clothes never made it past the back door. He was round to the Co-op the following morning for a new outfit. Careful she might have been, but my mother was nothing if not hygienic.

5

Going Up in the World

'Our Edie's got a car.'

'Is it a posh one?'

'I'll say. Four ashtrays and a steering wheel cover.'

Tom Chambers, *Fur Coat and No Teeth*, 1966

It was ages before television influenced us. Grandma Titchmarsh got it first. We were taken round to her house and, from the outside, asked if we could see anything different about it. It took a while before we noticed the X-shaped aerial strapped to the chimney. We got our own set six months later. I was probably about eight years old.

I remember, like the rest of my generation, newsreaders and presenters with posh voices – Sylvia Peters and Richard Dimbleby – puppets like Bill and Ben and Muffin the Mule, cowboy adventures like *The Lone Ranger* and *The Range Rider*.

We had a Pye television in a wooden cabinet with a sloping glass screen at the front, a natty sort of affectation which was the televisual equivalent of the Ford Anglia with the sloping rear window. It had four small knobs on the back – contrast and brightness, and horizontal hold and vertical hold, which you turned to stop the framed picture from moving side to side or up and down – and two bakelite knobs on the front. One was on/off and volume, and the other a tuning knob. Not that we had much to tune in to. One BBC channel, and that was only in the evening. Nothing during the day except a test card with lots of black, white and grey patches and patterns on it. ITV came along some time later, along with its ATV three-note vibraphone signature tune and Robinson's Lemon Barley jingles, but my mother didn't really approve. It was, to her, a 'common' station. Auntie Bee's family watched ITV a lot, but they lived in a council house. Mum would never watch the news on ITV. The BBC was what you watched the news on. They got it right. My mother never was and never will be a snob, in the accepted sense of the word. As she would see it, she just has standards.

To this day she still watches the BBC news, though *Coronation Street* and *Emmerdale* have wooed her over to the other side now, for part of the evening at least. From time to time there is talk of me moving to ITV. 'Ooh, Ala! You wouldn't, would you?'

What can you say?

It was shortly after we had the television that our first means of transport arrived. It was a van, a big, dark green Austin A35 pick-up, registration number UWU 581. I've always had a problem remembering number sequences (something I've handed on to my youngest daughter) but I can remember the numbers of our first van and our first car. This one had a bench seat in the front where, perched between Dad, driving, and Mum on the passenger side, my sister and I would be taken on Sunday afternoon runs up the Dales or even to the Lakes.

It was on the corner of the main road at Bowness that we had our only family accident. A motor cycle shot across the traffic lights, collided with our offside wing and deposited its rider in the back of the van. He leaped out and began swearing at my father who, to his undying credit, asked him to moderate his language in front of the children. Nothing came of the encounter.

We were stationary at the time, and the motor cyclist realised he was in the wrong, but I remember feeling sick for the rest of the day, and my dad didn't say much.

William Lawson (Ilkley) Limited, the plumbing firm for which my father worked, kept the big green Austin van for a few years, eventually replacing it with a brown Austin Mini pick-up van with a plastic cover over the back. There was now no room for my sister and me to sit in the front. The bench seat went with the bigger model and now we had two almost bucket seats and a floor gear stick instead of one on the steering column. Added to which, we were growing. As a result Kath and I were moved outside, under the plastic cover where, with a few cushions to soften the steel floor, we travelled with our backs to the cab, trying not to get a numb bum and doing our best not to inhale the exhaust fumes which had a habit of backing up, especially going up hills. But were we bothered? No! We were out 'on a run', and saw the likes of Bolton Abbey and Grassington, Pateley Bridge and Burnsall, usually with a picnic at the side of the river or on the edge of the moors.

And then, one day, came the first firm's car rather than a van, though what my dad did with all the copper piping and ball-cocks he needed to take to his jobs I'll never know. It was a green Austin Mini and from now on Kath and I had our own seats. After the Mini came a red Austin 1100. We toured Scotland in that. It was great, except that at the factory they hadn't fitted the rubber bungs in the floor properly and my sister and I looked down, a few miles north of Inverness, to discover that our feet were under water.

'Dad! We're wet!'

'Yes. Well, it's raining.'

'No. I mean we're really wet.'

'Doh!' It was my dad's word long before Homer Simpson.

We pulled up, lifted the carpet and poked a stick through the hole in the floor to let the water out, then fitted the misplaced rubber bungs and set off again.

We didn't really care. We were independent. We were on holiday, and to this day I am not certain how a plumber and his wife, who stayed at home to look after us rather than go out to work, managed to give us a holiday every year (only a week, mind) and provide us with Christmas presents and new clothes and a feeling of being special. Well, I do have a vague idea. It was all down to good accounting. My mother would have nothing on 'tick' or the 'never-never'; everything had to be paid for in full when it was bought, even if it meant waiting. And it often did.

I looked enviously at the Kensitas gift coupons saved by Mickey Hudson's parents from their cigarette packets and stuffed behind the mantelpiece clock in his house. Every so often some new household luxury would arrive, courtsesy of Kensitas, and I would wish, ever so slightly, that my parents smoked the right brand.

My dad was a Senior Service man, though not in the house. In later life he smoked Castellas, believing that cigars were better for you than cigarettes. I longed to tell him that this was only if you stopped inhaling, but then I think he knew that anyway. He tried a pipe once, but realised in the end that he was smoking more matches than tobacco. Mum didn't smoke, but would occasionally have a single Peter Stuyvesant at parties. She held the cigarette aloft very elegantly between index and middle finger and drew in the smoke and blew it out all in one breath. She never really liked it; it was more of a fashion statement.

Every Friday my father would hand her his wage packet. She took out the housekeeping and put it in assorted tins and jars for the butcher, the grocer and the insurance man. Mr Knight from Pearl

Insurance came to collect his dues once a week. Tall, with a moustache and glasses, he doffed his trilby as he came in the front door, then sat in our easy chair and smoked his pipe as he took the money from my mother and filled in the book to show she'd paid.

On Friday night my father would be given his pocket money for the week, and my mother would eke out the rest of the contents of his pay packet, baking our own cakes, making clothes for us children and generally doing-it-herself.

In the Fifties and Sixties she made all her own dresses, cutting out the material from the remnant shop pinned to paper patterns on the living room floor. She had a lovely full-skirted evening dress made from peach brocade, and another floral number with a skirt shaped like a tulip. There were two-piece woollen 'costumes' and dirndl skirts, as well as coats and trousers for my sister and me. Only once do I remember my mother coming downstairs in trousers, taking one look at me and shooting back upstairs to take them off. That was in the Fifties. It would be another five years before she was able to pluck up the courage to wear them every day.

My dad did his bit, too. In the years before my electric train set arrived at Christmas there were, in turn, a wooden garage with Dinky toys, a fort with a lifting drawbridge and soldiers, and a zoo with cages that had sliding doors and contained lead animals. Each December the cellar at 34 Nelson Road was declared out of bounds. My sister and I never enquired why; we just accepted it without question. There were no suspicions. Father Christmas was to do with chimneys, not cellars. I remember December as smelling of new paint, the aroma drifting up the cellar steps into the sitting room. Only now do I think of my dad labouring on his woodwork every night when he came home from work.

We did things together when I was little. One of the bosses

Dad worked for was a Burnley Football Club supporter and we'd sometimes go to Saturday matches at Turf Moor. Dad taught me how to swim, how to ride a bike, and even how to shoot a bow and arrow. He was left-handed and I am right-handed, but I am a left-handed archer. When the need arises.

Dad played cricket for Ilkley fire station, where he was a part-time fireman, against other stations up the Dales – Beckwithshaw and Barnoldswick, Skipton and other rural towns and villages – and we'd all turn up and watch. He was a passable batsman, a better bowler. On Armistice Day he would march with the rest of the firemen in the parade behind the Hammond's Sauce Band to Ilkley's Cenotaph, and sometimes he'd lay the fire service wreath. I'd nudge my sister and we'd swell with pride. He looked smart in his uniform. When he wasn't in uniform he sometimes looked like Columbo. A bit crumpled.

He loved singing in the church choir, and ringing the bells, playing dominoes at the Legion or the Station Hotel, but, above all else, he loved reading the paper. My father could make a newspaper last for hours. I've even watched him read the small ads and the situations vacant. I think the technique was probably born out of necessity. To get a bit of peace and quiet from the wife and two kids.

I suppose housekeeping was always a question of priorities. I never had a new bike until I started work, but I always had new shoes twice a year – sandals with white crepe soles at the start of summer, and Clark's shoes in winter (our feet measured on a strange sort of X-ray machine that you looked into and saw green outlines where your feet had been). But I do remember, at school, wondering if I would ever have a jumper with a label in it. Mine never did; they were always hand-knitted.

6

Unwillingly to School

'Those who claim that their school days were the happiest days
of their lives are to be pitied. Such sentiments are invariably used
to camouflage a lack of fulfilment in later life.'

Ernest Sanguinetti, *The Origins of Terpitude*, 1953

Although during my school days my mother never went out
to work, she clearly thought that a break from her son during
the day would give her a bit more time to herself and a chance
to catch up. Added to which, my newly born sister would
benefit from a bit more individual attention. The result was
that I was packed off to nursery school. Now in case you think
the story has suddenly shifted up a gear and we had come into
some old family legacy, let me explain that the nursery was
council run, and it was free. I went there for several days each
week from mid-morning to mid-afternoon, probably for less
than a year.

The things I remember about it are that it occupied a single-
storey building at the end of my grandad's allotment on the banks
of the Wharfe, and that we had to have a sleep after lunch – on
canvas stretchers laid side by side on the floor. It seemed an odd
thing to me. I was always bursting with energy and they would
make us lie down and go to sleep. Daft!

There was a great deal of painting and wearing sun hats on

bright days, and we played a lot. I quite liked it. Apart from the sleeping bit.

And then, when I was five, I went to the New County Infants School, down Leeds Road. The playing field at the back of the school abutted on to Dean Street where Grandma Titchmarsh lived, but I don't remember seeing her during the day at all. She was probably out working at the Bluebird Café, and Auntie Alice would be either cleaning or in bed.

I enjoyed my first years at school. They became progressively less enjoyable, but between the ages of five and ten I was reasonably happy. At infant school I remember gentle Mrs Osmond with her white hair teaching sums and encouraging us to read *Janet and John*. There was robust and energetic Miss Outersides who was very good at sports, the kindly but strict Mrs Lambert, and the fierce headmistress, Miss Howker, short and squat, with iron-grey hair and a leg at each corner.

We took meals in the school hall – brand new but unbelievably lofty and with a clock which had coloured numerals. Here I learned to hate rhubarb and custard. Well, school rhubarb and school custard. I quite like it now, but I remember sitting hunched over one unappetising mound of red, green and yellow while my schoolmates played outside and a teacher stayed behind until the last morsel disappeared. It was to no avail. I brought it all up again and she had to mop the floor. I was excused from eating rhubarb for the next three years. 'No! Don't make him. He'll only be sick!'

It was at infant school that the first hint of a child's embarrassment with its parents manifested itself. It was sports day. There was to be a parents' race. I longed for my mother to enter it and win. She was a good runner and younger than a lot of other mums. She arrived with a scarf wrapped around her mouth and an inability to speak. She also lacked any inclination to run, having been at the dentist's to have a tooth removed. And so I stood and watched while Mrs Brown, not nearly so good a runner as my mum, won the race and the admiring looks of my fellow pupils. My mum peered silently over the top of her woollen yashmak. She fared little better when my sister was at infants' school, as Kath's school diary relates: 'Mum could not enter the parents' race because she was in the toilet.'

It makes you suspicious, doesn't it?

At eight I moved up a school. Ilkley All Saints Junior School was not simply for those children of a heavenly disposition, it was a church school, Ilkley Parish Church being dedicated to All Saints. It was a Victorian building, one of those classic northern schools made of stone that had been blackened by a century of soot and now usually brightened up with turquoise doors. They don't fool anybody.

If the infants school had gentled me into education, junior school shook me to the core – or rather the teacher of the first class did. Her name was Mrs Richardson. She was a robust woman with short legs and an even shorter fuse. Within moments she could transform herself from a well-spoken, bespectacled educationalist into a fiery ball of venom, spitting out the words 'You big blockheads!' and managing, with the deft manipulation of her plump thumb and forefinger, to transform the curl of wispy, silken hair at the back of my neck into an instrument of torture thanks to a simple screwing motion.

She had a lot of spit, did Mrs Richardson. Most of it airborne. But she was hard to dislike. You just ended up trying not to upset her for the year you were with her.

It was while I was in her class that I added another item of food to my list of hates: school milk. I loved milk at home, but at school it came in bottles that carried one-third of a pint, and it seemed sort of off-white. Even the cream was grey. When the weather was cold it was not too bad, but when the weather was icy they would stand the bottles on the low, fat school radiators to thaw and then it tasted sour. And anyway, Avril Thwaites once sat next to the milk on the radiator and accidentally did a wee and I never felt the same about it again. Mrs Thatcher may have been branded 'milk snatcher' by a nation of parents when she was Minister of Education, but millions of schoolchildren had reason to be grateful to her.

Then came my favourite teacher of all time. Mr Rhodes. Harry Rhodes was well spoken and jolly. It seemed that he was always smiling, always enthusiastic and always – most importantly – encouraging. Where other teachers would be of the 'Sit down and shut up' school of education, Harry Rhodes was the 'get up and show me' type. If you showed the slightest aptitude for anything, he fanned the flame. It's down to him, as much as anyone, that I became a gardener.

Mr Rhodes – six feet, with a Roman nose on which perched a pair of rimless glasses – was a keen gardener. Cacti were his speciality. He would bring them, in tiny pots, to the school bring-and-buy sale or the church bazaar, selling them for sixpence apiece. Always he would give you a few handy hints on their cultivation: 'Not too much water, drier in winter than in summer. Try it on a windowsill, Alan; it likes good light.'

He was the only teacher who occasionally called boys by their Christian names. With the rest it was always surnames for the boys and Christian names for the girls. It was not a problem. We accepted it. But Harry Rhodes marked himself out as being all the more human because of his friendliness.

Not that he was a pushover. Oh, no. He could maintain discipline with practised ease, and could achieve silence by the raising of an eyebrow both at Sunday school, where I went on Sunday afternoons when I was little, and at school. It was he who was in change of the music at morning assembly, held in one of the central classrooms, made larger by the folding back of heavy sliding doors. He would stand to one side of a large and ancient gramophone in a white-painted cabinet with a raised lid, and with almost military precision lift the needle into the groove with a sideways movement of his arm without ever seeming to look down. It was as smart a manoeuvre as shouldering arms in a military tattoo, and it heralded the arrival of Miss Hickinson, a tall, grey-haired lady with a regal bearing and a mouth that went down at the corners.

Miss Hickinson would make her entrance to a slow movement from Handel's *Water Music,* or to 'Greensleeves' or, if Mr Rhodes was feeling a little brave, to *The Arrival of the Queen of Sheba,* at which she would look at him accusingly over the top of her glasses.

We would sing a hymn, and then Mr Rhodes would say – and I can hear him still – 'Hands together . . . and eyes closed,' and we would pray, before listening to Miss Hickinson's message of the day and singing another hymn.

I remember her, once, picking us up on the pronunciation of the word 'peculiar' in a line that ran, 'peculiar blessings to our King'. A hundred northern voices kept ringing out 'pick-yu-lee-er' until she gave up and swept out again to the strains of Handel while Mr Rhodes kept his inscrutable face fixed firmly on the wall ahead.

But she had a kindly side. Aged eight I fell over in the school playground – an everyday occurrence and not particularly spectacular. I was running and someone put their leg out. I tripped over it and crashed to the ground, sat up, cried and announced that I'd broken my left leg. 'Nonsense,' said a grown-up voice. But they took me to hospital, X-rayed the offending limb and discovered that I was right. My leg was plastered up and I was sent home.

Within a day or two a large envelope arrived, containing crayons, colouring books and a simple book of sums. It was from Miss Hickinson. Her letter said: 'Dear Alan, Here is a lucky packet for you . . . Don't try to do too much in one day . . . We look forward to seeing you soon. Yours sincerely, E. Hickinson.'

I felt very special. And I still have the letter. Somewhere.

It was when the plaster came off that I discovered a new emotion. That of grief. I remember gazing down at the weak and withered limb that was my left leg, its dry and scaly surface sporting wisps of cotton wool, and looking upwards to see my mother weeping. While I had been at the hospital having my plaster painfully removed with an enormous pair of clippers, Grandma Hardisty, who had been in another hospital, had died. I remember crying for my grandmother, and crying for my mother. I had never seen her weeping before. Tears yes, but sobs, no.

During my grandma's stay in hospital they had, unbeknown to her, admitted my grandfather who had also become ill. An ulcer, they said. I was taken to see him. He had a brown rubber tube coming out of his nose. I remember thinking how poorly he looked. He died within a few days of my grandmother. Mum said that Grandma had called for him, and that Grandad had never let her down.

Looking back at my mum's parents, whom I knew for only eight years, I realise now how much Kitty and Herbert Hardisty taught me about love. Not effusively; just indirectly, by example. They were quite ordinary or they certainly seemed so. My grandad would go to the British Legion for a drink with my dad, and they'd play dominoes. Grandad worked at the Liberal Club in his retirement, cleaning and serving behind the bar, with a robust couple called Mr and Mrs Boyle, whom I remember smoking a lot. And in the house he would, more often than not, be sitting smoking his pipe full of Condor in his big armchair, pulled up by the fire that glowed in the massive kitchen range, shiny black with steel handles. Grandma would occasionally snap at him, 'Move your feet, Herbert,' or tut at him for slurping his tea out of the saucer while she buttered the teacakes, but there was always a magic between them. I can recognise it now.

I have a black-and-white photograph of them taken on a day trip to Hornsea on the Yorkshire coast not long before they died – Grandad in his flat cap and suit, a coat folded over his arm, and Grandma, wearing a strange felt hat, the bandages showing under her stockings, her arm linked through that of my grandad. There's a tired, almost haunted look about them, as though they are on the brink of a journey into the unknown. I suppose they were.

Even now, when people talk of grandmas and grandads, I feel nothing but a warm glow of remembrance. I can still hear my grandfather singing 'My Old Dutch' to my grandmother; still see her looking away so that no one would notice the tear rolling down her wrinkled cheek.

7

Bells and Smells

'If music be the food of love I must improve my diet.'
Eleanor Weill, *Earthly Passions*, 1928

I passed through Mr Rhodes's class and moved on to Mrs
Rishworth. Tricky Mrs Rishworth. She taught us how to do
joined-up writing. Hour after hour we would copy letters off
the blackboard until all our calligraphy matched her plump,
round hand. The we spent the rest of our lives trying to give it
a character of our own. Mrs Rishworth was in charge of our
musical appreciation, too. Not that it included anything special.
The only instruments we had were ones that you could hit –
triangles, tambourines, bells, drums and castanets which were
called, at this early stage in our musical development, 'clappers'.
Perhaps 'castanets' was too complicated and foreign-sounding a
name, or maybe we'd have trouble reproducing it in joined-up
writing.

There were also cymbals – my favourite. I loved playing the
cymbals, until one day when my aim faltered and I succeeded in
slicing off part of my left thumb. I still have the scar.

But the cymbals were eclipsed by one other musical activity –
conducting. Armed with a short wooden stick which Mrs
Rishworth had borrowed from a ball-bearing bagatelle, we were
allowed to take it in turns at beating time. I loved it, but put in

rather too much expression for Mrs Rishworth's liking. She preferred one of the girls' more restrained styles, rather than mine which was based on Sir Malcolm Sargent at the Last Night of the Proms. I could not understand why she rated this ploddy girl, who simply drew a triangular shape in the air, better than me, with my sweeps and twirls. But she did, and I was relegated to a triangle in this clearly pedestrian percussion orchestra.

The only time I ever saw Mrs Rishworth in awe of anyone was when she was in the presence of the man who was the Sir Malcolm Sargent of Wharfedale – Charles Bainbridge. He was tall with chiselled features and Brylcreemed hair, and he dressed every day, I was sure, in the white tie and tails in which I saw him conduct. He waved the baton – a proper white one with a cork handle – at the Wharfedale Music Festival, held in the King's Hall at Ilkley, and at concerts throughout the West Riding. We were scheduled, along with other local schools, to take part in a concert at Otley Mechanics Institute, a building which made the King's Hall look like the Royal Albert Hall. Among the songs we were to perform was 'Westering Home':

> Westering home and a song in the air,
> Light in the eye and it's goodbye to care,
> Laughter o' love and a welcoming there,
> Isle of my heart, my own one.

There was, at one point, a reference to 'Isla', and in the final rehearsal at the Institute, Mrs Rishworth, having been unsure of how the locals of the Western Isles would pronounce the name of the home to which they were westering, put up her hand.

Charles Bainbridge lowered his baton and looked sternly over the top of his half-moon spectacles.

'Mrs Rishworth?'

I had never seen simpering before. It was not too over the top, but it was simpering nevertheless. 'Mr Bainbridge,' and a girly giggle, 'do you think you could tell my class whether to pronounce it "Eye-la" or "Iz-la"?'

He paused. 'Yes. Eye-la.' No expression. He turned, he took up the baton and we westered on home. I never saw Mrs Rishworth simper again, and I also noticed that Charles Bainbridge's conducting was very similar to my own.

I did succeed with one instrument. The voice. I inherited a quite passable treble. My father had sung since his childhood, even making it as far as a choir festival at the Royal Albert Hall, and I found that my own voice was capable of getting me through an audition into the church choir – head-boy eventually – on account of seniority as much as vocal dexterity. But I wasn't bad. I even managed the first, solo verse of 'Once in Royal David's City' from the back of the church for a few Christmases.

Choir practices were taken by Mr Atkinson, a lovely old man with bandy legs and a gold watch chain in the waistcoat of his grey suit. Every week I would cast covetous eyes over his two-tone grey Rover 90. As our treble voices trilled and soared he would bravely warn 'Don't force it!', but he was hopeless at keeping control and the cry of 'Boys, boys!' would echo up into the rafters of the church on Mondays, which were 'boys only' rehearsals, the men joining us on Thursdays. Then things were more disciplined and my dad and my uncle George Pennock (uncle on account of him being my godfather) would help to keep order, along with a local garage owner, Harry Chambers, who had a high tenor voice and a quick temper, slapping the back of the head of any boy who misbehaved within an arm's length. We weren't riotous, just spirited. Especially on Mondays when 'Acky' couldn't keep control.

After practice we'd sneak out across the churchyard to a tomb with a 'V'-shaped lid, a bit like the roof of a house. A cross was embossed on its green and mossy lid and it was known as the 'Devil's Grave'. I suppose every churchyard has one. It was probably the final resting place of some well-to-do harmless spinster, but to us it was far more scary. New boys would be given their initiation rites pinned down on the Devil's Grave. What were these unpleasant customs? They were tickled until they couldn't stand any more. Tough, eh?

And then there were the conkers. The churchyard was surrounded by chestnut trees, and autumn saw us throwing fat sticks up into them to send the shiny brown fruit raining down into our waiting hands and on to our heads, along with the occasional stick.

There were special, secret conker treatments to make them hard. My own forty-sixer was soaked in vinegar and dried in the oven. It eventually succumbed to the church choir tearaway's conker which wasn't a conker at all, but a steel nut, relieved of its bolt and tied to the end of a piece of string. By sleight of hand he would deftly swap a rather pathetic-looking conker on the other end of the string for the steel substitute and the last I saw of my forty-sixer was a few ivory-coloured fragments soaring over the graveyard.

He was mad, this red-haired lad, but we were all secretly in awe of him. He was the first of us to have 'cow-horn' handlebars on his bike and he could give vent to a belch that could be heard three streets away. He could even belch tunes. He had a sort of henchman who tried to keep up with him, and failed, but then he was a hard act to follow.

He used to fasten the biggest threepenny bangers to the back forks of his bike on Bonfire night and then light them and proceed to cycle off down the street. When the bangers went off they lifted his back wheels clean off the ground. He's still alive. They tell me he's settled down. Shame, really. I wonder if he can still belch?

With choir practice on Monday and Thursday evenings and Matins and Evensong on Sundays, I seemed to spend quite a lot of time in church. Sermons were usually around twenty minutes, except in the reign of one Welsh curate who rejoiced under the name of Llewellyn Rees Howell. I liked Mr Howell, but his sermons were always at least thirty-five minutes long. You could read at least two *War Picture Library* books in that time, and get through two bits of PK chewing gum, the remainder of which was stuck under the pew for later. Much of it is still there.

Church, like most other undertakings in Yorkshire, was not some outspoken commitment of faith, it was just what we did – instinctive, natural – Dad in the back row of the choir and me in the front. Mum ran the Brownies and my sister was a Gnome. In Brownies, that is.

Because of this the church has always been a part of my life, not unthinkingly or unquestioningly, but certainly naturally, and sometimes more frequently than others. Having spent the best part of ten years in a purple cassock and white surplice, it came as a relief to have a break from it when I first left home. I wondered if I would bother going back. But it was only a half-hearted wonder, perhaps born of laziness, the prospect of having a lie-in on a Sunday morning. I still go to church on an irregular basis, sometimes to the little corrugated 'tin tabernacle' in our village, sometimes to the abbey up the road where a dozen Anglican Benedictine monks welcome the locals to partake of their morning mass, and sometimes to Winchester Cathedral where I can enjoy the singing of a fine choir. I suppose I'm a sort of C of E tart, putting myself about a bit. I go into churches and cathedrals when I'm away from home, seldom for a service, but mostly for a quick prayer. 'To send one up.' To light a candle for my dad.

Many churches have a majesty and a peace born of ages of worship and it is easy to feel at peace inside them, even if you only sit there for a few minutes and breathe deeply. Sometimes feeling is enough. It is not always necessary to express or articulate beliefs, and an ability to do so does not necessarily make for a greater depth of faith. I find the evangelical approach to Christianity too hearty for my liking, a bit embarrassing. I'm still uneasy with 'the peace' in the modern service, knowing that the person next to me is bound to turn the other way just as I'm offering my hand. But then I've always been a 'quiet churchman', if you see what I mean.

And I've always enjoyed the language of the Book of Common Prayer. I grew up with it. Familiarity in worship counts for a lot. And language. It is not necessary to understand every nuance of every word to be spiritually uplifted by the sound of the words themselves. Matins in Winchester Cathedral is especially comforting – the Venite, the Te Deum, the Magnificat – wonderful, wonderful words which, I suppose, evoke the security and comfort of childhood.

Anyway, that's my bit on religion, in a nutshell. It's a belief. A faith. Simple as that. I don't like going on about it, and in spite of the fact that I presented *Songs of Praise* on BBC1 for five years or so I don't like using my faith as some kind of banner. It's not that I'm ashamed of it; it's just that I've always believed it to be a personal journey rather than a corporate advertisement. And it is a journey, sometimes with a very distant destination. Sometimes I get lost. Or it's a bit foggy. I have bad patches, times when I can't seem to get through. I once heard a nun describe her difficulty in praying as 'firing blanks', and there are times when it does feel like that. I have spells of not going to church, then I pick up again. I pray some nights and not others – silently – but the deep, underlying belief is always there, if sometimes obscured by other things in life. I pray for my children, my family and my friends, always in the same order. A sort of personal litany.

If you were to put me on the spot and ask me what I really believed in, then the answer is a simple one. It is not an old man with a big white beard, though I seem to see Him and talk to Him now and then. It is not necessarily an unshakeable belief in every last word of the scriptures or all those conundrums that mightier intellects than mine struggle with. It is a belief, pure and simple, in goodness. And love. And thoughtfulness. Lord Hailsham summed it up for me in his memoirs, *A Sparrow's Flight*, when he said, 'Despite all the destruction and malevolence in the world, I do not believe in a malevolent deity. I do not believe in an irrational universe. I believe in goodness, truthfulness, loving kindness, beauty, generosity, loyalty. They all exist and are qualities which demand just as much explanation as malevolence, mendaciousness, cruelty, ugliness, meanness and treachery.'

That'll do.

8

The Call of Nature

'When you hear her call you, follow.
No good ever came of fighting nature.'
J.D. Fane, *The Simple Life*, 1923

I blame it all on my mother. If she hadn't whisked us out of the house for a walk almost every day then I'd never have noticed nature. As it was, I grew up with an insatiable curiosity about anything that crawled, flew, swam or grew. I don't remember the moment it started; it has always been there.

Those early days by the river, on the moors and in the woods fostered an interest in natural history in all its forms, and I can't quite say why plants and gardening were my chosen direction, rather than veterinary science. No; that's not true. I can. I was not academically bright enough at school. I'm not being modest, just realistic. I suppose I'm brighter now, but I was your classic late developer. My brain seemed fuddled at school, filled with fog. There was plenty of enthusiasm there – always has been – but not much in the way of intellectual back-up.

And I did like plants, and my dad always said I was a sucker for a lame duck. Perhaps I thought, even then, that plants needed my help more than animals who had quite enough champions.

At the age of ten there were two television programmes in particular that fanned my interest in nature: one was Peter Scott's

Look, and the other was a children's programme called *Out of Doors*. I was given the *Out of Doors* book one Christmas. I still have it. One of its features was about building a vivarium, a small tank filled with rocks and mosses and bits of twig, as well as a small pool of water, in which you could observe frogs and newts.

One of my greatest bits of good luck as a kid was having a dad who was good with his hands. Dad made me a vivarium, wooden framed with a glass front and sliding glass lid. I filled the inside with bits of moss from the wood, a glass bowl to act as a pool, and assorted gnarled branches and twigs. I never had the good fortune to find a newt, but a small frog, Gladys, seemed blissfully happy there.

I went on nature walks, at first with Mum and Kath, and later alone. Just looking. When I finally went to Kew the same sort of thing was encouraged, though then it was known as botanising.

Before long I realised that the books I had – including the *Observer's Book of Pond Life*, the three Ladybird bird books and W. Percival Westell's red and gilt-covered *British Birds*, given to me by Mrs Cunnington ('Cookie'), our next-door neighbour – were not answering all my questions, so I joined the Ilkley-based Wharfedale Naturalists' Society.

It was mindblowing. We had visits to Farnley reservoir near Otley to see great crested grebes and waders. We watched moorland birds such as grouse and curlews, and there were evening lectures in the winter where experts brought along 'lantern slides' and, if you were lucky, real, live specimens.

Walter Flesher was our most famous local naturalist. He had only one arm, but I remember him being completely carried away when he talked, and gesticulating wildly with the one that remained. He was an excellent radio broadcaster, too, with tremendous powers of description.

And then, one evening, we had as our speaker George Cansdale.

In the 1950s and 60s, when BBC children's television featured an 'animal expert' it was usually George Cansdale. He was a tall, well-built, well-spoken man with short grey hair, a grey suit and a grey moustache. It seemed strange to me that someone who was so much a man of nature should look exactly like a bank manager. But I forgot all that when, towards the end of his talk, he asked if some of the younger members of the audience would like to come to the front of the Congregational Church Hall and see what he had brought.

We duly obliged. He took three small brown sacks from his suitcase and pulled out three snakes, draping them around our necks. I can remember the thrill of it even now. I don't think I had seen a snake so close-to, and I'd certainly never handled one. It was dry and warm, not at all slimy. You could feel its scales, feel its muscle power. I was entranced. I hardly wanted to give it back. But I did, and George Cansdale popped it back into its sack and back into the suitcase.

I suppose that evening was my first real encounter with 'celebrity', or with someone I regarded as a celebrity. A few weeks later, when I saw George on television, still in the grey suit, I turned around boastfully to my sister and said, 'I've met him.'

What would be great, I thought, would be to have a sort of wildlife sanctuary in our back garden. I drew diagrams of rows of hutches peopled by different breeds of rabbit and guinea pig. My sister and I had two rabbits – Lulu and Wilmer – and I reasoned that adding to them would not be too difficult, if I had a shed with these rows of hutches inside. But sheds cost money. So I built a greenhouse.

It was a simple structure, three feet wide, six feet long and five feet high. Inside it I grew half a dozen geraniums, a couple of spider plants and a false castor oil palm. Oh, and I had two mice in a cage, just to keep the animal dream going. One morning I rolled back the polythene door, only to discover that a cat had got in during the night and frightened the two mice to death. Thinking about it, this is probably the one event that influenced my decision to be a gardener rather than a vet – plants clearly had much stronger constitutions.

I began with a small piece of garden just outside the greenhouse. I sowed a patch of carefully raked earth with mesembryan-themum seeds. But I forgot to tell my dad. They grew up with a perfect footprint shape in the centre where Dad had trodden just after the seeds had begun to germinate.

I sowed alyssum and was surprised when the plants that grew were only three or four inches high. In the picture on the packet they had looked to me as big as the hydrangea that grew in the corner of the garden. Or the 'Lone Ranger' as we called it.

My mum was the gardener at home and it was she who encour-aged me. And discouraged my sister and me from damaging what was already there. 'Mind the Lone Ranger!' was her frequent cry as Kath and I careered around the garden on our bikes.

But my gardening activities were not confined to our own back garden. Mickey Hudson, who lived opposite, had a larger patch of ground than we did, and his dad was a greengrocer so he got free wooden tomato trays for sowing his seeds in. Now we were both regular lads – football in the street and cricket against the bus-garage wall at the bottom of the road – but we really took to gardening. None of the other kids bothered to join in, but neither did they try to dissuade us. They just shrugged and left us to it. It was what we did, and never once did they criticise our efforts. We grew marigolds and clarkias, godetias and alyssum – hardy annuals in the main – and produced quite a decent show with them. I had already decided – aged about ten – that I was going to be a gardener. Mickey had a better idea. He said he was going to be a postman. Postmen got up early, but they were finished by lunchtime and he could then garden for the rest of the day.

He ended up working in a bank. But then earlier this year I bumped into his sister Janet on The Grove. 'How's Mickey?' I asked.

'Oh, he's fine.'

'What's he doing nowadays? Still in the bank?'

'No,' she said. 'He's a postman.'

It's good to know that he fulfilled his ambition, even if it was late in life. I completely forgot to ask her if he still liked gardening.

Every Saturday morning Mickey and I would exchange views on the previous night's television viewing: *Gardening Club*, with Percy Thrower or, as we used to call him, Percy Chucker.

'Percy said . . .' would begin our conversation. Or there would be some covetous remark about a particular plant. 'Wish we 'ad one o' them.'

There was little chance of us ending up with anything exotic. The local nurseries were small and basic. Garden centres did not come into being until a good five or ten years later, and anyway we didn't have that kind of money, so our range of plants would be strictly limited to what the packets of Mr Cuthberts or Bees Seeds from Woolworths could produce for us.

Every year in the King's Hall there would be the Trades Fair, when all the local shopkeepers and tradesmen, from florists to cabinetmakers, would show off their wares for a week. Mr Oliver was the local florist, and his stand was an Aladdin's cave of dried flowers, massive arrangements of foliage and rubber plants. How I wanted a rubber plant! It was my first Latin name – *Ficus elastica*. It had to be a rubber plant with a name like that. But it cost five bob. That's 25p. No chance. I looked, and I drooled. Every year.

Pocket money was a shilling. You could buy two or three packets of seeds for that. But I do remember being jealous of a lad who had three shillings' pocket money a week and used it, quite extravagantly I reckoned, to buy a small, red plastic propagator with the seeds already sown in the vermiculite it contained.

What was wrong with a biscuit tin and a sheet of glass? Better to spend your money on decent seeds rather than on one small gadget. But I did envy him that red propagator. And it didn't last. He was into stamps by the following week.

My sister's arrival in 1954 – shame about our back garden.

Mum holding Kath and Auntie Bee holding Arnold (her younger son). Behind are Martin and his father, my Uncle Bert, me in a smart striped tie and David, Auntie Bee's elder son.

Kath, bored, Mum, apprehensive and me, smiling.

Right: Grandma Titchmarsh gets to hold the baby. I am not smiling anymore.

Above: At Blackpool Pleasure Beach, aged 6.

Left: A photo that stands on my bedside table – walking down by the river in the 1950s. My dad's is the only shop-bought coat.

Our first transport – the Austin pick-up. The only vehicle in Nelson Road.

With Kath and Cindy on the moors. We always walked on Sundays.

Me, and my valentine Jill, in our first year at
Secondary School.

The reluctant scout at the lock
gates on a hike.

The same beret in use at a music
hall. Not much has changed then.

Sweet children: Me and Kath aged about 11 and 6.

Right: Butter wouldn't melt – the choirboy at Ilkley.

On holiday at Butlins in the 60s.

9

A Bit of a Nerve

'They say that knowledge is power. But knowledge is power only when given away; then it empowers. Knowledge retained is knowledge squandered.'

Professor A.T. Sparks, *Cultural Evolution*, 1948

I can remember the conversation quite vividly. 'So are you really going to be a gardener?' asked Mickey. 'There's no money in it.' (The banker in him was coming out, though he probably didn't recognise it.)

'Yep. I wouldn't mind being Percy Chucker.'

'Fat chance. Do you know 'ow many people there are in Britain?'

'Nope.'

'Fifty million. And there's only one Percy Chucker. What chance 'ave you got?'

'Not much, I suppose.'

'So why don't you be a postman like me?'

I didn't answer. Was it really impossible for me to do what I wanted for a living rather than simply settling on gardening as a hobby? I wanted to be in a garden all the time. And Percy Thrower? Oh, I knew I hadn't a cat-in-hell's chance of getting his job. But I could watch him on the box and dream about what it would be like. Like all children I was entranced by the glamour of telly, but stronger than that was the love I had for gardening, and a need to share that passion and not just keep it to myself. That's what Percy did. I wanted to do it, too.

I wanted to feel special – all children do – but I never set out to be famous or even considered the implications of fame. I came from a small Yorkshire town. Telly was something that happened in London – or America – a million miles away. I was a realist. Oh, a dreamer, yes, always – I still am – but always with at least one foot firmly on the ground, or in most cases in it. My mum and dad brought Kath and me up to believe that life owed us nothing, but that if we were lucky and worked hard we might get a chance to do something special. Some people never get that chance, but there are others who get it and just don't notice it. They're too busy looking the other way.

Sir Dirk Bogarde had a neat way of putting it. He said that many people are too single-minded. They go through life with one burning ambition, their sights set on some distant goal – a sort of door at the end of a corridor. They don't notice the other doors down the side of the corridor that are wide open, often with unexpected opportunities beckoning them in. Determinedly they march on to that final door, and when they get there it is bolted. However hard they hammer, it will not yield. But if only they had taken a diversion through one of the side doors, they might have discovered that it led to the same destination. It's a persuasive sort of argument.

I suppose that's what happened to me. I took a few side doors along the way – *Pebble Mill, Songs of Praise* – because the prospect looked interesting. And I had a bit of luck, too. I had the good fortune to meet one or two people who could see what I was good at, sometimes when I couldn't see it myself.

The trouble is I have never been blessed with much in the way of self-confidence. I still wait to be rumbled; still wait for the voice saying, 'Come away! That'll do!' But over the years I suppose I've found that two good substitutes for confidence are punctuality and reliability. If you turn up on time and do a decent job you don't let people down and they might employ you again.

There are pitfalls, of course. You've got to maintain your own standards, which might sometimes make you a bit exacting, but that's only to be expected. It's when you start being tricky to prove that you're the boss that things begin to go wrong. Life can throw up its own problems without bringing in those of your own invention, and bitterness, if allowed to grow, eats away at you from the inside until you're left with a hollow shell. Better by far to smile sweetly, go home and rant to her indoors. That way you get it off your chest and nobody's any the wiser.

It's not a saintly approach, just a practical one. I've worked with people who have astounded me with their generosity, and I've worked with mean buggers, too. I realised very early on which of these two groups of folk lasted longest and found it easier to live with themselves, and which ones turned into miserable old sods.

And anyway, success is a journey, not a destination. My accountant told me that.

10

Moving on Up

'There comes a point in every child's life when he suddenly real-izes that life is a conspiracy. A conspiracy, moreover, that everyone else is in on except him.'

Dr James Teal, *First Principles of Growth*, 1953

The eleven plus baffled me. It seemed to be couched in some sort of code. I don't think that from the moment I picked up the paper I expected to pass. My memory is of a classroom of boys and girls silently hunched over individual, ink-stained desks, and of a loudly ticking clock. John Brown, the boy who was really good at knitting, seemed to be beavering away. I tried to make a stab at things but clearly it was futile. It came as no surprise when I failed. John Brown passed.

Did I feel a failure? Yes, I did. But then I think it confirmed my suspicions that there were those in life who had brains that could cope with arithmetic and verbs and dates and facts, and there were others who had different sorts of brains. I was one of them. But I did feel things. It didn't seem to matter. Not in exams, anyway.

My final teacher at All Saints Junior was Mr Swann. He was a good sort, thorough and robust in his delivery and ace at reading poetry and stories. I remember him reading Rider Haggard's *Alan Quartermain* and leaving us late each afternoon with a cliffhanger to make us eager to take up the story the following day. But I did think that Umslopogas was a strange name for a native. Affirmation of Mr Swann's brightness came when he stood as a candidate in the General Election. I remember being hugely impressed seeing him pictured on his handbill with Hugh Gaitskell. Not that I was in any way knowledgeable about politics, or interested in them, it's just that I'd seen pictures of Gaitskell on the television news. Mr Swann was clearly a clever man.

It was a pretty unremarkable scholastic career so far. No prizes to speak of, except one for a pressed wild flower collection – each dried and withered bloom fastened into a scrapbook of rough grey paper with stamp hinges. Spidery writing with my first fountain pen annotates things likc 'Evergreen alkanet' and 'Jack-by-the-hedge', and tissue paper that would have been wrapped around our daily loaf of bread is interleaved to stop the pages from sticking together.

I bought the *Observer's Book of Wild Animals* with the book token that was my prize, and had it autographed by the great and the good who came to talk to the Wharfedale Naturalists' Society.

The nerves began to build during the summer holidays. I sat on large boulders by the river, while the amber water swirled around me, and wondered what a new school would be like. Ilkley County Secondary School. Why county? Ilkley was a town. I didn't care much. Tried to put it out of my mind.

At the end of August my mother took me to the Co-op for my first school uniform. Mr Hay came out from the back of his shop, through the swinging door fitted with a mirror, finishing off his lunchtime sandwich. He was tall and thin, balding and pale, probably on account of never being allowed to finish his lunch. He was despatched through the door once more by my mother, and returned carrying a navy blue blazer with a badge on the breast pocket, grey shorts, grey shirt and navy blue tie with a diagonal mid-blue stripe. And a cap. Scary.

I would need something to carry my books in. Leather brief-cases and satchels were too expensive. We settled, instead, on a small cardboard suitcase that was coloured mid-brown, as if to simulate cowhide. Over the next year it revealed its true colours of grey, as the outer coating was bumped off on my bike, and washed off by rain. The leather briefcase was, in the end, the only way forward, and the soggy cardboard was consigned to the dustbin.

The new building of Ilkley County Secondary School was due to be finished after Christmas, so our autumn term, as first-formers, would be in a large stone-built house at the top of Oakburn Road. It's name was 'One Oak', and it gave me my first taste of school proper. School that meant business. School that was work, not fun.

So what sort of lad was this Alan Titchmarsh, aged eleven? Small of stature, and skinny. Crooked teeth (no change there). A bit silly. Boundlessly enthusiastic about anything to do with nature, and art, and completely clueless about anything to do with numbers.

And art? Where did that suddenly come from? Oh, it had been there all the time. I liked painting, though was not especially good at it. And I liked the theatre – not that we went a lot, except to the pantomime at the Bradford Alhambra or the Leeds Grand. I had a small part in the 'Pace Egg' play at Junior School, the Easter one about St George and the Dragon. I played Little Devil Doubt, clad in yellow tights, a green tunic and a yellow hat with horns poking through it:

Here am I, Little Devil Doubt,
If you don't give me money, I'll sweep you all out;
Money I want, and money I crave,
If you don't give me money, I'll send you all to the grave.

And I then proceeded, with my mother's dustpan and brush, to sweep up the coppers that were flung by appreciative parents on to the school playground. It was not a large part, which is probably why I can still remember it, but it must have sown the performing seed: I got a laugh. I rather liked that.

I liked the company of girls, though as yet had little experience of them. I liked the company of boys, but being small and enthusiastic I was painfully aware of the fact that I was prime bullying material. And I liked my own company. In my attic bedroom of an evening and at weekends I would make models of theatres and television studios, with miniature cameras cut from balsa wood. Why? Just because it fascinated me, not because I longed to be on television. I loved making small and miniature worlds into which I could disappear. With a strange irony, those studios and stages eventually became the means by which my world would be enlarged, replacing my privacy and solitude with national recognition. Funny twist, really.

I made miniature gardens, too, with tiny borders, a pool and a greenhouse from something called 'Floral', which was a sort of gardening equivalent of the Airfix kits out of which most normal lads made aircraft and ships. Oh, I made them, too, but I was too impatient to read the instructions first, and so there were always a few bits left over at the end.

And I was, in spite of being something of a loner, a chatterbox in company. 'Vaccinated with a gramophone needle,' my dad called it. But when you're passionate about something, it's hard to be quiet. It was this that led to my downfall at 'One Oak'.

It was a grey and drizzly day. Showery. But we were sent out to 'play', nevertheless. And when you were out you stayed out. The school porch was out of bounds. And then it bucketed down, and I was so deep in conversation with one lad that we ran, unthinkingly, into the porch for shelter. The next sensation was one of flight. We were both elevated by our collars by Mr Melville, a tall, athletic guy who taught English and games. The girls all fancied him to death. The boys all thought he fancied himself.

'What are you doing, Titchmarsh, Bradley?'

'Talking, sir.'

'No change there, then.'

'We were just sheltering, sir. It was raining.'

He looked out of the window. 'It's not raining now.'

'No, but it was, sir.'

'The porch is out of bounds.'

I don't think we saw it coming. I think we just thought we were in for a telling off.

'Hold your hands out.'

There was a moment, just a fleeting moment, when I wondered if he was going to give us a sweet. And then I saw the cane. Long. Sinewy. New.

Our hands were out in front of us, held there by a kind of horrorstruck paralysis. I heard the swish, and I saw Mr Melville lower the cane before I felt any pain at all. And then it came, stinging, penetrating, biting through to the bone in its agony. The tears sprang uncontrollably to my eyes and my fingers curled inwards.

'Again!' he instructed.

It was hard to straighten your fingers when you knew what was going to happen. Two thwacks later we were ejected into the playground with hands wedged firmly into our armpits, trying to look like brave victors in some kind of battle of wills, but feeling stupid. And hurt. God, it hurt. A deep, searing, throbbing pain through palms and knuckles. Writing, for the rest of the day, was an uncomfortable process.

The only sensation remotely close to it came a few years later in the Parks Department nursery while I was emptying flower-pots of their compost on a dark, icy, winter afternoon, when my hands, so chilled with cold, began to throb in that same, bone-numbing agony. For now it was enough to try to wipe away the tears with a sleeve, and hope your mates didn't notice. Stephen Bradley said nothing. And neither did I.

I didn't tell them about it when I got home. I might have got another clout for getting into trouble.

There were two sorts of parents, it seemed to me: those whose kids could do no wrong – who would be around at the school complaining that little Johnny had been chastised when he was really a little angel – and those who, if you were punished at school, would punish you again when you got home for getting into bother. There didn't seem to be a middle ground.

My parents were of the latter school. They weren't strict in Victorian terms, but they expected good manners and good behaviour. Just because we hadn't much money didn't mean that we didn't know how to hold a knife and fork properly. We were expected to say 'please' and 'thank you' and not answer back. It was hard sometimes.

'There's nowt wrong wi' good manners,' would be the expla-nation. As a result, I can only walk on the outside of the pave-ment when accompanying a female down the street, and the deft move of passing behind her to swap sides when we cross over the road has resulted in more than one friend looking around to find out where I've gone. Heigh-ho.

When physical punishment did come at home (and it wasn't often), the instrument of application would be a whalebone hairbrush. It sounds barbaric now, but it was a swift slap to the backside, not the hands, and I can honestly remember it happening on no more than two or three occasions. God! How we used to run up the stairs in front of whichever parent was brandishing that brush! I don't think it has tarnished my life. We don't have a whalebone hairbrush now, but I've probably exercised the laying on of hands about the same number of times with my own kids. I never enjoyed it, and I always seemed to end up apologising half an hour later in a flurry of hugs and tears.

At 'One Oak' we were introduced to cross-country running over the moors. I liked that. I was nimble of foot and fairly good over long distances, being wiry. And I enjoyed the scenery. I was less good at sprinting. Sports days were never much of a chance for Titchmarsh to shine; not a natural competitor. Or sportsman. Even today, when I can occasionally be persuaded to play cricket for the Lord's Taverners, my wife coaches me in bowling and batting a week in advance. It's a heavy cross for a man to bear, having a wife who once had a trial for the Surrey County Ladies Cricket Team. Still, Sir Colin Cowdrey was once caught out off my bowling in a Lord's Taverners match. I wish my dad had been around to see it.

But back to school. We did art, properly, rather than daubing, with Miss Gill. Ah, Miss Gill. Shirley Joy Gill. The first teacher who ever aroused any kind of . . . well . . . you know . . . feeling in me. She was in her twenties, tall and elegant, wrote very artistically with a fountain pen containing red ink, and would bend over her desk just a little too low in a crisp white blouse that was perfectly respectable when she stood upright. When she bent down, concentration became more difficult. It was not at all sordid; just, well, rather lovely.

She used to play badminton with another teacher, round and jolly Miss Williams, and it was rather a comical sight – the long and the short of it.

Miss Gill took us for art appreciation as well as art itself, and we filled book after book with articles from newspapers on Augustus John and Pablo Picasso, learning how Van Gogh had cut off his ear and staring into the mirror of Van Eyck's Mrs and Mrs Arnolfini, and looking at the details of the hairs on the dog. I owe Miss Gill a lot, and I did rather fancy her.

In the New Year, the new school was finished and we moved down to Valley Drive. Instead of walking to school, I now caught the bus, or went on my bike, the new building having come complete with bike shed. There was a brand-new stage with lighting, a large and airy art room, a science lab with gas taps on the benches and a science mistress with a booming voice who was built like Andy Capp's wife, Flo, in Reg Smythe's cartoons. Improper fraction, we called her. Top heavy.

I looked forward to science as a chance to see behind the façade of natural history. The inside workings, if you like. Cutting frogs up and things. Like Beatrix Potter used to do when she was drawing her characters from life.

Our first lesson consisted of writing out the rules of the laboratory on the back page of our exercise books. The last of these, to be written in capital letters, followed by three exclamation marks and underlined three times was: ACIDS MUST BE RESPECTED!!!

I felt excited. I smelled danger. We were going to deal with acids and things like that. Real science and chemistry. Over the next four years I saw nothing more exciting than a bunsen burner and a Petri dish. Oh, and lead shot. The science mistress was very big on physics in general and specific gravity in particular. 'Come and get an S.G. bottle!' Oh, God! Here we go again.

One misdemeanour by any pupil and that was it: 'Okay, take out your books and revise.' It seemed to happen every week. What she did with the acids I have no idea.

Maybe I'm being unfair. Maybe we did more biology than I remember. But I know that I didn't enjoy her lessons, and I should have done.

It was the thin end of the wedge. My eagerness to learn was gradually being replaced by a sinking feeling. My stumbling blocks were: Maths (numbers always a mystery), French (good ear for oral but too thick for the intricacies of verbs), Geography (loud teacher with boring voice).

Of the subjects I liked: Science (see above), English (one of those picky teachers for whom you could never do anything right. The biggest crime in essays was to use your imagination), Rural Studies (you're in the A stream so you can only do it for the first term of the first year, after which it is reserved for the B, C and D streams), Woodwork (ditto).

History had always inspired. There was a kind of magic about it. To visit an old castle and touch its stones was to be in touch with people who had gone before. Somehow they did not seem so far away. Bolton Abbey was a real place, and the de Romilly lad who had drowned in the river, and his mother who had died of a broken heart, were real people. History was not old and dusty, it was alive, and it was responsible for the way we were now, it seemed to me. But the flame was not fanned, it was smothered. We were just spouted at, and made to write down lists. The teacher of history was the same man who had charge of geography. He did his best to fit us into his busy schedule. I tried hard to remember the Kings and Queens of England from 1066 in order, but failed. If only the teacher had given us a mnemonic. I found it thirty years later:

Willie, Willie, Harry, Ste,
Harry, Dick, John, Harry 3.
1, 2, 3, Neds
Richard 2,
Henry 4, 5, 6, then who?
Edward 4, 5
Dick the Bad,
Harrys Twain
And Ned the Lad.
Mary,
Bessie,
James the Vain
Charlie,
Charlie, James again.
William and Mary
Anna Gloria
Four Georges
William
And
Victoria

All of which is added to the list of things I know now that I wished I'd known then.

So, setting aside the things I was useless at, and the things I liked but which didn't like me, I was left with Art and Drama, both in the hands of David Wildman who turned from an encouraging teacher into an encouraging friend for the rest of his life. He could be grumpy and crusty on a bad day, but he had a prodigious talent and was a fine artist and draughtsman. He would write plays for the school, and design sets and costumes. He was the driving force behind the Ilkley Players until his untimely death a few years ago, and he encouraged me in Art and gave me opportunities to tackle Drama both in school and with the Players.

Along with Harry Rhodes from Junior School, he remained a great influence. Now they are both gone and I remember them happily and with gratitude.

It's easy to blame your teachers when you don't do well, and to be fair to them all I was immature for my years; my mind probably wandered more than it should have done. But like all kids of that tender age, I needed encouragement more than anything else. I was an eager puppy, intellectually younger than my age, and all I seemed to be getting, poor, over-sensitive little soul that I was, was the 'shut-up and sit down' approach.

I was interested, but it seemed to me that most of my teachers weren't that bothered – apart from Mr Rhodes and Mr Wildman; they were both encouragers and enablers. When you thought that you could not do something, Mr R and Mr W would be the ones to say you could. Others who were taught by them will feel the same, and every pupil that ever there was will have fond memories of those teachers who made their subjects come alive.

Good teachers somehow manage to rise above the low pay, the ridiculous demands on their time and those disruptive kids who just don't seem to want to learn. They are at the other end of the spectrum from the teacher who bumped into me on Ilkley car park a few months ago.

'Titchmarsh!' she said, as though she couldn't believe her eyes. 'Yes?'

'Well!' she said, accusingly. 'We never thought you'd amount to much!'

I felt as though I'd disappointed her.

11

Girls and Stuff

'Girls are like fags; you wish you could give them up but you know that's about as likely as the Pope chucking it all in and setting up a hostel for fallen women. I wish I was the Pope.'

Mike Upjohn, *Slightly Soiled*, 1987

Having a sister does have its advantages as far as I can see. It's easier to form relationships with the opposite sex when you've had a chance to observe them at close quarters before committing yourself. Not that it made things any easier when it came to asking them out. And loving someone in a brotherly way is quite different from falling in love hook, line and sinker.

The first time it happened I would lie awake at night wondering if the object of my adulation – the local chemist's daughter – would ever whisper three little words in my ear. She did, eventually. But they were not the ones I had in mind.

'You disgusting thing!' There was an echo about them. It was probably the water in my ears – that and the lofty roof of the swimming baths. Every Friday night I went there, to the Grammar Baths, attached to the school up Cowpasture Road.

Hardly Olympic sized, the indoor pool was fifty feet long and twenty-five feet wide, but it had a shallow end where I could just get my nose above the water and a deep end that I had just proved I could not stand up in. The daft thing was that I could still feel embarrassed even though I'd nearly drowned. Pathetic really, but then I did have a tremendous crush on her. She was dark and slim, eleven years old. Her lips and cheeks were pink, her eyebrows neat and black, and her eyelashes and sleek bob of hair darkened by the water. I can see her now as I saw her then, clear as day in her green swimsuit. Not that she'd ever looked twice at me – except to sneer. Now, here I was, lying on the cold, wet concrete surround of the pool, shivering and sodden, holding her hand and struggling for breath. I'd thought quite a lot about holding that hand, but I'd never thought about drowning.

She pulled me out of the pool after I'd gone under three times. I finally decided that although I might draw attention to myself, waving would be marginally less embarrassing than drowning. I slithered on to the pool surround like a lump of wet cod. Having fished me out and delivered her opinion, she reclaimed her hand and that was it: my first and last physical contact with the object of my dreams, over in a matter of seconds.

I knew that the reason I'd gone under was that someone had jumped on top of me. One of the bigger lads at the swimming club probably. But then they were all bigger than me. Not exactly a hunk at eleven and a half. Not exactly fanciable either; sluttering and panting, trying to rid my lungs of the burning sensation of water. But I did wish she hadn't found me disgusting, even if she had saved my life.

I don't remember seeing her again. We just grew apart. Well, she did. I met her mum a year or two ago and plucked up the courage to ask about her. She'd moved to Canada and become a tax inspector. I stayed here and became a gardener, but ever since then I've wondered idly if my interest was kindled by the fact that her name was Heather.

To claim that Heather was the first object of my affections is not strictly true. She was the first girl I fancied physically. There had been others, but they were more like friends who were girls rather than girlfriends proper. At five, in Mrs Osmond's class at the New County Infants school, there was Kathy who wore a fluffy white cardigan with pink pom-poms. I went off her when she pushed one of them up her nose the day she forgot her hanky.

At nine there was Gin, short for Virginia. A blonde beauty. She lived at the top of our street and we used to sweep up the clippings from our privet hedge together. She bought me a box of Newberry fruits one Christmas – it was the first time I blushed. I don't remember the second.

At ten, at Junior School, there was Anthea, whose father was a farmer. She'd arrive at school every morning in the Dormobile that picked up the kids from the outlying farms at Langbar and Addingham moorside. She had glasses and plaits. I liked her because she gave me a notebook with BOCM Cattle Foods stamped on the front. We swapped love letters written on scraps of paper, an envelope full of them once a week. It lasted a fortnight. Maybe three weeks. Until I ran out of paper, and enthusiasm.

At eleven, at Secondary School I had my first kiss. Two of the girls in the class had decided we needed a Christmas party, but one that was strictly for the kids, not the grown-ups. They managed, though I've no idea how, to book a church hall. The party was to start at seven thirty in the evening. There would be games and something to eat and drink. The food I cannot remember, nor the drink, though I know that alcohol didn't figure at all.

In true Titchmarsh fashion I was first to arrive. Punctuality is a disease, and it's incurable. I have suffered from it ever since I can remember and am now a chronic case. In an adolescent, no other complaint, except acne, is less cool. But on this occasion it paid off. Dorothy (dark, curly-haired and no slouch when it came to a fag behind the bike sheds) greeted me with open arms, shrieking with relief at my arrival and explaining that she thought no one would come. I was given a smacker full on the lips and spent the next half-hour convinced that this would be a party like none I had experienced before. Auntie Edie and Uncle Bert gave cracking Christmas parties over their grocer's shop, but postman's knock never figured largely, and even if it had you couldn't do much with a cousin five years younger when you were only nine yourself.

By eight o'clock there were around twenty of us there; the doors were closed and the curtains drawn and I waited to see what we would play. Pass the parcel, perhaps? Or musical chairs – both of which I was well versed in, thanks to Sunday school parties and my uncle and auntie's bashes.

No. The first game would be spinning the bottle. We all sat round in a circle. The idea of the game was that a bottle would be spun in the centre, and when it came to rest the person pointed at by the bottle would have to get up, cross to the person opposite and give them a kiss.

That was all there was to it. Pretty simple. And I knew in my heart of hearts, as sure as eggs is eggs, exactly where the neck of the bottle would stop first. I have never won the lottery. I have hardly ever won a raffle. I am lousy at cards. But I knew to the nearest millimetre precisely where that bottle would stop. And it did. There was no denying that the pointed end of Mr Barr's bottle of cream soda was pointing right at me, and opposite sat the most fancied girl in the class. Sally. Long, blonde hair, lusted after by every boy in the school, including me, and frequently to be found in the stationery cupboard with a beefy boy from one of the B forms. He wasn't here tonight. This was the A stream party.

I stood up. Among the cheers that were worthy of an FA Cup Final I made tentative steps towards her as she grinned and advanced towards me. My heart thumped in my undeveloped chest. We were face to face now in the middle of the circle. I could see clearly into her pale blue eyes. Oh for a quiet corner! Oh for this situation to be repeated but without all these people watching. I looked at her hair – fair and gleaming, held back by a golden bandeau. Her high-necked cream blouse was decorated with lace. Her skirt . . . well, I didn't look that far down. Instead, with the shrieks of my classmates ringing in my ears, my fear got the better of me. I picked up her hand and lightly kissed it. To howls of derision from the hall, she looked me in the eye and, like Heather before her, whispered three words. A different choice this time: 'You soft thing!' Then she returned to her seat and waited for the next spin and better fortune.

Half a dozen spins later, when I had watched the rest of my classmates getting stuck in, my own embarrassment had quite disappeared, but when, once more, the bottle pointed at me, Sally had moved along and the opposite end pointed at a girl who had done her best but was hardly in the same league. There was no way I could try the hand kissing stunt again, though for different reasons I would have dearly loved to do so. I closed my eyes (the better to imagine Sally) and kissed her full on the lips, and to my profound surprise she was a cracking kisser.

I think we played the game for another ten minutes or so, before it was decided to dispense with the bottle and stick to the snogging. Each guy would approach a girl he fancied, and if there was a nod rather than a shake of the head he'd lift her up on to one of the wide windowsills, draw the curtains in front of them for privacy, and snog away until one of the parties got bored, at which time a swap-over would take place and the process would be repeated.

I did manage to persuade Sally to come behind a curtain, and I can remember that first queasy feeling in the stomach as our questing, tentative tongues explored each other's mouths. There was no groping; it was all very innocent; a French kiss being as much as one hoped for or desired at eleven years of age in the Congregational Church Hall. I walked home at ten o'clock with my feet hardly touching the ground.

By eleven o'clock we were all in bed – alone – and never again did I feel embarrassed about kissing. Sally, after all, had agreed quite happily to come behind the curtain.

There was another party the following year, in the room over the Essoldo cinema. This time we didn't bother with the bottle – just got straight down to it. I wasn't much hunkier, still four foot six or seven, one of the two smallest lads in the class. But it didn't bother me now. My current favourite was Anne, a tall girl, but she didn't seem worried by the fact that I only came up to her shoulder. We sorted it all out very amicably. I sat on her knee. It seemed to work better that way.

12

Getting Out a Bit

'I'll tell you what you want, our Malcolm; you want to get out and meet people of your own age. It's not good for you, stuck in here with all these old farts. Before you know where you are you'll be wearing Hush Puppies and a fawn anorak.'

Derek Roberts, *The Doncaster Diaries*, 1969

I'd like to report a misspent youth. Give myself a bit of street cred. I was a child of the Sixties, after all. A newspaper interviewer gave up on me a couple of months ago when the most impressive credential I could summon up from my teenage years was that I was the first person in my street to buy 'She Loves You'.

I didn't feel deprived. My bit of flower power happened in our back garden. London seemed like another country, a place you saw on the news. It might have been where the action was at but I felt no need to go there. I did go once when I was twelve. On a Scout trip. We went camping at Gilwell Park in Essex, and Uncle Bert Hardisty (rejoicing in the rank of Group Scout Leader) took us to see Big Ben and Piccadilly Circus. I took a few black-and-white photos with my Brownie 127 (only eight pictures to a film) and remember being impressed. But I didn't especially want to go back.

I was not a natural Scout. It all seemed a bit artificial. I'd been perfectly content as a Wolf Cub, but I was younger then, and you could wear a warm green woolly rather than a short-sleeved khaki shirt. When I was eleven Uncle Bert gave me a copy of *Scouting for Boys* by Baden-Powell. It was full of handy hints on making fires (which from my back garden efforts I could do already) and following a map, but I knew the moors like the back of my hand, and it seemed pointless to keep stopping to check contour levels and trig points.

One thing about the book irritated me more than any other: it showed the correct way to walk. The 'healthy boy' (who was pictured as a handsome youth with a square chin and bulging muscles) walked properly, striding forward with his arms swinging, his head and shoulders back, his mouth fixed in a rictus grin, his eyes gazing directly ahead of him. The unhealthy boy (his arms hanging limply by his sides like the missing link in one of Darwin's evolution engravings) was a chinless wonder with buck teeth, a sullen expression and a stoop. He was walking badly, dawdling along looking at the ground. This was plainly daft. Anyone interested in natural history will always walk along looking at the ground – it's where the wildlife and the flowers are. And, anyway, what if you were born with no chin and buck teeth? Did that make you a second-class citizen? I've never been impressed by political correctness, but *Scouting for Boys* turned prejudice into a fine art.

We would meet once a week in a dusty hut. The small kitchen smelled of burnt milk and Brillo pads and had a greasy sink and ancient gas oven which exploded into life every time you lit it. There were rows of black encrusted billy cans and dixies for making watery stews. The cupboards were stuffed with uneven hanks of rope and old boxing gloves. We would play British bulldog and shipwrecks, which I enjoyed, and learn to name the parts of an axe, which I didn't.

Scout camps were uncomfortable exercises, where childhood rivalries and boyish rituals could be played out in *Lord of the Flies* fashion. I tried to look enthusiastic at the prospect of ganging together and rubbing black boot polish on to another boy's bollocks in the name of 'initiation', but I was at best half-hearted and at worst a bit embarrassed. I stood on the edge of things, trying not to get involved, and hoping that no one would notice and do it to me.

One of the lads, a podgy, pasty-faced youth, would always wear flowery shorts and take a particularly close interest in such activities. I could never work out why. Not till much later. But then I don't believe anyone else thought anything of it, either. The rest of the troop were all refreshingly normal, and so were our leaders. I think if any scoutmaster with an unhealthy interest in boys had ever tried anything on in our Scout group he'd have gone home with the boot blacking brush inserted where it felt most uncomfortable.

Scout meetings were just about tolerable; camps were more difficult. The very first one I endured was at Pateley Bridge, about fifteen miles from Ilkley. It could have been on the moon. It was only a long Whitsun weekend, and my parents came to visit on the Sunday. I was fine until then. As they left, I remember sitting on a rock high above the campsite and watching their van lumbering off down the track. I have never felt so alone before or since. As they disappeared from view, I frowned hard and gritted my teeth. It was to no avail. I brushed angrily at the tears that ran down my cheeks. But I made sure my face was dry before I went back to the tent.

Homesickness. A rite of passage. A part of growing up. It made me more understanding of others in the same boat. Some of them didn't even know what it was. Later on, I remember persuading a younger lad than me to have an aspirin every day, endeavouring to convince him that it was a special tablet that would cure the sort of feelings he was having, feelings that resulted in him bursting into tears. He was a brave little soul who didn't really know why he felt the way he did. It worked for a couple of days, but he couldn't understand why it was less effective as the week wore on.

'I'm never like this at Tenby,' he stammered bravely through the tears. I longed to tell him that it was because his parents were with him when he holidayed in Tenby. In the end he had to go home.

I soldiered on at Scouts in a half-hearted sort of way, wondering if I was odd not to fully enjoy it. It was years before I realised that I didn't have to do it; that I could have more fun elsewhere. Oh, it wasn't all bad, and some of the lads were great fun. I am not ashamed to say that I did enjoy sitting round camp fires, swathed in a blanket, singing 'Ging-gang-gooly' and 'The Quartermaster's Stores', and building aerial runways that would let you fly over ravines, but I never enjoyed the cooking – all those twists of dough wound round a stick and burnt to a cinder – and sleeping in a tent with five other lads farting all night until the air turned green. I even became an assistant Scout leader when I was seventeen, but it didn't last. I think my Uncle Bert felt a bit let down. And most of his knots are still a mystery to me.

Family holidays were much more fun. We usually had a week in Bispham, what my mother would call 'the select end of Blackpool'. We stayed for just a week in Mrs Schofield's boarding house – 'Pendennis', in Hesketh Avenue – which came recommended by my childhood friend Virginia's mum and dad.

It was a smart, neatly painted terraced house in a street just off the promenade, where the cream and green trams hummed and clanged their way to classy-sounding destinations like Thornton Cleveleys and Gynn Square, the Norbreck Hotel and South Shore. 'Pendennis' had a woodgrain-painted front door, freshly leathered windows with clean net curtains, and around half a dozen bedrooms. Old Mrs Schofield, a plump, grey-haired old biddy with glasses, would sit in her apron just inside the kitchen door, overseeing while her daughter-in-law cooked the meals and her son, Clifford, wearing a cream jacket, waited at the tables in the dining room at the back.

The kids who were there (and there can only have been room for a couple of families) would vie to see who could get the bottle of Vimto with their evening meal. Clifford would stagger in with a wooden crate of a dozen pop bottles, and only one of them would be Vimto. I don't remember liking it much, it was just that its rarity value made it more desirable.

We'd go on the beach during the day, swim in woollen costumes that threatened to drag you under, make sand castles topped with paper national flags, bury Dad up to his neck and ride donkeys. Lunch would be egg-and-sand sandwiches and a bottle of pop; Mum and Dad pouring their milky coffee from our own Thermos, filled up in the Schofields' kitchen each morning. In the evening they would leave us in the care of the boarding house proprietors while they went out to a show – Ken Dodd or the Black and White Minstrels – or to a pub for a drink.

I suppose I must have been about ten or eleven, and my sister five or six, but I remember every evening in the holiday, sitting with my dad in the tiny lounge at the front of the boarding house, with its antimacassars and 'Magicoal' fire, having milk and biscuits before going to bed. There would always be one evening when we'd get the giggles. Poor Dad. There he was, in his suit and tie, doing his best to get us upstairs to bed so that he and

Mum could have a night on the town, and my sister and me completely losing it.

'Will you get on and drink your milk!'

The more angry he became, the less we were able to control ourselves. You know what it's like – one glance at each other would be enough to send milk and biscuit crumbs spouting forth like a waterfall, all over Dad's suit trousers then he'd get cross and we'd try even harder to control ourselves.

'Right. That's it!'

In the end he'd storm out, and Mum would come and put us to bed; two kids, crying with laughter and exhausted from half an hour of hysterics.

We tried Butlins a couple of times when we got older. At Filey. I remember entering the 'Mr Debonair' competition and coming nowhere. I was bitterly disappointed. I had a new jumper and tie which I thought made me look particularly suave. I was about thirteen. The man who won was portly with a suit and a moustache. But he did have a nice smile. Other than that I can remember nothing, except breakfasts in a massive canteen-like dining room, and the smell of the regale lilies that stood in the corner of the Hawaiian bar. Butlins was quite posh then.

During the rest of the year there were Sunday excursions up the Dales in the van or the car when 'going out for a run' was all the rage. We'd have high tea of ham and eggs at the Hopper Lane Hotel, or a picnic on the moors with sandwiches (always egg) and home-made rock buns and flapjacks.

Sometimes we'd go with Uncle Bert and Auntie Edie and their children Martin and Valerie, all piling into Uncle Bert's Dormobile – a sort of minibus which could just about contain a family of eight, but which had a primitive heating system. In summer it was fine, but in winter he'd have to boost the temperature inside by opening the lid of the transmission box between the driver and the front seat passengers. You could hardly hear yourself above the roar of the engine – especially on hills – but you did feel warmer. We'd stop off at places like Castle Howard and Bolton Abbey, Burnsall and Grassington. Dad and Uncle Bert would talk about things that dads talked about; Mum and Auntie Edie would spend their time fielding four children and two dogs – Cindy, our dare-devil mongrel, and Tracy, Auntie Edie's blue roan cocker spaniel with ears that were always decorated by burdock seedheads.

'Tracy! Come out of there!' shouted Auntie Edie, retrieving her dog from a bush or the middle of the river.

'Cindy! Get off your bottom!' shouted Mum at our dog, whose manners sometimes let us down. She did seem to enjoy pulling herself along by her front legs and using her bum as castors. Worming tablets were often suggested but not, as far as I can remember, ever administered.

As I grew older, Mum and Dad clearly thought it would be a good idea if I socialised a bit more. It's only writing now that I realise how self-contained my life must have been then. It makes me sound a bit sad. Billy No-Mates. But it didn't feel like that. I was a member of the church youth club, and we played tennis once a week in summer and ping-pong in the church institute in winter, but I didn't go out with a gang of mates, roaming the streets. It never occurred to me that I was missing out. My greatest friends are those that I made in my twenties – and we have remained close for thirty years now – but what happened to my school friends I don't know. David Martin and Stephen Bradley, Richard Bailey and Steven Feather, Sally Boocock and Jill Clapham – all names from the past that conjure up memories of playing out and falling out, first kisses and early passions, but all lost in the mists of time.

So when I was fourteen or fifteen my mum and dad took me
to fire station socials. For years we had a bell at the bottom of
the stairs, and when it rang, and the siren wailed over the town,
Dad would drop whatever he was doing and, sometimes still
wearing his slippers, would sprint the three streets to the fire
station in Golden Butts Road.

I never worried about the danger; it never occurred to me. I
suppose my mum did. We were surrounded by woollen mills and
I remember Dad taking us all to see the devastation at a mill the
morning after a fire. It had taken them hours to bring the blaze
under control. We gazed down on a tangled mixture of machinery
and brickwork, massive girders twisted like snakes by the fierce
heat. My mother looked pale and taut, then she nodded in the
direction of the mangled remains of the mill and asked, 'What
do you think about when you're tackling something like that?'

My dad just shrugged.

'You must think about something,' she persisted.

'Do you really want to know?'

Mum nodded.

'Stupid, really.'

'What?'

'Well, I stood at the top of a ladder squirting water on that lot
last night and thinking: "Someone, somewhere wants a letter from
you."'

Mum shook her head. It was the quietest sort of bravery. On
both their parts.

Sometimes, when we were little, Dad would take me and my
sister to sit on the engine. It was one of those open-topped ones,
all scarlet paintwork and gleaming chrome, with canvas hoses
wrapped around reels, and a huge extending ladder with red,
wooden wheels at the back. He'd let us ring the bell and put on
a helmet. My sister disappeared under hers and had to walk

around with her arms in front of her, bumping into the row of tall leather boots, with their leggings already attached so that they could be jumped into and pulled on in a hurry. I still remember the smell of the fire station – rubber and metal polish and petrol.

The socials were held once a month in the room above the engines or, as my dad called them, appliances. This always made them sound faintly surgical. It was basically 'housie-housie' – bingo – with a good supper afterwards. Sometimes they had a 'beetle drive', throwing dice and adding limbs to the body of a plastic beetle, the first to complete their insect winning a prize which would be a box of Quality Street or a couple of bottles of beer.

The first prize I ever won was a box of tulip bulbs, and I could not have been happier. Darwin hybrids they were. I can still remember the box. Maybe it was the half-pint of cider that made it more exciting.

13

A Bit on the Side

'There is nothing like a little extra income for raising a man's expectations.'

Thomas Craddock, *Willy Eckerslike and the Girl Next Door*, 1958

You can't live on a shilling when you're in double figures. Anyone knows that. I needed a few extra bob. There were discos at the King's Hall and the Scout hut. If I didn't go to them I'd never meet a girl. Oh, I met them at school, but you couldn't be intimate with a girl at school. Not with everybody else looking on. And those early spinning-the-bottle parties seemed to have fallen by the wayside. Dorothy clearly had a boyfriend of her own now and didn't see why she should organise everybody else's social life. You were on your own. What you needed was a job.

My cousin was giving up his early morning milk round to start work full-time. It meant getting up at five but you were done by eight and then had time to get ready for school. I started in the middle of winter. I lasted a day. It was cold, you couldn't see what you were doing, and the milkman was a miserable bugger who spoke only half a dozen words during the whole three hours. The prospect of seeing him every morning filled me with gloom.

So I did a paper round instead. I was still only about four and a half feet tall and I had about thirty papers to deliver, over a round that went up and down Ilkley's hills for about two miles. I reckon it must have stunted my growth. I was ages growing. But I could do it in an hour and a half. The only day that just about finished me off was *Radio Times* day when the bag doubled in weight. In the end the paper shop took pity on me and gave me a trolley. Five shillings a week I was paid. I stuck at it for a couple of years and enjoyed the luxury of a small private income.

I was measured for a suit a couple of months ago. The tailor told me that my right shoulder was a good inch lower than my left. I blame it on the *Radio Times*.

The church helped with finances, too. Singing in the choir wasn't highly paid but it did yield a few coins every six months in a small brown envelope. But whenever we sang at a wedding we got half a crown.

And then there were the bells. Eight of them. Dad had been a bellringer for years. They were short on numbers. Did I want to have a go? I looked at him, and then down at my puny body.

'It's all right. We'll put you on the treble. You'll be able to manage that.'

I wasn't so sure.

I went along to practice on a Thursday night, climbing the cobwebby spiral stone steps up to the ringing chamber, where ropes with red, white and blue 'sallies' disappeared up through holes in the ceiling. In the centre of the floor stood a pile of wooden boxes.

'Come over here,' said Mac Crawshaw. He was a portly man with a red face and a pipe. 'We'll measure you up.' He wore a tweed waistcoat and trousers, and his shirtsleeves were held back with shiny arm bands, a sort of bellringer's symbol of office.

He piled about three boxes on top of one another and then lifted me up and stood me on top. I could reach the middle of the rope now, where the longer of the two sallies was joined to it.

Now ringing bells is, in itself, quite a simple operation, but if you make a mistake the results can be quite spectacular. In the void above the ceiling of the ringing chamber, the bells are hung on massive girders. The treble is the lightest bell and strikes the highest note, and the tenor is the deepest-toned and heaviest at around fifteen hundredweight – three quarters of a ton. Each bell swings on a central pivot and the bellrope runs up through the ceiling and then around a sort of cartwheel, attached to the end of this pivot. Stick with me; it will all make sense. You pull on the rope to dislodge the bell from its upright position, and then take the strain when it has gone through 180 degrees so that it doesn't continue to travel round and round.

A wooden stay, made of oak, allows the bell to be rested in its upright position, but it's not strong enough on its own to stop several hundredweight of cast iron from revolving. So, if you fail to take the strain in time, the stay can snap, and the rope will be pulled up through the hole in the ceiling. If this happens, it is important to let go. If you don't, you'll hit the ceiling. And it hurts.

They say you're not a bellringer until you've broken a stay. They would, wouldn't they? I am a bellringer.

It was a scary moment. It didn't happen when I was learning. I'd been at it for a few months. But I got the number of boxes wrong. I added one too many. I pulled the bell from its upright position and expected to feel the strain as it reached the top of its arc. I didn't. There was a crack, and a bang, and twenty feet of fluffy bellrope disappeared through the hole in the ceiling like a rat up a drainpipe.

The rest of the ringers looked at me, then stood up their bells. I wasn't in a position to hide. I was standing about three feet off the ground on a series of wooden boxes, looking like a gold-medal-winning athlete at the Olympics. Except I didn't have a medal.

The silence seemed to last ages. It felt like eternity. I waited for the telling off. It didn't come.

Mac Crawshaw spoke first. 'Well, laddie, you're a bellringer now!' A round of applause followed, and some slapping on the back and ruffling of hair. For the rest of the week the treble was out of action, until the stay was replaced. They gave me the old one as a souvenir – a three-inch square spar of oak, snapped clean in two like a matchstick.

You learned respect for bells. There was something about them that commanded it. It wasn't just the weight, or the noise, though both had something to do with it. On New Year's Eve we'd pull the bells down to their hanging positions and then go further up the spiral staircase and into the bell chamber itself. There was no light; only our torches. We would each be allocated a bell, under which we would sit, gripping the metal clapper in one hand and bashing it against the side of the bell to play carols. 'O Come All Ye Faithful' and 'O Little Town of Bethlehem' would clang out from the tower and across the town on the freezing air. By the end of half an hour your head would be buzzing – it was impossible to hear conversation – and your hand would be almost frozen to the clapper. It would take ages to get your fingers to move again. Then we'd pile down the stairs for a glass of sherry and a mince pie.

Half of me loved this annual ritual, the other half found it a bit scary. It was as if the bells were alive, menacing monsters that seemed to have secret lives.

There were compensations: if you rang the bells at a wedding you got another five bob, and you could run down the belfry steps as the bride was going into church on the arm of her father, nip round the back to the vestry, put on your cassock and surplice and be standing in the back row of the choir stalls by the time she made it to the bottom of the chancel steps.

I wasn't a mercenary child. Just practical.

I suppose there were around a dozen of us who rang the bells. There was Geoff, who was a body-builder and didn't say much. He rang the tenor. He said he'd have joined years ago if he'd known how good it was at building arm and stomach muscles. My mum came along later. She, and a pretty girl called Carol who was a good five years older than me, were our only female ringers. I quite fancied Carol, but she was way out of my league. And older. And anyway she emigrated to Canada. Mac Crawshaw and Geoff Featherstone – another bespectacled pipe smoker – shared the role of 'captain' and would be in charge when we rang peals.

These were incredibly complicated permutations of numbers that involved timing the strike of your bell to fit into a prearranged pattern. My total lack of numeracy meant that anything more complicated than 'Grandsire Doubles' and 'Call Changes' – when you would ring in a shouted, rather than a pre-arranged order – were beyond me. Later, when I'd grown a bit, I did ring the tenor whose job was to bring up the rear. I could just about manage that.

I only got my hands on the big bell when Martin Hewitt left. Martin was a couple of years older than me, and full of all the confidence that I seemed to lack. He came to youth club as well. He could count to eight in German and he was the first person I ever knew who became famous. Well, in my eyes.

He went and joined the Household Cavalry in London and had one of those red uniforms with a gold helmet and a plume. Then came his moment of glory: he rode in Winston Churchill's funeral procession. We were all very proud, trying to spot him on the telly.

I asked him about it a couple of years ago. He laughed. 'We had to get on our horses at eight o'clock in the morning, and we couldn't get off them again until four in the afternoon,' he said.

I asked him what happened if they were taken short. You know, being practical. He said, 'We were told that if we dismounted we'd be on a charge.'

'So what did you do?'

'We went in our saddles.'

Whenever I see the Household Cavalry trotting down the Mall, now, I keep a weather eye open for steam.

14

The Call of the Boards

'Show me a nervous youth who will blush at the mere mention of his name, and I will show you an actor who can command the attention of a packed auditorium.'

Aston Waterlinks, *The Roar of the Crowd*, 1938

Now I don't want to go on about this size thing – the fact that when I left school I was only five foot and a bit. But when you're small it does mean that you need some weapon in your armoury to make up for a lack of strength if you're to survive the slings and arrows of an outrageous secondary school. It might be humour or speed or a temper.

I'd never thought of myself as having a temper. Still don't, really. I'll walk away from an argument – anything for a quiet life. Until something snaps.

It happened in the school playground. The lads in another class had been making seagrass stools, those things with a seat made of a sort of woven hemp. Like all lads do, they'd pinched a few lengths to muck about with, and at breaktime they emerged into the playground with their plunder, each length knotted at the end, all the better to flick at the back of your bare legs. We wore shorts until the fourth form. Short shorts.

There was one particularly surly youth who had it in for me. It was the lad who snogged Sally in the stationery cupboard when nobody was looking. I think he must have known I fancied her. I watched him walk over, flicking his length of seagrass in the air and making it crack. I knew what was coming.

'What yer lookin' at, Titmarsh?'

It still rattles me when people call me that. Why is it that people who can say 'switch' can't say 'Titch'?

Anyway. He knew what he was doing. He cracked the length of twine in the air again, stared at me, then lowered his arm and flicked it at the back of my knees. It stung. I winced. He did it again. I pulled away, and then he started running towards me, whipping at my now reddening legs.

We ran past Sally, who was standing at the side of the play-ground with a group of girls. They stopped talking, turned and watched. I felt myself blushing. Then I just stopped running and turned to face him. I can remember my knees shaking with anger. Before he could lift his arm again, I had the hank of seagrass out of his hand and lashed it across the back of his own legs.

If I had stopped to consider the probable consequences of my actions I doubt that I would have done anything other than run for cover. Instead, I gave him three good licks of the twine and then lobbed it over the fence and into the school field.

He stared at me. I stared back; quivering with rage, but silent. He turned. He walked away.

He never spoke to me again. I never did make it with Sally. But then I never saw him in the stationery cupboard with her again either. I just wonder sometimes . . .

I saw him again about ten years later. He was running his own building firm by then. Doing well for himself. We met at a wedding reception and he was wearing a very smart three-piece suit with a gold watch chain. I went up and introduced myself.

'I'm sorry,' he said. 'I don't remember you.' And he turned on his heel and went to get a drink from the bar.

The temper couldn't be counted on to get me out of trouble on a regular basis. It only erupted once every couple of years, unbidden, like an erratic volcano. Making people laugh was more reliable. Nothing hugely witty. Just stupidity mostly. Clowning. 'Titchmarsh, sit down and shut up.' It was a daily instruction. I wasn't uppity; just naturally chatty. And silly. But it made the girls think I was 'cute' so it had its uses.

At sport my lacklustre performance was unlikely to get me noticed. I still maintain that Barry Hines must have based the character of Billy Casper in *Kes* on my own appearance on the football field. Always the last to be picked – along with the fat boy – me with my spindly legs and my ancient brown leather football boots, bought at a jumble. Antique fair, more like.

I used to play centre half. Mr Bailey, the sports master, used to explain to me that the centre half was the 'kingpin of the defence'. Well, he was when anyone else was in the role. As far as I was concerned he was the one who took the blame from the goal keeper when he missed a save. That was Richard Bailey, no relation to the master, who used to call him 'namesake'. He supported Norwich and wore a yellow Canaries shirt and woolly gloves. Odd for a Yorkshireman. I remember him being good at kicking the ball halfway down the pitch, but he never seemed to stop many of them getting into his goal. Not to worry. He had a fine line in tragic head holding when they got past him.

The only time I ever caused a stir on the cricket field was when I ran out to take the opening batsman his 'box'. He'd left it in the dressing room, so he beckoned me over and whispered in my ear. 'Fetch us me box, Fred – it's somewhere in the dressing room.' (They used my middle name as my nickname at school.

With a surname like Titchmarsh it could have been worse, but fortunately my older cousin was already known as Titty. I was called Fred to avoid confusion.)

I went to the dressing room, eventually located the protective item under a pile of evil-smelling socks, and ran out on to the field, waving it over my head to signify my success. The straps streamed out behind me like a banner, and the batsman snatched it from me with a red face and stuffed it down his trousers. You'd have thought he'd have been grateful.

Half a dozen girls on the boundary line lay on their backs, kicking their legs in the air, and laughed until they cried.

With such a marked lack of distinction on the sports field there had to be another way of geting noticed. I discovered it in school plays.

They were a legitimate way of showing off. I had a good memory for lines, a reasonable stage presence, and I could be other people – school masters and pirates, doctors and Shylock in an abridged version of *The Merchant of Venice*. I got to wear the beard all day. And I fell in love with Portia. Both of them.

Jill and Julia took it in turns to play the part. Jill had sent me a Valentine card two years running now. Oh, we never went out. Just swapped Valentines. And smiles. (I mean, what was I on?) And Julia? She was a new girl. Tall. Very pretty, with dark curly hair, and eyes that flashed. And she chewed gum like I've never seen anyone chew gum.

There I was, standing in the wings with her, waiting to go on; me dressed in grey robes, a floppy hat and a grizzled beard, carrying a cardboard knife, and she in a full skirt of green silk and a white, off-the-shoulder blouse. She bent down to stick her chewing gum under a chair and I missed my cue.

I wish I'd had more courage with girls. God, I was slow! But then most of the girls were fairly slow, too. Apart from a select few. We didn't use the word 'slapper' in our school in the early Sixties. The most derogatory term you could apply to a girl was 'prozzy', and that was reserved for an ugly lass from the back end of Burley. There were a couple of lads who had a fumble behind the bike sheds at thirteen, but they were way ahead of the game. And yes; there was a girl who was removed from school under mysterious circumstances and who was seen a year later pushing a pram. But only one. A lot of lads talked about sex, but if they talked about it you could be certain they weren't getting it. Not at fourteen, anyway.

Most of them had a nifty way of getting rid of a girl they didn't want to go out with any more. Instead of plucking up the courage and telling her to her face, they'd just put their hand up her blouse. That was usually enough to see her off.

I did once get a girl to show me her knickers at junior school, but she refused to show me any more. I'd said that I'd show her my willy if she showed me her thingummy-whatsit, but I intended to rat on her at the last moment. I think she knew. She didn't oblige. It was all very innocent by today's standards.

I can still remember my first view of a pair of breasts. One of the lads in the street had a sister who caught measles. She must have been past the infectious stage because we were talking in her back kitchen and she said her belly was covered in spots. I opened her cardigan to have a look and she wasn't wearing anything underneath.

I didn't say anything. Just had a good look, then closed the cardigan and carried on as if nothing had happened. Well, only a few months earlier I'd seen her in the paddling pool on the moors wearing nothing more than a pair of shorts. How was I to know that things had happened since then?

Acting in plays gave me a new sort of courage. It was the first time I was aware of being able to do something well, other than growing plants, which didn't count. At least not as far as my schoolmates were concerned. The lads who were good at sport were often embarrassing in a play, passable impersonations of a plank. I could get laughs. It was glamorous. And you got to see girls in a different light.

David Wildman, the Art and Drama master, asked my parents if I could take a role at the Ilkley Players. He wrote them a letter. I sneaked a look at it. The play was by André Roussin. It was called *The Little Hut*, all about a married couple who were ship-wrecked on a desert island, along with the wife's lover. There were only two huts, a larger one that could be occupied by two, and the smaller 'little hut' in which the third person must sleep alone. It was a comedy about who slept where.

The letter explained that the play was 'outspoken' – lovely euphemism – and would my parents mind if I was in it? They said that they did not, and that I would have to learn about this sort of thing some day. Bless 'em. Their biggest reservation was that there was only one dressing room at Ilkley Playhouse in those days. Men and women changed in the same space. My dad knew that. He did the plumbing. But they kept their worries to themselves and let me go.

I was to play a monkey who comes on in the very last scene of the play, just before the characters are rescued by a passing cruise ship. It was not a large role. There were no lines. I just had to run up a tree and pelt them with nuts. But I got a good laugh, especially on the last night when I threw a banana. The bug had bitten.

I would become an actor.

There are two reasons why I didn't. For a start, I reckoned that I might not have enough talent. But the more important thing was that I was the son of a Yorkshire plumber. I think it might have been a bit difficult for my dad to cope with. I mean if your son is a sensitive sort of soul anyway, who isn't exactly built like a brick shithouse and doesn't appear to have much luck with the girls, you could be forgiven for thinking that he might turn out to be a nancy-boy.

My father became concerned about me when I came home from Leeds one Saturday with an umbrella. I knew he would. I hid it behind the settee so that he wouldn't find it. When he did spot it, he went quiet and read his paper. As far as he was concerned, umbrellas were for poofs. In this respect he was no different from other northern men of his generation. He was a kind and gentle man, but very masculine. And umbrellas were not.

The funny thing is that five years later I wouldn't be seen dead carrying that umbrella. But by then, if the weather looked at all doubtful, my father would never leave the house without it.

I never had any real doubts about my sexuality. Well, no more than your average youth. I remember admiring the legs of the lad who was playing Lysander in the school production of *A Midsummer Night's Dream*, and suddenly being scared that I might be turning that way. But then along came Rosemary Pickering, a cute redhead with dark brown eyes. We met at a dance at the King's Hall. In spite of the snogs at school parties, I'd formed no lasting relationship. Rosemary was the first girl I ever crossed a dance floor for who said yes. Then we sat down and had a Coke. I put my hand underneath the table and held hers. She didn't pull it away. I felt like a king, and my stomach wouldn't stop churning. We kissed properly when we said good-night. She was a lovely kisser. Our tune was *Groovy Kind of Love*.

I don't remember introducing her to my parents, but they must have bumped into her at some point. My mum wasn't too keen. She didn't say a lot, I just got that impression. My dad said nothing for weeks, until one day when he spoke to me from behind his newspaper.

'That girl . . . Rosemary . . .'

I wondered what was coming. 'Yes?'

He lowered the paper. 'Very nice.' Then he winked and went back to his reading.

'Thanks, Dad.' I couldn't stop smiling for ages.

I was a bit worried that she was too young for me – I was two years older than she was. It lasted three months and ended rather sadly when she turned up late for my sixteenth birthday party and said she'd forgotten my present. It wouldn't have seemed nearly so bad if it had been a good party. But it wasn't. About eight of us just sat round in a circle and talked. It was very stilted. I'd never thrown a party before. I noticed that Rosemary was wearing suspenders. I never saw her again.

15

The Great Escape

'The man who could call a spade a spade should be compelled to
use one. It is the only thing he is fit for.'

Oscar Wilde

Things were not looking promising at school. Drama was fun,
but I lacked the conviction to make it a career. Science should
have been interesting but the shouting Improper Fraction took
the joy out of it. Neither did I fare especially well in English, but
one essay in particular netted me 22 marks out of 35.

It was entitled 'A Description of My Garden', and this is it, in
its entirety, spellings and all:

The garden as a whole is not very big, but manages to acco-
modate three flower-beds, a vegetable patch, and average
sized lawn and a very small polythene greenhouse.

At the top left hand corner is an old sycamore tree which
gives shelter in winter and shade in summer and is greatly
appreciated as it gives the rest of the garden a character.
Along its side is quite a wide flower border with many
perrenials and oily leaved jungle plants. Down the right
is another border, this time containing many tall plants;
such as the tall tapering lupin and a clamber of dogroses
on the fence. Down at the front of the border we have

lobelia and alyssum, adding a neat touch to the edge. Next comes a small border of flowers and opposite it a vegetable patch, on which various salads such as lettuce, raddish, spring onions and other tasty dishes can be grown. Then comes the thing which I like best; the greenhouse. It is only a very small, polythene one, which I built myself, but it is just right for growing seeds in boxes and one or two pot plants. I also bought a thermometer, and it has recorded a temperature of 108 F in summer, and it has no means of heating. There seems to be a lot in my garden but there is still room for a spacious lawn in the centre. This is very useful in summer and gives the garden a less cluttered up look.

252 words. Well, it was to the point.

Though it might not be abundantly evident from this example, I liked writing, loved words, and found that if I improved my vocabulary by looking up in the dictionary any long words I heard I had another way of impressing my friends. But none of this impressed my English teacher.

We were asked to write a précis of *A Midsummer Night's Dream*. I made what I thought was a pretty good stab at it, though looking back now it was rather a pathetic sortie. At the bottom of my essay, in red ink, were the dreaded words 'See me'.

Miss Weatherall was a perfectionist. Not always encouraging. I went to see her after class. She sat behind her oak desk and pointed to a paragraph with her pen. 'Read that.'

I read out loud: 'Helena, whose love is not reciprocated by Demetrius . . .' I began.

'What does that mean?'

'It means that she loves Demetrius but that he doesn't love her.'

'How do you know that word?'

'I looked it up in a dictionary.'

'I see.' She bent down and wrote in the mark. Eight out of ten.

I can confess now that I fibbed. I hadn't looked it up in a dictionary. My mum had told me. But I used it. And I knew what it meant, and that day I learned that words gave you power. They could even silence Miss Weatherall. They were another weapon in the armoury. I still love dictionaries.

And I still love the outside. My interest in gardening began to grow during my teens. I don't think it was simply because I wasn't much good at anything else; it was just that it felt comfortable, natural, almost easy. I took on more of the back garden at home, built a slightly bigger greenhouse and filled it with more pot plants. To this day the aroma of newly unrolled polythene in a hardware shop still induces a frisson of excitement and whisks me back forty-odd years to my little greenhouse. They were simple but raw pleasures then. I sent off for seeds in catalogues from companies which have long since ceased to trade: firms like Asmer, Clucas, and Carters, famous for their 'Tested Seeds'.

Although I was not allowed to attend rural studies lessons after the first term at school because I was in the A, rather than the B, C and D streams, I was still encouraged in my endeavours at home by Mr Heath, the rural studies teacher. He was a tough cookie, Mr Heath. He had announced himself in stentorian tones during that first term. He sat us down at either side of a long table in his classroom and he himself stood at the head of it. He was a short, stout man, almost wider than he was high, with a bullet-shaped head, purple cheeks, iron-grey hair and a thick moustache. He wore a Harris tweed suit that seemed to be made of steel wool, and carried a thick rod of willow about two feet long whose frayed ends were bound with Sellotape. 'My name is Heath; Ernest Wilberforce Heath.'

His voice was loud enough to silence the most recalcitrant boy, and he always suffered from sinus trouble so that he said: 'By dabe is Heath; Erdest Wilberforce Heath.'

Even his middle name was impressive. Better than Fred.

He continued. 'And if eddy of you think you are going to get the better of be id by lessods, you've got aduther think cubbing,' at which point he whacked down the willow rod on the centre of the table and thirty-two pairs of hands were withdrawn faster than the speed of light. He never needed to do it again.

In his sergeant-major-like fashion he would give short shrift to time-wasters, yet never failed to offer encouragement when he saw a glimmer of hope and interest in a pupil. But after that first term I was never in his class. I had more academic subjects to tackle.

I battled on until I was fifteen. My proposed O levels were a year off by then, apart from Art, which I was allowed to take a year early. Lined up for my future delectation were the delights of Maths and French and Physics, and English where my prowess seemed not to impress my teacher. I would sit in the classroom and gaze out of the window at the distant purple of the moors, longing to be out in the fresh air. If I were a gardener I could be.

We had no careers talks that I can remember. It was my dad I confided in. I told him I wanted to be a gardener. He didn't say much, and I thought he hadn't really taken it in.

Without telling me, Mum and Dad went to see the headmaster, Ernest Braban, a poker-faced man who always looked as though he carried the weight of the world on his shoulders. It was a large school, packed with eleven plus failures from the near-misses to the no-chancers. To his enduring credit he suggested that they did not discourage me.

'There are too few gardeners in the world,' he said. 'If your son wants to be one of them, it might be best to let him try.' They came home and told me so. I can remember feeling relieved. And scared.

'What about my O levels?'

'He says you can leave this summer, if you want. You don't have to take them.'

This didn't seem right. I had listened to enough teachers who warned of the perils of not taking your GCEs. Of how you would be unemployable. How for the rest of your life you would regret your earlier misdemeanours when all your friends were doing well and you were struggling at the bottom of the ladder.

My dad said, 'It's up to you,' and then, 'I'll see what I can do.'

A week later he came back from his cleaning stint at the fire station. 'Wally Gell says they've a vacancy at the council nursery for an apprentice. You can start in August, if you want.'

Did I want?

I couldn't believe my luck.

I passed my Art O level at fifteen, and began work at Ilkley Urban District Council Parks Department nursery during the first week in August 1964.

On my first morning I was interviewed by the Parks Superintendent, Hector Mutlow, a small, neat gent with a khaki-coloured mac and a flat tweed cap. He had a reedy, creaky voice and asked me, very sternly, if I was sure that this was what I wanted to do. I told him it was. He cleared his throat, put his hands behind his back and leaned against the side of the grey van that bore his name on the offside valance: 'Ilkley U.D.C. Parks Dept. H.L. Mutlow, Parks Supt.,' it said, in neat, black letters.

'I don't want you to do anything hasty,' he said gravely. 'Anything that you might regret later.'

I shook my head obediently.

'So why don't you come and work a fortnight for nothing to see if you like it. If you do, I'll take you on.'

I thanked him profusely. It was years before I tumbled to his ruse. But I did like it. It came as a revelation that I could make a living out of my greatest passion. Even acting didn't give me the thrill that I found in growing plants.

With Mr Mutlow's words of warning ringing in my ears, I was put into the care of the Parks foreman, Ken Wilson, who gave me a denim apron (woe betide my mother if she called it a pinny), a budding knife and an instruction to follow him.

He led me to a long, white-painted Victorian greenhouse, the central section taller than the two lower ends. He turned the brass doorknob and ushered me in. 'These are yours,' he said.

I stared at him, disbelieving. 'What do you mean?'

'These are yours to look after. They'll be a bit bigger than the ones you're used to.' He smiled and left me alone in the cathedral-like silence of the ancient greenhouse on whose gravel-covered staging stood serried ranks of celosia – Prince of Wales' feathers – and geraniums. All I could hear was the drip, drip, drip of water falling from the freshly watered pots into the sunken tanks beneath the staging where I would dunk my watering can for the next four years.

For a while I couldn't move. I just stared. Then I walked slowly down the path, looking at the plants to right and left, occasionally touching a pot, or a flower. I stuffed my hands deep into the pocket of my apron. Mine. To look after. Like the clear dawning of a day, I realised at that moment that I could spend my life in the fresh air, growing plants, and that I would even get paid for the pleasure.

The wage packet confirmed it. For my first week's work I was given three pounds, eight shillings and sixpence. I gave it to my mum, and she gave me back ten bob.

16

Alan the Gardener

'Most of us imagine that we can choose the particular job we want
in life. In my experience it is the job and the life which chooses us.'

Ernest Asher, *Early Aspirations*, 1962

Little Lane nursery was a ten-minute bike-ride from Nelson Road.
Handy. But work began at 7.45 a.m., so I was up at seven, out by
half past and parking my bike under the loam shed by twenty
to eight.

It's hard to overstate the sense of freedom I felt on starting
work. It was tough, yes; my fellow apprentice Mick Ware saw to
that – he was the hardest worker I've ever met, and expected me
to keep up with him. Tea breaks were unheard of. You drank your
tea while you worked, shovelling compost, potting plants, or
sowing tray after tray of bedding plants. But I was doing a job
that I loved, and my brain, once a confused rag-bag of mixed
emotions and frustrations, turned almost overnight into something with the absorbency of a sponge.

I was sent to day-release classes in Shipley, near Bradford, to
study for my City & Guilds in Horticulture. It all came as a
surprise to Dad who imagined that, as in his father's day,
gardening was manual labour, not something that involved much
in the way of 'book learning'.

For the first time in my life I was coming home with progress reports which, instead of 'Alan means well, but his intentions are not always fulfilled', now said, 'An attentive student. By far the best in his class.' I even won prizes. And received letters of congratulation:

Clerk of the Council   *Ilkley Urban District Council*
Bertram E. Townend LL.B   *Town Hall*
Solicitor   *Ilkley*

                                             7th February 1967

Dear Mr Titchmarsh,
The Burial Board, Moor and Parks Committee, at their meeting held last month, were pleased to learn that you had received a prize for being head of the class in the horticultural course which you are attending, and congratulate you on this success.
Yours sincerely,
B.E. Townend
Clerk

Under the warm sun of encouragement provided by the lecturers at college and my bosses in the Parks Department I felt myself blossoming. There really is no other word for it.

Much of it was down to the daily environment in which I now found myself. It simply could not have been more to my liking. The nursery had thirteen greenhouses. My three were the oldest of the lot, but also the most characterful, with their white-painted glazing bars, brass doorknobs and stone staging filled with pea shingle. I grew geraniums (which my elementary botany now told me were really pelargoniums, geranium being the correct Latin name for the hardy varieties of cranesbill which grew outdoors).

I also had charge of grevilleas, *Primula obconica*, celosia and
other colourful pot plants destined for floral decoration in the
Town Hall. I'd not studied Latin at school, but botanical Latin I
took to quite happily. It seemed the most natural thing in the
world, a bit like a telephone directory, with the equivalent of the
surname first, and the Christian name to follow.

I used to make up songs with them. As I scrubbed my greenhouse paths every Friday afternoon with a stiff broom to remove
the green algae, I would sing, to the tune of 'La Donna è Mobile':

> *Parthenocissus tricuspidata*
> *Thuja plicata*
> *Fagus sylvatica*
> *Atropurpurea*
> *Pinus sylvestris*
> *Acer campestre*
> *Metasequoia glyptostroboides*
> *Rhus typhina*

Well, it kept me amused. I can still remember plant names
more easily than people's names, which is something of an embarrassment.

So keen was I to do well that I would sit up late into the night,
writing lists of the plants I'd learned that day. I was inscribing
the words *Aucuba japonica* in a notebook one evening when my
dad came to look over my shoulder. 'What's that?'

'Spotted laurel.'

'Yes, well, you'll be spotted if you don't go to bed. Come on.
You've to be up early tomorrow.'

We'd get up at the same time each morning, Dad and me. I
never felt like eating much at that time, but in winter he'd insist
that I have some porridge. He'd make it. He was good at porridge.

And cooked breakfasts, too, though if he'd cooked it he could never eat it. Funny. We didn't say much; both quiet first thing. Then I'd say goodbye and get on my bike, while he'd get into his van and motor off in the opposite direction. I wore jeans, a jumper and a donkey jacket. He'd wear a blue boiler suit, a tweed jacket and a flat cap.

I might not have eaten much in the way of breakfast, but for the rest of the day I could eat for England. By a quarter to nine, the van driver who took the men out to work in the public gardens would return with pork pies. These were not the tired, cold pies from a supermarket but fresh, hot pies from Thirkell's, the pork butcher. I'd have two of them, drinking the liquid through the hole in the top, then biting into the crunchy pastry and finally devouring the meat. God, how I loved those pies! There would be a mug of tea later in the morning, then I'd nip home for lunch – sometimes sandwiches, and sometimes something hot. I'd have an iced bun in the afternoon, then a hot meal when I got home, and a sandwich for supper. I weighed about eight stone.

I was five feet tall when I started work. I grew to five foot nine inches during a year under glass.

During four years on the nursery I learned my trade in every last detail. I was taught how to sow seeds and take cuttings – fifteen thousand pelargonium cuttings every summer. They would be brought into the nursery in great hessian sheets, and we'd sit in the potting shed week after week, preparing them until our thumbs were covered in black cuts, stained by the sap of the plants. At the end of every day we'd dib them in around the edges of four-inch clay flowerpots filled with well-drained compost and topped with sharp sand, to stop them rotting. Then they'd be barrowed to the propagating house to be kept warm until they rooted and were ready for potting up.

I was taught how to dig properly, and how to plant a tree. Mick Ware, Ron Jeavons, the propagator, and Ken Wilson, the foreman, were responsible for my basic education, but I remember being instructed in tree planting by the most senior of the gardeners, Harry Hollings. He was a big man, Harry, with white hair and a sizeable 'corporation'. He'd be in his sixties by then. In manner he was often curt, but good natured, and he knew his stuff. He always answered my questions, however stupid they might seem to him, until that moment at the end of the day when it all became too much and he wanted to get off home. 'Right.' He'd swing his leg over his bike and be gone.

Tree planting. He was quite specific in his instructions:

'Tha digs an 'oil. Then tha chucks some shit in, then tha plants t'tree, firms it in an' stakes it.'

I watched, and copied his technique. When the job was finished I turned to go and clean my spade.

'Where's tha goin'?'

'To clean me spade.'

'But tha's not done yet.'

I was puzzled. 'I've done all you told me.'

'Nay, lad. Tha can't go until tha's talked to it.'

This was long before Prince Charles's pronouncement on the importance of conversations with plants.

'What do I say?' I asked.

'Tha teks three steps away from it; tha looks at it sideways and tha sez, "Grow, yer bugger, grow."'

And I still do.

There were times when Harry's patience seemed to be in short supply, but then I learned why. His wife was suffering from cancer, and had now been moved into a local hospice. He went to see her every evening. It was only a matter of time, they said.

He came to me one day and started up a conversation. 'I hear tha's looking for a greenhouse. A proper one.'

'Yes. Why?'

'Tha can have mine, if tha wants. I'm going to be moving soon and it needs a good 'ome. I can't tek it with me. No room.'

I felt sad. And embarrassed. But thrilled, too.

'How much do you want for it?'

'I don't know. I'll 'ave to ask the wife. I'll let thee know.'

Harry's wife died a few weeks later. He sold me the greenhouse for a fiver, and I helped my dad dismantle it and take it home on a hand cart. With it came all manner of brass sprayers and syringes, dibbers and seed box firmers and sieves. I use them still. He always enquired after it, and took an interest in what I was doing. Even told me that I should go to college, and to Kew, to get a decent training. But for now I had to learn the basics of my chosen craft, the mysteries of pruning, and seed germination, the intricacies of air-layering, budding and grafting. How and when to water, and potting up, and pricking out, and potting on.

There were mundane tasks, as well as the more fulfilling kind – washing clay flowerpots in ice-cold muddy water, mixing mountains of John Innes compost, after heating up the loam in a massive soil steriliser. And then there was the boiler, an enormous coke-fired beast that heated the greenhouses.

I had a week on and a week off when it came to boiler duty. At eight o'clock in the morning I would go down the steps of the sunken boilerhouse to meet this glowering hulk that sat there like a massive fledgling, always demanding food. First the door at the front would be opened and the melted and congealed mass of ash waste in the bottom of the fire bed had to be broken up with a six-foot poker, on the end of which I would have to bounce my feeble frame to get the clinker to fracture. I'd lift out the lumps with a huge set of tongs and put them into two dustbins, followed by the ash that had to be scraped out from under the fire.

When that was done, the damper would be opened to create a through draught to get the fire bed glowing, and I'd then shovel in hundredweight upon hundredweight of coke, ramming the eight-foot chamber full with another long-handled tool, and then shutting down the damper once the flames had taken hold. I'd check to see all was well at midday, then stoke up again at night before I went home. Once a week the dustbins full of clinker would have to be carried up the boilerhouse steps and emptied on the ash pile. It was as good as being an engine driver. No wonder I weighed only eight stone.

Not all my training went smoothly. I was sent into a greenhouse one day to disbud carnations that were being grown to decorate the Town Hall. I was asked if I knew how to disbud. I said I did. I mean, it's a fairly straightforward word, isn't it – disbud? It means take buds off. So I did. All of them.

Now I'm older and wiser I know that when a gardener says he is disbudding something, he means that he is taking off the side buds to let the larger, central ones develop sooner and free of competition.

In my case it was later – much later.

In the mid-1960s, Ilkley Urban District Council Parks Department employed around a dozen men. First thing in the morning they would all meet at the nursery, some arriving on foot, others on bikes and Mopeds, and one or two in cars of ancient vintage – the Ford Popular belonged to the propagator, the ancient Austin van to Dick Hudson, the tractor driver, and the Hillman Imp to a man who didn't stay long. He seemed smart and well spoken. I think he thought gardening might be fun, but he didn't last.

They'd all have tea in the mess room, then be driven out to the parks around the town to plant and mow and cultivate the soil, before being rounded up and returned at the end of the day.

Three of us – the propagator, Ron Jeavons, and Mick Ware and me – worked in the nursery full time. Our job was to grow bedding plants for the town's flower beds, to provide floral decoration for the Town Hall and the public library, and to raise quite a few plants for the council's social event of the year, the Civic Ball, held in November in the King's Hall. We furnished troughs of flowers for smaller events, too – recitals for the Ilkley Concert Club, and the annual Wharfedale Music Festival – but it was the Civic Ball that was the Chelsea Flower Show of our year, and much of the content of our thirteen greenhouses was cultivated especially for it.

We had two greenhouses full of chrysanthemums, chest-high plants in massive clay pots with large incurved or reflex-petalled flowers as big as melons. Today, names like 'Fred Shoesmith', 'Town Talk' and 'Mayford Perfection' take me straight back to the Dutch-style greenhouse with its large panes of glass that rattled in the passing breeze, and the hundreds of pots of chrysanths that stood on the low, gravel-covered beds.

Chrysanthemums have their very own fruity smell – crush a leaf and the sweet and sour aroma of autumn will hit your nostrils. They needed weekly feeding, and regular staking and tying. In summer they would be stood outdoors, their bamboo canes fastened to horizontal wires that ran between posts so that they would not blow over on windy days. In September they came under cover for the final push – and the disbudding, by which time, fortunately, I knew what I was doing.

We grew cinerarias and cyclamen, an entire greenhouse full of tender ferns, hydrangeas, oh, you name it, we grew it, and in November, vanload after vanload would leave the nursery and make the ten-minute journey to the King's Hall where the precious cargo would be carefully unloaded and used to fill the balcony and the boxes, as well as the sides of the massive stage.

My job was almost always at the nursery end, loading up. The grandeur of placement fell to more senior members of staff. I rather wished I could have a go, too. But then, when the work was nearing completion, I was always allowed to travel with the last load and have a look, sitting in the back of the Land Rover, steadying the stems of the last few potfuls as we rattled up to town. I remember feeling very proud, the first time I saw the results of our efforts. The King's Hall had been turned into a botanic garden, the most wonderful fairyland of perfect flowers, banked up in a brilliant mountain of colour that would impress any visiting dignitaries.

'Not bad, eh?' asked Harry.

'No.' I couldn't say much more. I'd never seen so many flowers in one place.

There were those who considered it an extravagant waste. All those plants being grown simply for decoration; for pleasure. I never thought of it like that. It was a chance for those of us in the nursery to show off our skills, and to give pleasure, and that's what gardening has always been about – growing things to give pleasure. If cutting down on such extravagances really did make a difference to the health service and the education within the town, all well and good but, as everybody knows, when savings on such things *are* made, you never notice the improvement anywhere else. Life doesn't work like that. And life without flowers is a dreary thing.

During the summer I would be allowed out of the nursery early each morning to go and water the hanging baskets up the posh end of town. And I quickly realised that I was happier in the nursery. As I trundled along The Grove, I would see my mates walking to school in their smart uniforms. And there was I, pushing a water cart and shinning up a ladder in my denim apron to water the lobelia and the alyssum, the ivy-leafed pelargoniums and petunias.

Gardening was a job I had always longed to do but, at fifteen, running this gauntlet of my schoomates was a tough baptism of fire. I'd try to time it so that I could get done before they passed, or delay my arrival until they had gone, but it never seemed to work, and they would shout at me across the street as I bent double, pushing my wheeled tubful of water: 'Yeah! Go for it, Fred!'

I'd smile back ruefully, and pretend I didn't mind.

'That's 'im! Alan the Gardener!'

And it was. I had made my choice. And apart from that one job, I never regretted it for a moment.

I worked in the nursery for four years. After I left, they converted the boiler to oil. Then Ilkley Urban District Council became part of the Bradford Metropolitan area and the nursery stopped growing a bit of everything and became a staging post for bought-in pelargonium seedlings.

The Civic Ball is no more. The chrysanthemums are just a memory.

Eventually my old greenhouses, along with all the others, were pulled down, and the staff were dispersed to Burley and Menston and other little outposts. The nursery is now a housing estate. But the metal gates leading off Little Lane are still there, and I glance through them every time I pass, hoping that the people who tend the gardens appreciate the state of their soil. We dug a lot of manure into it over the years.

Hector Mutlow died last year, aged a hundred. Ken Wilson is retired and Ron Jeavons has moved on, but I still see Mick from time to time when I go back home. Harry Hollings died as well, a few years ago, but in his last year I went to Ilkley to open a Sensory Garden on The Grove. No hanging baskets to water now, and no passing schoolchildren shouting obscenities. Just friendly locals.

Quite a crowd turned up. I was asked to plant a couple of fragrant rose bushes. I was gardening on The Grove again, but not wearing my apron and jeans – instead a pale yellow jumper and grey trousers.

'We've got someone to help you,' they said. I looked up and saw Harry, in a grey suit. Thinner now, and older, but the same Harry, with the same shock of white hair.

'You look smart,' he said.

'So do you.'

'Want a hand?'

'If you like.'

We planted the bushes together, then I looked at him. 'Will you say it or will I?'

'Go on then,' he said.

And I whispered it, softly, so that only the two of us could hear: 'Grow, you bugger, grow!'

Harry nodded and chuckled, then stood up and wiped the soil from his hands.

'You know, lad,' he said, 'I'm right proud of you.'

It was the last time I saw him.

17

Stepping Out

'You can hang on to a daughter – a bit. But you've got to let go of a son.'
Steven Grace, *Brought Up Proper*, 1966

Leaving Nelson Road was not something that I ever thought about. But my parents, having lived there and saved there for fifteen years, decided they could afford to move to something a bit better. Dad was now the manager of the plumbing firm – albeit a manager who still fixed ballcocks and radiators – and they could afford to spread their wings. The terraced house they had bought in 1950 for £400 was sold for more than twice that amount and the money was used as a deposit on a brand-new semi-detached house that we all liked up 'the posh end of town'. It was pebbledashed, and had an integral garage, and glazed sliding doors between the dining room and the lounge.

The front and rear gardens were not much larger than those we'd left behind, but there was room for Harry's greenhouse, and I had a new garden that I could properly get my teeth into. Dad was happy to let me get on with it.

The move was less of a wrench than I imagined. We left behind the long thin garden and the sycamore, the midden that we never did dare to enter, the back lane and all the neighbours that I could name from the bottom to the top of our terrace in a kind of childhood litany – Beaumont, Lettern, Cawood, Evans, Barker, Francis,

Cunnington, Titchmarsh and Dinsdale. We moved into a close of twelve houses. I suppose I should have hated it, but it was really very pleasant. The neighbours were polite, there was room to park a couple of cars and, anyway, I knew I wouldn't be there for long.

That's why I didn't make too much fuss about having the smallest bedroom. From originally sharing with my sister the back bedroom at Nelson Road, with its floral-papered walls and oval cardboard print of Holman Hunt's *Light of the World*, I had been elevated to the lofty attic bedroom of my own with the dormer window, the duck wallpaper, the electric train track and the built-in desk unit crafted by my dad. But now we had moved and the train set had gone. At sixteen I was billeted in an eight-foot-square box at the end of the landing, but at least it had a view of Beamsley Beacon, Ilkley's heather-covered equivalent of Mount Everest.

Kath would have the larger back bedroom. She had passed her eleven plus and gone to the grammar school and, being a girl on the cusp of her teens, she would need more wardrobe space, as well as a desk for her homework. I didn't demur. In my box of a room there was space for a bed, a built-in wardrobe, a book-shelf and a very small table with a lamp.

It gave me just enough room to study for my City & Guilds, but with nursery work all day and one full day and evening at day-release classes, my social life was not exactly awesome. I could have taken more of an active role in the Ilkley Players, but the commitment was more than I could manage. Several nights' rehearsal a week would be hard to fit in among the swot's studies. I had enough plant names to learn without having to cope with pages of lines. I think I was also a bit scared of their repertoire, having been sent a script of Max Frisch's *The Fire Raisers* to read, and not understanding a word of it.

So what was the alternative? One night a month at the fire

station and choir practice on Thursdays? At least my voice had broken now. It took an embarrassingly long time. I had school friends who were grunting in a deep bass at fourteen, but I was still piping away reedily when I left school. I moved into the back row of the choir with the men when I started work, to avoid further embarrassment and prevent myself from being thought of as Ilkley's answer to Jimmy Clitheroe. Gradually, over the space of a year, my voice began to deepen, though it never did 'break' in the true sense of the word. I can still sing in a quite passable falsetto, but not in public. Not much in private, either.

My mates were all involved with their studies, and we had never really 'socialised' anyway – just played out in the street as kids, and then gone to school together. That bridge between being a child and an adult had been crossed now, and my school friends were still on the opposite bank; either that or they had crossed the water by a different route and ended up in another country. I find myself trying to think of an excuse as to why we grew apart. But I can't. Perhaps it was nothing more sinister than the simple fact that we now had different interests – they embroiled with their GCEs and A levels, and me wallowing in horticulture.

But how to find a social life? There was the tennis club down by the river, but they always seemed a bit stuck up. When you walked the dog along the riverside you could hear them shouting 'Yours!' in shrill, patrician tones. No. Not for me. And the tennis I used to play with the youth club on the public courts in summer was hardly of club standard. A pair of Dunlop Green Flash plimsolls and a Slazenger racket do not a Wimbledon champion make. How about the bowling club? Too old. The rugby club? Too rough – I'd have my head knocked off. And, anyway, I'd never been much of a ball player.

There wasn't much in the way of water skiing or hang-gliding around us. Not many opportunities for scuba diving. Listen at me going on, as though I really wanted an athletic pursuit. Of course I didn't. That's why I joined Ilkley Amateur Operatic Society. Homely, rather than impressive.

It was all Joyce's fault. She was our next-door neighbour. She had twin boys and a warbling soprano voice – you could hear her using it when she was cleaning. As she shook her duster out of the window you'd be treated to a snatch of *The Merry Widow* or *Die Fledermaus*, and over the drone of the Hoover she would implore, 'Tell me when you've got an hour to spare, then we'll fix up when to meet and where.'

As it happened, Joyce and I met up the following Tuesday. She said they were short of men and did I want to join? It was a completely resistible invitation, but the prospect of getting out of the house one night a week and doing something different swung the balance. What had I got to lose? So, with a vocal score of *Oklahoma!* tucked under my arm, and Joyce offering words of encouragement, I went with her, on that Tuesday evening, to the King's Hall to rehearse.

You're probably thinking by now that my entire life revolved round the King's Hall. I suppose it did. A lot of things happened to the Titchmarsh family in that great Edwardian pile. My parents first dated there; I first dated there. It's where the Civic Ball was held, and where we sang 'Jerusalem' once a year on the last night of the Wharfedale Music Festival, trying not to be embarrassed when Dad sang too loud. I went to dances there, to art shows and flower shows, and even to a concert by The Hollies, Ilkley's only brush with the Top Ten.

But on that Tuesday in October 1966 I wasn't exactly full of hope. I mean, an operatic society. Not exactly groovy.

I walked up the steps. The King's Hall has a proper stage, with lighting and crimson velvet curtains. There is a balcony at the

As Sir Joseph Porter in *HMS Pinafore* (1978) . . .

. . . and Ko-Ko in *The Mikado* (1976) at Richmond Theatre with
Barnes & Richmond Operatic Society.

Schachen, above Garmisch – Partenkirchen,
where I lived for three weeks in 1972.

The best view from a loo that
I've ever seen. (Taken standing
on the seat!)

Mum and Dad in their prime
during the early 1970s. Love the
sandals and socks, Dad.

The Kew student on the look-out for a squeeze.

Mum, Dad, Kath and Cindy at Bolton Abbey, taken on a weekend home from Kew.

Left: Cross-country running at Kew. With legs like these it's a wonder I could stand up. They are more robust now, and so is the rest of me.

Above left: Tramps' ball at Ilkley Fire Station
in the early 60s.

Above right: Bring on the dancing boys. *Oklahoma*
with Ilkley Amateur Operatic Society in 1967.
'Uncle' Harry Batty, Andrew Walbank and me in a
delightful paisley-patterned tie.

Left: The gloom of the potting shed – my first week
at work in the council nursery.

With Harry Hollings (who taught me how to plant a tree) planting roses
on the grove at Ilkley – 'Grow yer bugger, grow!'

Growing for gold – the *Woman's Own* Country Kitchen Garden won
me a Royal Horticultural Society Gold Medal in 1985. The awnings
belonged to the NatWest Bank next door.

The boy with his hero – on the 'Amateur Gardening' stand
at Chelsea Flower Show in the 1980s with Percy Thrower.

Celebrating 50 years of gardening at the BBC in 1981 with (*left to right*)
Geoffrey Smith, Arthur Billitt, Clay Jones, Professor Alan Gemmell, Percy
Thrower, Geoff Hamilton, Frances Perry, self, Roy Hay, Peter Seabrook
(hidden) and Ken Ford (producer of *Gardeners' Question Time*).

BBC *Nationwide* in 1980, thrust upon an unsuspecting
public from a studio potting shed.

At home in the greenhouse – rugby shirts
seemed like a good idea.

Better, perhaps, than Fair Isle
Sweaters. With Lulu, our first yellow
Labrador and a real star.

Saturday 26 July 1975. The sun shone, and the bride looked lovely.

back, and boxes with velvet-padded rims down either side. There is a ballroom floor that can be used for dances or, with its rows of what were then tubular steel seats with green padded backs and bottoms, it can be used as an auditorium.

On this particular Tuesday a shiny black grand piano had been pulled into one corner of the floor, and the padded seats were arranged around it in a horseshoe formation. I hung my coat on the mobile rack, already suffering paroxysms of agony. Seventeen, a bit spotty, total lacking in self-confidence, and about to plunge into I knew not what. I gripped the dog-eared vocal score tightly, turned round, took a deep breath, and then had it knocked out of me by the hardest back-slap I can remember.

'Nah then, lad! What's tha doin' 'ere?'

Jimmy Elder was the King's Hall caretaker. He was built like a hard rubber ball, every bit as round and every bit as resilient. He was always tanned, always full of vigour and, some said, always a bit too full of himself. He ran the King's Hall and Winter Gardens like a mini-empire, though the same some said that the place was really run by his wife Mary, a quiet, bird-like woman who seemed always to be dressed in a woolly headscarf and coat. And she was always carrying a mop and bucket. She looked like a woman who was always slightly disappointed in life. Not so her husband. They were an unlikely pair.

Jimmy (never James, unless you wanted belting) used to run weekly discos at the Hall, dressed in a shiny silver suit with a sparkly bow tie. He had his own miniature stage set with 'Jimmy' painted on it in stylish script. If you wanted middle-of-the-road musical entertainment in Ilkley at that time, you had two choices: Jimmy and his disco, or Bradley Hustwick and his trio, with Bradley (a small, hook-nosed man with slicked-back grey hair) on piano, a man with a lopsided toupee on drums, and a deaf carpenter on violin and saw. It was acquired listening.

Jimmy must have been pushing fifty at this time, but his favourite trick was to get you to punch him as hard as you could in the stomach. He could take this punishment without batting an eye. You'd do it once, and he would grin, 'Go on!' And you'd do it again. He seemed satisfied only when you had hurt your arm. Tonight he stood, in his customary fashion, in a set of all-in-one maroon-coloured overalls, with his hands on his hips and his stomach sticking out. 'Come for a sing?'

'Yes. Just seeing if I like it.' I didn't want to commit myself.

He beamed. 'Good for you! See you at tea time,' and with another slap that knocked me sideways he went off in the direction of his simmering urn.

As things turned out, I did like it, mainly because everyone was so laid back. So pleasant. It sounds rather pathetic to say so, but I was bowled over by the good-natured sociability of it all. I sat with the tenors and learned the line, but found myself, a few weeks later when music rehearsals turned into floor rehearsals, being asked to join the ranks of the 'dancing boys'. Just a minute; I joined to sing, not to dance. But it seemed churlish to object. I looked at the other men, hoping to spot somebody better qualified, physically, but most of them were the choral sort – all chest and legs like telegraph poles. I was an obvious choice – no chest and legs like rubber. Now this was a real worry. I had mastered my fear of joining an operatic society, and of singing on stage instead of in the choir stalls, but to dance in public? As a 'dancing boy'? And what would my dad think? It would be the umbrella incident all over again.

There is a moment in Rodgers and Hammerstein's *Oklahoma!* where Laurie, our heroine (that was Rita, a housewife from Ben Rhydding), has a dream about the hero, Curly (a portly man of forty-something called Brian, from Guiseley), and several male dancers trot across the stage pretending to be horses.

There were three of us: Andrew Wallbank, who was a local scoutmaster, myself, a local gardener, and the tall and urbane Harry Batty, whom I always knew as 'Uncle Harry'. Harry was a friend of Mum and Dad's. They had grown up together and stayed friends right through their lives.

Picture, then, suave, silver-haired Uncle Harry, a tall and angular Andrew Wallbank, and a small embarrassed gardener performing a sort of human dressage to the music of 'chicks and ducks and geese better scurry' – pause – 'when I take you out in the surrey' – pause, get off your horse and slap your thigh, pause – 'when I take you out in the surrey' – pause, fire your gun, then blow down the barrel, pause – 'with the fringe on top'.

I did it, but at every performance I thought I would die of shame during that particular scene. And my dad never made a comment. Perhaps he was speechless.

The following year we performed that memorable off-broadway hit, *The Quaker Girl* by Lionel Monckton, and I landed my first speaking role, that of William, a waiter at The Chequers Inn. A few days of listening to *The Archers* furnished me with a suitable accent with which to deliver my opening line, which was a sneeze, followed by the words: 'The moth do nesty so in these dress things.' Shakespeare it wasn't, but fun it was. In the second half I got to play a guest at the British Embassy in Paris, and joined in lustily with 'Come to the Ball', sung by a stout man from Burley pretending to be a ladykiller of a prince. Maybe that's what appealed to me about operatics (or, as Mum called them, 'your amachers'). The escapism. The dream. The romance.

Mick Ware in the nursery said it was daft. 'No one ever starts singing like that in real life – in the middle of a conversation.' I couldn't argue. Didn't want to.

In *The Quaker Girl* Uncle Harry played the part of Monsieur

Duhamel, a debonair French diplomat, which he carried off perfectly in white tie and tails and a silken sash sewn for him by my mother.

Harry was always referred to as 'a ladies' man'. He was handsome and distinguished, always smartly turned out, and had the most infectious laugh of anyone I have ever met. If Harry was in the audience you would always know. If a line were well timed, or a joke well placed, it would be rewarded with Harry's wonderfully aristocratic 'Har-har-har', coming from the heart and guaranteed to get the rest of the audience in the mood. People would have paid Harry to be in an audience.

When I was young, I could never work out why he was so well spoken, having grown up in Yorkshire with my parents who said 'bath' and 'grass' not 'barth' and 'grarse'. Harry's vowels were rounded, not flat, but there was no hint of snobbery about his delivery – it was just courtly. I've no idea what he did for a living.

When I was nine or ten I watched my mother make Harry a costume for a fancy-dress party. He had decided to go as a Maharaja, and Mum created for him an outfit that would have done a real Maharaja full justice – all turquoise silk and gold lamé, and sashes and jewelled orders.

I sat at her feet as she fitted him out with the silvery grey sash (which was actually a length of car seat belt, frayed at the ends), and Harry presented to my mother two round pieces of material which he asked to be stitched into the armpits 'because I perspire rather freely'. I remember particularly the elegance of the phrase. Not 'I sweat a lot', but 'I perspire rather freely'.

I had always liked Uncle Harry, right from being small. Apart from the fact that he laughed a lot, he was always encouraging in anything you did, and his conversation was witty and sharp. He dressed elegantly, and turned cigarette smoking into a fine art – not effeminate, just classy. It had never occurred to me to bracket him in any other category than that of 'Uncle Harry'. But when I started work in the Parks Department, I would hear them refer to him, from time to time, as a poof.

At first I thought they must be talking about another Harry. But no. Then I thought there must have been some mistake; they were wrong. It was just a misunderstanding and I wanted to tell them so. But I didn't. I just kept quiet. When it finally dawned on me that Uncle Harry really was gay, I remember the deep feeling of sadness. I wasn't sad that he 'wasn't normal', I was just sad that those who were sneering at him couldn't simply accept him for what he was – a lovely man who was tremendously good company.

There were, if I am honest, several weeks when I thought I had better avoid him, in case the guys at the nursery thought that I was a 'poof', too. But the feeling of awkwardness did not last long. I got over it, thank God, and until he died – all too suddenly just after I left home – Harry remained a valued and highly rated influence in my life, even if, just once, he caused me a certain amount of anguish.

My parents never referred to his sexuality. I thought that my father must have known, though he never said anything. My mother reiterated, perhaps just a touch defensively, that Harry was 'a ladies' man'. I bit my tongue.

Harry was friendly with another guy who was in the Operatic Society, a sweet, gentle soul who worked in the bank. More than that I do not know. Whenever Harry was in our company he was always alone. He had a small, terraced house in Brewery Road, a few streets along from Nelson Road, and one Christmas at a family party Harry put away more than his usual quantity of booze. He was legless – still laughing, but slurring away and having considerable difficulty in remaining vertical.

At the end of the evening Mum and Dad decided that we three

would take him back home to Brewery Road. I was not at all sure that this was a good idea. What if 'someone else' was in the house? Supposing we got there and found 'company' in Harry's divan? I went hot and cold at the thought. I offered to take him home myself. No; they said. I wouldn't be able to manage it. He was too heavy.

And so, with my heart thumping in my chest, I helped my mum and dad get Harry back home. We let ourselves in the front door with his key, located after much fumbling in the pocket of his tailored mac, with Harry still laughing away. We stumbled up the stairs to his bedroom where a large, double bed sat in the middle of the floor. It was empty, and we took off Harry's shirt and trousers and tucked him in.

My parents returned home as if nothing had happened. I was a nervous wreck. In my mind's eye I can still see the other guy sitting up in that bed wearing a frilly nightie. I'm glad it was just my imagination.

18

I Believe I Can Fly

'Gardening is a basic instinct. It is not so much learnt as uncovered.'
Tom Derwent, *Getting Down to Earth*, 1974

They gave me an alarm clock when I left home. To help me get up. And for doing well. But I'd have left earlier if I could. It's not that I was anxious to leave home, just keen to learn. I applied to Askham Bryan College near York when I was eighteen, just three years into my time in the nursery. But they turned me down.

The interview seemed to go well. But I was a bit puzzled. The principal of the college saw me for just a couple of minutes after I'd been comprehensively grilled by the Head of Horticulture. He asked me about bellringing.

The letter arrived a few weeks later:

Dear Titchmarsh,

With reference to your application to attend the Institute, I have carefully considered this matter and it is with very great regret that I have no alternative but to place your name on the list of reserve students for admission to the course commencing in September 1967.

I am very sorry to take this decision, but I know that you will understand that the places are limited by residential facilities, and until these are expanded it is necessary to restrict the number of places available.

Failing my ability to provide a place for you this September your name will be transferred to the list of applicants for admission to the following course.

Yours sincerely,

L. Gilling

Principal

There was no room in the inn. I would have to wait another year. But what if there was no room then, either? I had better hedge my bets. The following year I applied to another college for the National Certificate in Horticulture course scheduled to begin in autumn 1968. The Hertfordshire College of Agriculture and Horticulture at Oaklands, near St Albans, offered me a place. I accepted. A week later the letter from the Yorkshire (W.R.) Institute of Agriculture arrived. They would take me on their 1968 course.

For the first time in my life, I turned my back on Yorkshire and went down south. To tell the truth, I felt a bit of a traitor.

Nineteen is a suitable age to be measured for your first suit. I went to Easby's Gents Outfitters on Leeds Road with my mum, and Mr Flower measured me up. An appropriate name, I thought, bearing in mind my destination. The suit was charcoal grey. My waist measured twenty eight inches.

I needed work clothes, boots, wet-weather gear, and the suit. I think I only wore it once, for the group photograph of the yearly intake. There must have been about a hundred and fifty of us. I had never posed in one of those photographs before, where they stand you in tiers, and use a camera that moves from side to side to produce a long, narrow photograph. I knew they did it at universities, and posh schools, but it wasn't something they bothered about at Ilkley Secondary. In the photograph I look nervous; apprehensive. But then I was. I felt a bit like a small boy on his first day at boarding school.

The south did seem a bit impersonal at first. For a start, it was flat. And then there were the voices. As far as my mum was concerned, anyone who lived south of Sheffield was a Cockney. At the Hertfordshire college a lot of the students came from Essex and did seem to speak with what I imagined was a Cockney accent. Where I'd say 'plant' with a flat 'a', they would say 'plarnt'. But they were friendly. I steeled myself in preparation for the expected homesickness, but the pangs passed quickly, smothered by a mountain of work.

I had a room of my own in the hostel known as 'East Block'. No poetry there. No prizes, either, for guessing the name of the other accommodation building. They had probably been constructed by a group of architects whose previous commissions had included Parkhurst.

We ate in a large canteen, staffed by two Macedonian cooks, and there was always a queue for extra chips. Men of the land have hearty appetites, and the mood in the chip queue could become aggressive in cold weather. In the late 1960s, two thirds of the students were studying agriculture and the other third horticulture. Today the situation is reversed. Then, there were just half a dozen female students, shared between the two courses, and they resided in the big old house, under the watchful eye of Matron. The rambling, dreary, brick-built house was out-of-bounds to male students, except for the library, and the Principal's office, which you only saw if you were in trouble. Mr Pelham – 'Chunky' to the students – was a bulky man with a short fuse. He was not to be crossed. He only appeared in front of the students at occasional assemblies, and to teach meteorology.

Watching his massive bulk demonstrating the differing effects of veering, backing and katabatic winds was one of the highlights of the first term.

Matron was about five years older than most of the students. She was attractively built, with a short bob of dark hair, but her countenance was marred by a terminally bored expression. Always. In spite of this we all fancied her, but she would have none of it. She was of my mother's school of nursing – get out and get on with it. Anyone who requested her ministrations was a malingerer. She might give you some attention if part of your body broke off, but other than that you had to pull yourself together. Her equivalent of surgery was a brace of Anadin.

She came into her own in the second week of term when we all lined up for our tetanus jabs. Great burly agricultural students went down like flies at the sight of her needle. One after another they toppled from a great height, their eyes rolling into their sockets, and their lips fading to an icy white. She sighed, waited for them to stand up again, then stabbed their biceps and rubbed the wound with a lump of cotton wool dipped in methylated spirits, before poking them in the middle of their backs to send them on their way.

These muscular farmers' sons, previously intent on wooing her into their rooms, left her presence pink-faced and cowed. I waited, anxiously hoping that I would not suffer the same ignominy. I didn't look as she approached my arm with her instrument of torture. I felt a few sharp pricks and heard her tutting. I turned to see her face. She was biting her lip and screwing up her eyes, and seemed to be having difficulty finding the right spot.

'What's the matter?' I asked, risking her wrath.

'Hide like a rhinoceros,' she muttered, then finally pushed her weapon home, withdrew it and put my fingers over the meths-soaked cotton wool pad. I felt quite a hero, walking down the corridor with my sleeve rolled up, exposing my small but evidently steely biceps.

College days began with work in the fruit and market garden, the nursery, or under glass. Here the horticulture was 'commercial' rather than 'amenity', and I found myself working among acres of identical tomatoes and cucumbers, carnations being grown for cut flowers, apples and pears to be picked and graded, cabbages and cauliflowers that had to be harvested for market.

From 7 until 8 in the morning we had practical work, anything from washing leeks in cold, muddy water, to digging over nursery beds. From 8.15 until 9 a.m. was breakfast, then from 9 a.m. until 12.25 p.m. came lectures in subjects that were nothing if not comprehensive – botany, top fruit, soft fruit, crop protection, climate and soils, nursery practice, glasshouse construction, glasshouse food crops, glasshouse flower crops, machinery, records and accounts, extensive market gardening, ornamental horticulture, calculations and protected culture. Quite what the last-named covered I have no recollection at all.

At 12.30 we broke for lunch, and in the afternoon, from 1.35 p.m. to 5 p.m., we had practical work – learning the intricacies of budding and grafting, how to sharpen your knife properly, practical projects, nursery walks and, once a week, library tuition. How to find what you want in books. And how to hang a sentence together. The librarian was a gentle man called Colin Barley. He wore floral ties and spoke very softly, but he was no soft touch. What he lacked in volume, he made up for in vocabulary and sent bolshy students from his presence in embarrassed silence, wondering if they had just been insulted or praised.

In between times we made dried flower collections (my only first prize) and bottled insect pests in formaldehyde. We had an hour and a half of sport on Wednesday afternoons. I opted for cross-country running, but the scenery around the college wasn't really on a par with the Yorkshire moors. I played rugby once, and got concussed, and hockey once, and scored a goal. It seemed enough.

High tea was between 5.30 p.m. and 6 p.m., followed by private study (in your room) from 6 p.m. till 8 p.m. After that, you could go out, if you wanted, to the Bunch of Cherries down the road for a drink, and to chat up the landlord's two daughters whose strapping thighs were the talk of the college. But you had to be back in your room by 10.30 p.m. And we always were. Bless.

At weekends the rules were relaxed a little. We did practical work from 9 till 11 a.m., and had a weekly test – plant identification and the like – from 11.15 till noon, but then our time was our own, and we could be back as late as 11 o'clock. Midnight if we had a signed exeat form.

It was at weekends that we had our only chance to fraternise with the opposite sex. The half-dozen women at college were either spoken for or not interested in that sort of thing. So we cast our nets slightly further afield, in the direction of Watford, to two girls' colleges by the name of Wall Hall and Balls Park – the latter, on a bad night, being referred to as 'the Knacker's Yard'.

Here, at dances, we could try our luck with the local talent. Shrinking violet that I was, I was emboldened by the success of Dick, a fellow student who, in spite of being a country bumpkin from Somerset, with a slow delivery and an accent straight out of *The Archers*, seemed to pull every time he went out.

'How did you do?' I'd ask on the return journey, from the back of his minivan, after yet another evening of lost opportunities.

'All right,' he would say. 'Her face warn't up to much but she were good fer a grope.'

I'd catch sight of him, sometimes, at dances, necking in a

corner. He had this engaging way of holding a girl in one arm while he snogged her, so that he could hold his pint and his fag in the other. And he always leaned sideways, and lifted one leg off the floor. I hoped it was not a technique I'd have to learn.

Throughout the whole of my year at college I managed just two conquests – a one-night stand with a Chinese nurse, and a longer liaison with a girl who was deeply into horses. The Chinese nurse was lovely, with long, shiny, jet-black hair and limpid eyes. I dreamed of having to confront my parents, and of their possible reaction, being fans of the film *South Pacific*. But she wasn't called Liat, she was called Lyn. She left purple eye-shadow on the collar of my cream, drip-dry nylon shirt. I didn't wash it for a fortnight.

Dick was desperate to know if it was true what they said about Chinese women – you know – down there. Was it really sideways? I smiled knowingly. But I'd only kissed her. I hadn't a clue.

Helen was a different kettle of fish altogether. She was a petite blonde with long hair, held back by a black velvet band. She wore floral-patterned mini-dresses and had the best pair of legs I'd ever seen. And you could see almost all of them. We met at a dance, and Dick took up with her friend. He said he only did it so that I could get off with Helen. I didn't really believe him, but it was nice of him to say so.

She didn't try to escape before the first smoochy number. Instead, she rested her head on my chest, and then came to the bar for a drink. We snogged in the car park when it was all over, and she gave me her telephone number.

We went out four or five times, I suppose, and towards the end I even went round to her house. It was a smartly turned out sort of farm, and her parents were well spoken. Very Hertfordshire.

Helen seemed uneasy. She perched next to me on the arm of the sofa in her mini-skirt, and I remember my heart pounding. She was going on at her father about a horse.

'But I didn't want him cut; he should have been left entire,' she kept saying, tossing back her long blonde hair.

Her father grunted and said, 'Well, it's done now.'

I hadn't a clue what they were talking about.

We agreed to meet the following Saturday afternoon outside the prize cattle shed at the agricultural show.

I turned up at the appointed time – well, earlier probably, bearing in mind my punctuality problem. There was no sign of her. Half an hour I waited, until I heard a voice at my elbow. I looked down and hardly recognized the girl standing there. She had short-cropped hair and no make-up, and wore an army combat jacket and jeans. She didn't look very happy.

I wandered around the cattle pens with her, trying to enthuse about a heifer here and a bullock there, but her heart wasn't in it. Our little affair had clearly run its course. That afternoon I was given the old heave-ho by a sweet girl who thought there was no longer any point in wearing her long blonde hairpiece or her mini-skirt. To be fair, I suppose they would have looked a bit out of place at an agricultural show. But then, perhaps if I had been more sympathetic about equine castration the problem would never have arisen.

I studied, during my nine-month stint in Hertfordshire, for the National Certificate in Horticulture, and the following summer I left the college a qualified horticulturist. I even typed myself a few business cards: Alan Titchmarsh N.C.H. But only a few. They weren't really proper letters after your name, but Mum and Dad were pleased.

They were even more pleased that autumn. I was accepted by the grandly titled Royal Botanic Gardens, Kew, to be a Student Gardener on their three-year diploma course. Hundreds applied, they said. Only twenty were taken on. I was one of them. Mum and Dad bought me a transistor radio this time.

19

Infra-Digs

'It wasn't so much that the bathroom was dirty, it's just that it would have kept David Attenborough going in natural history programmes for a year.'

Tom Welland, *Leaving Home*, 1995

The student accommodation in East Block suddenly seemed like the Ritz. Well, it would have done if I had known the Ritz. It was all right for the poet Alfred Noyes, cajoling his readers to 'Go down to Kew in lilac time', but I came down in September, when the first nip of autumn was in the air, and finding comfortable digs did not prove easy.

There was no official provision for the accommodation of students at Kew. Instead, we were farmed out to assorted boarding houses and bed and breakfasts all over the London Borough of Richmond-upon-Thames. There were houses simply packed full of students – some two to a room – and there were 'normal' places where you would be treated as a house guest by a professional family who were happy to supplement their income by letting a room. But these cushy billets were few and far between.

A month before your impending arrival you would be sent a list of 'Approved Accommodation'. The identity of the inspector was never disclosed; probably for fear of reprisals. Neither were the grounds for inclusion explained in what turned out to be a hopelessly out-of-date set of details.

I knocked on the door of one house and discovered that the family listed as living there had moved out a year previously. The newcomers had not the slightest intention of taking in boarders, and I scuttled down the garden path feeling alone and unwanted in the big city. One woman, with folded arms and a face that could chop wood, explained that they no longer took students on account of 'problems'. Whether these problems were her own, or belonged to the students, she did not say. And I didn't like to ask.

There was only one name left on the list: Mrs Spurling. That's all it said. I plodded wearily along to the address in Mortlake Road and rang the bell. It was some time being answered, and before the door was opened I had to identify myself to the woman on the other side.

'Hallooo?' she enquired.

'Mrs Spurling?'

'Who is it?'

I shouted through the letterbox, the better to make myself heard against the din of the traffic. 'I'm a student. From Kew. I've come to enquire about a room.'

'Just a minute.' There was a rumbling of assorted bolts and locks, and finally, after the withdrawal of an armoury that would not have disgraced the Royal Mint, I beheld an elderly lady in an old-fashioned pinny, with grey hair and glasses over which she peered at me. The accent was Geordie, softened by years in West London.

Mrs Spurling squinted at me. 'Who did you say you were?'

'A student. From Kew Gardens. Your name is on this list.' I waved the piece of paper at her, rather like a white flag.

'Oh, yes. Well, you see, I don't take students any more. On account of . . .'

'Problems?'

'Yes.'

'But I'm very quiet.'

It was all I could think of. She eyed me up. Maybe she recognised a fellow northerner a long way from home.

The face was kindly, if puzzled, and the voice was sing-song in its rhythm. 'I see. Well, I might be able to squeeze you in.'

A trio of double-decker buses thundered past and all conversation stopped. I winced at the din.

'You'd better come in,' she said.

I stepped over the threshold into a dark hallway, decorated with even darker Victorian wallpaper, and she ushered me up the stairs at the end of the passageway.

'This is all I've got.' She pushed open the door of what amounted to a cupboard, with a small window and a smaller wardrobe. It overlooked the road and had two sources of illumination: a 25-watt bulb suspended from the ceiling, and the mercury-vapour street lamp directly outside.

'I see. Er . . . how much?'

'Four pounds ten shillings a week.'

I smiled weakly and ran my finger down my list. There were no more names to try. No more places to go. Mrs Spurling smiled back, knowing she'd got me over a barrel.

'You'd better come and meet Fred and Jack.'

I thought they must be her cats, but they turned out to be her lodgers, two elderly men who hardly spoke to one another but who had been with her for years. Jack worked in the civil service. He had a swollen face and thick glasses, and spent every evening, when he came back from the Coach and Horses, crouched over the gas fire in his room, smoking Woodbines. He was a quiet soul, but then Fred made up for his deficiency.

Fred worked for the post office. He was a strapping man with a broad chest and a bald head. When he went off to work in the morning he wore a grey Homburg and a grey coat over his suit and tie, and he left the house like a whirlwind – all huff and bluster. He smoked a pipe, which he used to puff on maniacally every time he lit it. He could have taught Uncle Bert a thing or two about camp fires.

Fred was Mrs Spurling's right-hand man. He even wore a frilly-necked pinny over his waistcoat and tie when he came home, and had a way of addressing you that assumed you were both hard of hearing and slow on the uptake.

'Cold out tonight, I say? COLD OUT TONIGHT!'

'Yes, Fred. Very cold.'

He was paranoid about gas fires being turned out properly, on account of the fact that Jack had once forgotten to light the one in his room after putting another shilling in the meter. I listened to his lectures every evening during those first weeks, hardly daring to point out that I hadn't got a gas fire in my room, so the rules didn't really apply.

It made no difference. Polishing away at the dishes hard enough to rub off the pattern, he reiterated the importance of turning off the gas fires and mastering the locking of the front door.

'There's a ring, do you see? A RING!' He demonstrated the security system, which was clearly of his own devising. It involved the removal of a curtain ring from a hook on the hat stand when you went out, and its replacement when you came back in. You were given a Yale key to let yourself in during daylight hours, but when Fred and Mrs Spurling retired – she to the back room downstairs, and he to the first floor front – the door would be bolted unless one of the rings had not been replaced on the hook, showing that you were still out. If yours was the last ring to be replaced, you bolted the door after your return, knowing that everyone was safe inside.

'It's important, you see? IMPORTANT! THAT YOU DON'T FORGET YOUR RING!'

It was clearly important that I didn't forget my ring. If I did, there would be no way of getting in, without waking the entire house and causing Mrs Spurling, who was a nervy sort, to imagine that burglars were trying to break in. In such circumstances she had been instructed, by Fred, to scream as loudly as she could so that he could run downstairs with the poker. He promised he would do that. I heard him one evening over the smoked haddock. Well, he had the smoked haddock. I had to make do with beans on toast, because Mrs Spurling had promised the final yellowing bit of fish to Fred.

He rubbed his hands and picked up his knife and fork. He was the noisiest eater I have ever met. A prince of mastication. Grandma Titchmarsh always said that you should chew each mouthful thirty-two times. Fred went into triple figures. With his mouth open.

Then he'd put his knife and fork on the plate and beam at Mrs S. 'Tickety-boo, dear?'

'Tickety-boo, Fred.'

Then he'd light up his pipe and the finer features of the room would disappear from view.

I paid for bed, breakfast and evening meal. Not dinner – evening meal, which provided Mrs S with a bit more flexibility if funds were running short by Friday. I 'enjoyed' tripe and faggots on countless occasions, and large helpings of boiled potatoes cooked, for the most part, *al dente*.

And then there was the bed. The first time I turned it down I noticed some small creatures on the lower sheet. In spite of my two light sources and a college education in entomology I was unable to identify them with the naked eye. They disappeared quite quickly and I thought that maybe, in the anxiety of being away from home, I had imagined things.

I woke up the following morning with an impressive selection of pink spots that itched like mad. I broached the subject with Mrs Spurling and she said that it must be the moth. I accepted her pronouncement, until my reasoning (clearly slowed down by the ever-lowering temperature in my icy room) told me that moths had caterpillars, not fleas.

She obligingly changed the sheets.

For several weeks I laboured in the gardens during the day, and retired to Mrs Spurling's in the evening, battling with the Incredible Exploding Geyser in the bathroom, and the livestock in the bedroom, until the one night when the inevitable happened. I forgot to move my ring.

I returned at midnight to discover the house in total darkness and the front door bolted on the inside. It was November. I spent the night on a deck chair in the coal shed, and only managed to gain entry to the house at 8.30 the following morning.

My parents had come down from Yorkshire to see me and had arrived at the Coach and Horses the night before. It did occur to me to see if I could stay with them when I found myself locked out, but then I would have had to explain about the front door, and my room, and Fred and . . . well . . . it seemed easier to sleep with the coal.

I heaved my bent and freezing frame from the deck chair and quietly let myself in through the now unbolted front door. Fred had gone for his paper, and I nipped to the bathroom, had a wash, changed my clothes and ran out of the house clutching my break-fast for the day – a banana. I was starving. I unzipped the banana and leaned forward to take a bite. It fell out of my hand and rolled down a drain. I stopped and looked after it. Crestfallen.

Over bacon and eggs at the Coach and Horses my parents agreed that I really had better try to find somewhere else to live. Either that, or Mum would come and sort Fred out.

I decided on the former course of action. The prospect of my mum and Fred in mortal combat did not bear thinking about. I said, DID NOT BEAR THINKING ABOUT!

20

Joining the Kew

'The Royal Botanic Gardens are one of the jewels in London's crown. Founded by Princess Augusta, widow of Frederick, Prince of Wales, and mother of George III, they are not simply a public park, but rather the country's premier seat of botanical learning and expertise.'

Aurelia Tennyson, *About London*, 1894

If the Parks Department opened my mind, then Kew blew it. Where once I had had cultivated bedding plants and geraniums, I was now given charge of orchids and giant palms, rare cycads and ancient trees. My three Victorian greenhouses in the nursery were replaced by Decimus Burton's Palm House. I felt like a provincial bit-part player who had landed a role on Broadway.

Unlike college, where the days were divided in two, with lectures in the morning and practical work in the afternoon, at Kew there was a solid block of lectures lasting three months. These were followed by exams and then by nine months of work in the gardens. There were no terms, just three weeks' holiday a year. This was a job, but a job like no other.

There were plant identification tests every week in the futuristic-sounding Jodrell Laboratory – twenty specimens drawn from Kew's unrivalled collection, all to be named in detail: family, genus, species and variety. The lectures majored on botany, now divided into more specific categories such as anatomy, taxonomy, structural botany, genetics and plant physiology. Our lecturers were doctors and professors. We studied fungi – mycology – and insect pests – entomology – and even the more prosaic staff management which bored me rigid. But practical gardening and landscaping figured largely, and we spent the nine months we were not incarcerated in lectures, working in one of the five departments: tropical, temperate, herbaceous and alpine, decorative and arboretum.

By the time the course finished in three years' time we would have worked in every single department and have accrued an all-round plant knowledge. With any luck we'd also have a diploma to prove it.

The first lecture block was mind-numbing in its intensity, but stimulating in the extreme. It was the horticultural equivalent of the Grand National, and there were four or five fallers. After the first year, most stayed the course, but it was not for the faint-hearted.

Manual labour came as a welcome relief after those first three months of academia, even though the plant identification tests continued on a weekly basis. We had no choice in the ordering of our place of work; that was decided upon by Leo Pemberton, the lean and diplomatically adept Supervisor of Studies in whose charge we remained during the lecture block.

Getting a decision out of Leo Pemberton was sometimes about as likely as getting the Elgin marbles back to Greece. I have never met a man who could so successfully see both sides of an argument, but he was scrupulously fair and a great champion of the students, even when it came to them securing employment at the end of the course.

When we were farmed out into the gardens themselves we

became a part of the workforce, and as such reported to department heads; men with the deliciously archaic title of 'Assistant Curator'.

The gardens are now governed by a board of trustees, but at that time they were a part of the Ministry of Agriculture, Fisheries and Food and even the students were civil servants. The hierarchy was carefully structured. The boss was the Director – at that time a dour Scot, Sir George Taylor.

At a cheese and wine party – then Kew's only officially recognised form of social intercourse – the new students were gathered together in the laboratory with senior members of staff to break the ice. Sir George was in attendance. Short of stature, with a beady eye and iron-grey hair, he was not a man of copious small-talk, as I was about to discover. He marched up to me (as the first student in his line of vision) and barked in his clipped, Scottish tones, 'Any complaints?'

'No sir!' I blurted out. 'I wouldn't dare,' and laughed maniacally to cover my embarrassment.

I had hoped that the conversation might have ended there, with my pathetic and not entirely original rejoinder. It did not.

'Why?' he asked.

I can't remember how I got out of the hole I had so neatly dug for myself, but I remember his incredulous expression as he turned on his heel and strode off in search of someone of finer intellect and a greater command of the English language.

Under Sir George Taylor came the Deputy Director, J.P.M. Brenan, a gentle and well-spoken man of impeccable manners. Pat Brenan was also the Keeper of the Herbarium, Kew's unique collection of dried and pressed plants. These are the specimens from which, in the main, the flora of the world is classified. Botanists are sent all over the globe by Kew's herbarium to carry out research, to hunt for new plants, and to otherwise add to our knowledge of the plant kingdom.

On their return, their desiccated plunder is fumigated, sorted, classified and stored in row after row of cupboards that stretch from floor to ceiling in the wings of the herbarium – they keep building new ones as the collection grows. And it grows at a staggering rate: botanists bring back in excess of 30,000 dried and pressed plant specimens a year to add to Kew's collection of around seven million. They also bring back seeds which are deposited in the Millennium Seed Bank, a genetic resource aimed at ensuring the sustainability of world vegetation in perpetuity.

The herbarium is one of three major departments at Kew. The second is the Jodrell Laboratory, the home of botanists and plant scientists who work on living plant material, as opposed to the dried stuff, and whose task is to discover more about the internal workings of plants as well as the taxonomy (classification) which is the main focus of the herbarium. Bringing up the rear (and sometimes it did feel like that) was the gardens department, which has since been elevated in its title, and its status, to the Living Collections Division. I ask you; what sort of name is that?

The Jodrell Laboratory was presided over by a highly sociable Welshman, Dr Keith Jones, again with the title of 'Keeper', and the Gardens by a wry, dry Scot, Dick Shaw, whose rank was that of Curator.

Each section of the 'Gardens' had its own Assistant Curator, and under them came the Gardens Supervisors, a name which, in the late 1960s, had recently replaced that of foreman. Gardens Supervisors were the first rank of the hierarchy, and to prove it they each had a bike. Some had baskets on the front, some had tatty saddlebags, but each was a badge of office, and one to be treasured. The gardens comprise 300 acres and, apart from an occasional rise or dip in the ground, they are flat. Riding a bike there must rank as one of life's greatest pleasures. But that would come later.

I was sent, first, to the tropical department, to work in the orchid houses, under an exacting, no-nonsense Assistant Curator called Stan Rawlings. Stan had a London accent that I found hard to grasp at first.

It is always assumed that people from the shires are the ones whose accents require translation, but that is the received wisdom of Londoners alone. The rest of us – be we northern or West Country – can also struggle to comprehend the vernacular of the Metropolis. (All right, so *EastEnders* might have helped us a bit, but back in the 1960s we were weaned only on *Coronation Street*, and for us northerners, that was telling us what we knew already.)

I had been made aware of my inability to interpret the local lingo on my way down to London by rail. It was an evening trip, and I had decided that I would have my tea on the train. I enquired of the steward as to when I could eat. His reply, so far as I could make out, was 'Din rartid arpy'. It was only after the third time of repeating the phrase that he slowed down enough for me to understand that he meant 'Dinner after Derby'.

I was quicker on the uptake when Stan Rawlings, using similar native woodnotes wild, reprimanded me for sleeping in two days running, suggesting that if I did the same the following morning my contract would be terminated. I think he used the phrase 'Yarra ta vere', which I was more easily able to construe as 'You're out of here'. I got the message and bought a new alarm clock to replace the one given to me by Mum and Dad. Its bell was clearly on the blink.

The orchid houses were part of a complex glazed structure known as the 'T-range', on account of its overall shape. It comprised houses for epiphytic and terrestrial orchids from trop-ical and temperate countries, cactus and succulent houses, Cape heathers from South Africa, and one large, central glasshouse which was devoted to the giant waterlily – *Victoria amazonica* – named after the late Queen by Sir Joseph Paxton who, apart from being the architect of the Crystal Palace, was clearly a dab hand at sycophancy.

There were guppies in the vast, waist-high tank in which this massive plant grew, its plate-like leaves fully six feet across. Top up the tank too zealously of a morning and it would overflow, leaving hundreds of little grey fish flapping all over the pathway. Getting them off the floor and back into the warm water was like spooning treacle with a feather.

Plants I had reckoned on encountering at Kew; the livestock came as a bit of a surprise and, in some cases, a shock. If you were to rearrange the rockery stones in one of the beds of tropical plants, you would discover earth that was simply alive with cockroaches. I'm not generally squeamish about insects, snakes, spiders and things of that sort, but I do not like cockroaches. They move too fast for my liking, and they make a nasty crunch when you tread on them, oozing with creamy-grey pus. Enough! Eughh!

But the orchids were a more pleasurable eye-opener, plants of incomparable beauty and unparalleled diversity. I discovered how to grow those exotic show-offs the cattleyas and cymbidiums, got to know dendrobiums and paphiopedilums; I learned the difference between terrestrial (ground-growing) orchids, and epiphytes (which grow on trees). And it was here that I had my first taste of the uniqueness of Kew's plant collection.

Aerangis rhodosticta is not a particularly flamboyant orchid, as orchids go, but it is one of the rarest. The botanist who collected it had been told of its existence, and its location, by local natives on some distant tropical shore, but was sceptical of their story that the flower itself was small and white – maybe an inch across

– but the reproductive organs in the centre of the bloom were scarlet. It was a combination hitherto unknown in the orchid world. He went in search of the plant and was shown it growing in the mist underneath a waterfall. It was not in bloom. He dug it out of its misty niche and sent it back to Kew, suggesting that the story was probably a fairy tale. Before he himself could return, the botanist fell to his death down a ravine. The orchid later bloomed at Kew and proved the natives right.

I tended that orchid – a plant barely four inches across, strapped to a piece of cork bark, with its roots wrapped in moss to simulate its natural environment – and gazed upon the flower that its collector never saw. Plant collecting may, on the face of things, seem a sedentary pursuit, but most plant collectors could teach Indiana Jones a thing or two about danger.

Many of these men (and they were mainly men in the early days) lost their lives in search of their botanical quarry – either in avalanches, rock falls or at the wrong end of a native's spear. Others got their plunder back home safely and it continues to survive. Provided the students don't cock things up.

The Palm House was my third stop during my time at Kew. I managed to stay there for a whole year, which is a long time in a plant's life. When you look at the Palm House from the large pond that sits in front of it, the long, low, left-hand end is where the cycads are grown. These are primitive palms which grew on the planet when dinosaurs ruled the earth. (So did marestail, but that's a garden weed and so is less exciting.) I was given charge of that left-hand end.

Among Kew's collection of cycads was a plant of *Encephalartos woodii*. It grew in a wooden tub four feet square and four feet high and was, itself, a six footer, with a spreading head of downward-curving fronds that had all the apparent toughness of an armadillo's scales. I was shown it, and instructed on its preferences: not too much water, just enough to keep it damp. Too little or too much and it could perish. Oh, and it was the only one of its kind in cultivation in the world.

The labels on many of the plants at Kew, as well as giving the plant's family and full botanical name, also show the date of the plant's introduction to the gardens, and the name of the collector. As I recall, the name of the collector of this particular plant was Francis Masson, and the date was 1775. I knew from this that the plant had been brought to Kew in the time of Sir Joseph Banks. It bears a label stating that it is 'The Oldest Pot Plant in the World,' and it was down to me to keep it alive.

I can honestly say that I have never been so glad to get out of a greenhouse than I was at the end of my year in the Palm House. While the work might have been a joy, the responsibility was sometimes just a touch on the heavy side. There is, on balance, quite enough pleasure to be had in growing a potted geranium.

21

Mutual Improvement

'Some wear their learning lightly; others use it like a club, to beat you around the head.'

Robert Colborn, *Oxford Anthology*, 1944

Sometimes fate is obstinately unhelpful, and sometimes it smiles. In November 1969 it smiled, and one of my fellow students got married. As a consequence he moved out of his digs in a small house in a neat terrace leading down to the Thames, and recommended me as his replacement.

I checked out the room. It was clean and pleasantly scented of geranium leaves (there was a home-made pot stuffed with them on the bedside table). A huge, polished mahogany wardrobe stood against the end wall, there was a gilded mirror and two Victorian glass paintings on the dusky green-painted wall, a Pembroke table and chair provided a work place, and there were bookshelves and a comfortable wing chair. An Indian rug covered the stained floorboards.

I turned back the bed. The sheets were clean and crisp, and there was no sign of a flea. Or a moth.

The house itself had a Bloomsbury feel about it. Over one of the downstairs cupboards, a nude reclined on a bed of grapes. A peke yapped behind a door, a cat purred alongside a wood-burning stove, up to which were pulled an overstuffed sofa and a fat armchair, and Mrs Bell, with her glasses on the end of her nose, and an artist's brush in her hand, asked if I thought I might like to be her new lodger.

I said I would, and for the next three years, under Mrs Bell's roof, I would enjoy my cultural education. Eileen Elizabeth Jefford Bell was an artist and an author. While I was in residence at 1 Willow Cottages she wrote two children's books: *Tales from the End Cottage*, and *More Tales . . .* , about Mrs Apple and her collection of animals who lived in an idyllic Suffolk landscape. She painted, too – in oils on canvases and boards that were stacked in her studio which sat over the next-door building that doubled as her husband's office. They were expressive sort of pieces, some abstract, some figurative, but all of them packed with energy. She'd give me a canvas from time to time: 'Titch, do you want this, because I don't?' I was always 'Titch', to Mrs B.

She was in her sixties then, and would beaver about in thick tights and tweed skirts, a baggy brown sweater and a green gilet. Heating was her one economy: 'It's much cheaper to put on another sweater than to turn up the stove,' she would growl. But I don't ever remember being cold. Perhaps I put on an extra sweater, too. And I ate well: wonderful soups and stews and her own brand of moussaka, and wine – sometimes home-made (her oak leaf had a particularly detrimental effect on the legs) – drunk from unmatching, artful glasses. She would talk to the dog and the cat in a strange squeaky voice, pushing her thick bob of grey hair out of her eyes as she cooked, or painted, or clattered away at her typewriter bashing out her stories.

I have one of her books, inscribed, 'For Titch, who waits patiently for his supper while these masterpieces are being knocked off.'

It was under Mrs Bell's roof that I had my first bash at writing fiction. Only one chapter of a book with no plot and no title. I asked her what she thought of my efforts. She read, and considered briefly. 'Exactly as I expected,' she snorted. 'Rather juvenile, and not very good.' On a bad day, when a book or a painting was not going well, she could be particularly sharp. I caught glandular fever towards the end of my time under her roof. Mrs Bell was completely unsympathetic. 'I don't want that,' she said, and packed me off home. I drove all the way up to Yorkshire in my Mini, and on my arrival I was confined to bed for two days with exhaustion.

Mrs Bell's pet name was 'Cat' and her large and larger-than-life husband, Randall, was known as 'Badger', a round, ruddy, bespectacled colonel of a man, with a laugh that shook his whole body. He was a consultant surveyor, and a man whose morning started in an armchair with a rug over his knees, a pint pot of tea on the table beside him and *The Times* on his lap. For an hour he would scrutinise its contents, then he would bathe, dress and go to work next door in the little office under a sign saying 'Consultat'.

The Bells' son, Sebastian, was the principal flautist with the London Sinfonietta. 'Bas' lived with his wife and family in nearby Twickenham. During the next five years I was treated almost like a member of the family.

Mrs Bell, while never saying so in as many words, clearly regarded it as her duty to improve my artistic and musical education. I was taken to concerts, and to art galleries.

Driving to the Royal Festival Hall one evening, Randall Bell enquired, 'Have you ever heard a row before?'

I though we must be in for some raucous concert of modern music. My repertoire of Gilbert and Sullivan, Rodgers and Hammerstein, Lionel Monckton and Holst's *Planets Suite* had already been supplemented, thanks to Mrs Bell, by Ligeti and

Schoenberg, and I imagined we were in for another ear-bashing.

'What sort of a row?' I enquired.

'Claudio Arrau,' he replied.

I marvelled at Fragonard's *Girl on the Swing* in the Wallace Collection, in Manchester Square, stood at the top of the Albert Hall during promenade concerts, read Tom Stoppard and went to see Paul Scofield at the National in *The Captain of Kopenick*. All these events, as fresh in my mind now as though they happened yesterday, gave me an insight into a world that I thought would never be my province. I became Eliza Dolittle to Mrs Bell's Professor Higgins, though she thankfully never attempted to round my vowels. Time alone did that, the longer I stayed 'down south'.

I'd get ribbed about it when I went back home. 'Goin' all soft, are you, down there? Talking posh now.'

My response was, and still is, that I am doing missionary work.

Southerners still regard me as northern (a hard 'bath' and 'grass' are still responsible for that), but northerners think I talk posh. I have become, through the vicissitudes of fate, a displaced person. My children say 'barth' and I sometimes hear myself say it, too. And then those feelings of being a traitor to my roots bubble up again. But not in a paranoid way; it is more a wistful regret. You can take the man out of Yorkshire, but you can't take Yorkshire out of the man.

Some people get very funny about it. 'Why is it that Yorkshire people always go on about their county? If it's that good, why don't you go back there?'

Well, because I've sort of ended up here. Just because I love Yorkshire, as my place of birth and my home until I was almost twenty, doesn't mean to say I have to be xenophobic, does it? I go back there often – three or four times a year. My family is still

there, but life led me to Hampshire, and that's where I now live
and work. I don't have a problem with that. But just as a Scotsman
will always be a Scotsman, I shall always be a Yorkshireman. Not
a 'professional Yorkshireman'. I find myself irritated by those
fellow countrymen of mine who appear on television and 'call a
spade a bloody shovel'. You know the sort. Meat and two veg
men, who'll have 'none of that foreign muck'. They'll stick two
fingers in the air and say, 'Take me as you find me and like it or
bloody lump it,' as if intolerance and a lack of flexibility are something to boast about. Yes. I can quite see why some Yorkshiremen
give the place a bad name. But we're not all insensitive to other
people's feelings, and we don't all grow up with enough arrogance to fuel an army. Some of us remain reassuringly baffled
by life and far too sensitive for our own good.

Not all of my metropolitan education was undertaken by Mrs
Bell. I got out on my own a bit, too, to galleries and museums,
concerts and theatre, discovering that there was more to London
than Big Ben and Piccadilly Circus, shown to me by Uncle Bert.

I took my English O level under my own steam while I was
at Kew. It seemed important to me that I should. My Grade A is
my only qualification for writing. It probably shows.

There was also scope for improvement in the gardens themselves. The 'Mutual Improvement Society' is a student-run organ-
isation of deliciously archaic title. It is now over a century old,
and during the winter it arranges lectures by visiting speakers on
all manner of botanical and natural history subjects. David
Attenborough and David Bellamy, Graham Thomas and
Christopher Lloyd have all spoken there, to an audience of
students and members of staff who turn up at the Jodrell Lecture
Theatre on Monday evenings to listen to the experts and ask
questions. I became the chairman during my time as a student,

and marvelled at the generosity of all these luminaries who would come and talk to us for no more than their train fare home or the cost of petrol.

Mind you, they kept us on our toes. I introduced Graham Thomas – a world authority on old-fashioned shrub roses – in rather too sycophantic a fashion, and ended by saying, 'Mr Thomas is about to give us a fascinating lecture . . .'

'How do you know?' were his opening words. After such a facile introduction, I think I deserved it.

Staying with Mrs Bell also adjusted my view on gardening. It was she, rather than the Royal Botanical Gardens, who opened my mind to a more relaxed style of planting. Where, at home and in the Parks Department, I had majored on lobelia and alyssum, pelargoniums and hybrid tea roses, she had a small garden where hardy geraniums were the ground cover, and massive shrub roses the dominant feature. In the garden of 1 Willow Cottages, I met for the first time cream-flowered 'Nevada' and pale pink 'Vanity', rampant 'Caroline Testout' and coppery 'Albertine'.

Under their boughs I sat and sipped home-made wine and ate moussaka. It was a pleasant change from cloudy water and under-boiled potatoes. The roar of the buses had been replaced by the thwack of tennis balls on the adjacent public courts.

The contrast between sleeping in a deck chair in a coal shed and in a decent bed in a clean room had never been more marked. Every time I inhale the aroma of the downy leaves of *Geranium macrorrhizum* I think of Mrs Bell. I owe her more than she will ever know. The last I heard she was living in Suffolk and holding occasional art exhibitions. She must be about ninety now. She hasn't exchanged Christmas cards for a couple of years, but I like to think that it's because she's too busy painting. She loved Suffolk. And the light there.

22

Up in the Air

'The Bavarians are a curious race. I do find it difficult to comprehend men who wear short leather trousers in all weathers and
allow a wooden cuckoo to tell them the time.'

Angus MacSween, *Travels With My Uncle*, 1936

In the last year of the Diploma Course at Kew, all students were
offered a chance to go on an 'exchange' visit overseas. The idea
was that it would broaden our knowledge of foreign plants and
enable us to acquire skills not obtainable in a British garden. In
my time the 'exchange' tag was something of a misnomer, as we
went over there but nobody appeared to come over here. The
choice of destinations generally comprised botanic gardens in
Europe, and one or two private establishments such as Les Cèdres,
a garden in the South of France owned by Marnier Lapostolle,
of Grand Marnier liqueur fame.

I turned my back on warmth and alcohol and plumped instead
for a three-week visit to Schachen, near Garmisch–Partenkirchen
in Bavaria, the alpine garden which is an outpost of Munich
Botanic Garden.

Why? Well, I was deeply into alpine plants at that time and
wanted to see them growing in their natural habitat.

Schachen is high up in the Bavarian Alps and is reached by a
full day's climb from the village of Garmisch, where the famous

Winter Olympics of 1936 were staged. I would go there with Trevor Savage, a fellow student from Burnley. He was a good lad, was Trevor. He wasn't exactly a chatterbox, but he had a wit as dry as sandpaper and a wonderful chuckle. Trevor polished his shoes more often than anyone I knew, and when you're sharing a small chalet with someone it's a relief to know that personal hygiene ranks high on their list of priorities. Comforting, from an olfactory point of view. Trevor and I would work up the mountain alongside the two members of staff for two weeks before coming back down and spending a week or so in Munich, depending on how long our limited funds lasted.

We travelled by boat and train, with our bulging rucksacks strapped to our backs, and I cut down a pair of tweed hipsters to make knee breeches that would hopefully look the part. They didn't much. I had to fasten the bottom of them with bootlaces which kept coming undone and tripping me up. I'd have been better off in jeans, all things considered.

In Munich we were shown around the botanic garden itself, and the elegantly proportioned buildings that housed its offices and museums. We were then taken to the picturesque village of Garmisch by a courteous official from the botanic garden, Herr Seidl, to buy food before making our ascent of the mountain.

Schachen is only accessible between June and September, when the snows recede. It enjoys a short growing season, but a spectacular one. We walked up, out of the village, past the grassy Olympic stadium and the ski-jumps over which Hitler had proudly gazed just thirty-six years earlier. Eerie. As the arena disappeared from view, we scaled the mountain slopes and picked our way between healthy clumps of rich blue gentians and pink androsaces, clumps of alpenrose and crags of granite.

On the edge of the snow line, tiny soldanellas pushed up through the white, melting crust to dangle their fringed and fragile pale pink bells in the chilly air. It was all breathtakingly beautiful. Chamois grazed on the massive rocky screes and, as we rose ever higher, Herr Seidl pointed out the distant speck that was the chalet where we would be spending the next fortnight.

We crossed alpine meadows, alive with the music of cow bells, and learned to greet loden-hatted passers-by with a cheery '*Grüss Gott*', and admire the feathery plumes that stuck out from the top of their headgear.

Above the pretty wooden chalet on its mountain knoll stood another, taller building with a pink roof. I asked what it was. '*Ah, der Schloss*,' our guide replied. My German was less than impressive, but I knew that a *Schloss* was a palace. The tall building, with its fretwork frontage, was relatively picturesque, but by no means a palace, more a sort of deluxe barn.

'What sort of palace?'

'A palace of King Ludwig.'

Mad King Ludwig of Bavaria. The man who built those fairy-tale castles. This was his alpine *Schloss*, an ornate shack crammed with everything he might need on a day out in the mountains. Including an organ. Well, you never know how the whim might take you at that altitude.

We reached the garden mid-afternoon and were introduced to the two men with whom we would be working over the next three weeks – Herr Dieter Schacht, the foreman, a robust man with leather knee breeches and bulging calves who greeted us with a courtly bow, and a labourer called Misha, a surly East European youth who did a fine line in grunts.

We were given a tour of the chalet, which took about thirty seconds, and shown the bunks in our shared room. The chalet was pretty, but basic – all shutters decorated with fretwork hearts, and cedar shingles on the roof. I looked for the loo. I found a few cupboards, and a store room. Nothing that looked remotely like a water closet. I asked Herr Schacht.

'*Der* loo?' he asked.

I mimed the pulling of a chain.

'*Ah, der Scheissenhause!*' He pointed to the bottom of the garden, where a small sentry box perched on the end of a cliff. '*Das is der* loo.'

Gingerly I picked my way around the little stone-edged paths of the garden, between edelweiss and saxifrage, to the cubicle on the clifftop. I opened the door and went in. There was nothing resembling a WC pan, just a hole in the raised wooden platform. Not to put too fine a point on it, when you go to the lavatory up there, you never hear anything hit the ground. It disappears over the cliff edge. I can only hope that no one was ever walking below. But I can confidently claim that the view from this loo is the best in the world. I took photographs of the panorama of the Oberreintal, the glacial valley thousands of feet below, taking great care not to lose my balance.

The summer work at Schachen consists mainly of weeding – reducing the competition to the cultivated plants, each of which was provided with a porcelain label, printed in ornate Bavarian script. There was a little planting to be done – bedding in new plants carried up the mountain track at the start of the season by an all-terrain vehicle – but not much, and we worked in all weathers.

I thought we were pretty tough in the nursery in Ilkley, but we did shelter from the heaviest downpours. Not so at Schachen. With a cry of '*Auf gehts*', Herr Schacht would don his khaki rubber cape and lead us out into the deluge to pull up weeds and topdress the alpine beds with grit.

In the evening, we would have our meal and then go on

mountain walks, taking photographs of perfect plants growing in rocky crevices. At least, they would be perfect if you snapped them quickly. I'd made a mental note one evening after my film ran out, to make sure that on the following evening's walk I took a photograph of a particularly elegant clump of *Allium victoriae* – an ornamental onion with perfect silvery-green orbs at the tops of eighteen-inch stems. Too late. A local cow had beaten me to it, and the centre of the clump was demolished by a hefty cow-pat. But then I suppose that regular manuring was the key to the plant's robust vigour in the first place. I just wish I'd got my photograph before the annual mulch.

Each evening we'd finish up the walk at the café alongside the *Schloss* for a beer. Trevor and I managed to do this about twice. Our funds were severely depleted on account of the food shopping, and it became clear that an unfavourable exchange rate would reduce our holiday at the end of the work stint to two or three days at most.

It was also galling watching the surly Misha chatting up the serving girls in German, when it was all we could do to get a word out of him all day. Maybe he regarded us as competition. He needn't have done. Our German was hardly O-level standard, though my bell-ringing friend Martin Hewitt's ability to count to eight in that language stood me in good stead when ordering beer.

We learned to eke out our food by eating plenty of stodge, but we never managed to adopt the custom of Dieter Schacht and Misha – that of crushing several cloves of raw garlic and spreading them thickly on bread. They wolfed down many of these stinking concoctions every day, until only a fool would have gone near their breath with a naked flame. For the best part of three weeks, our eyes watered whenever we came within breathing distance of our housemates. Trevor didn't say a lot, but he did a fine line in sideways looks and raised eyebrows. And I did learn the German for garlic – *Knoblauch*.

The weather on the mountain was almost as predictable as the weather in the tropics. Every afternoon at around half past three it would pour with rain for about half an hour, before the sun came out again and the mountain steamed and glittered. So clear was the air that you could feel your skin blistering if you forgot the Ambre Solaire.

On the one shopping trip that Trevor and I had to do mid-stay, we began our ascent back up the mountain at lunchtime, bent double under the weight of our packs of bread and spuds, tinned meat and pasta. Halfway up, I saw what I thought were giant snails leaping off the ground. It was amazing. I had never seen jumping albino snails before. I looked up to tell Trevor, and realised that the 'snails' were giant hailstones falling from the sky.

At the end of our stay we managed, as predicted, just two days in Munich, drinking the beer and eating the bratwurst before we came home again. Apart from the garlic, I'd rather enjoyed the fare, even if we could only afford one bowl of pea and ham soup, a plateful or two of sauerkraut and a few slices of knockwurst, bratwurst and a frankfurter. Trevor wasn't as keen. He was happy to get back to the supper that he insisted his Irish landlady at Kew provided him with every day of his life – HP baked beans on toast. He said it never had the effect on his digestive system that most people warned against, and that you knew where you were with a bean, rather than a strangely named sausage.

But then, you see, Trevor was from Lancashire.

23

Learning a Lesson

'We all know what thought did; thought followed a muck cart and thought it was a wedding.'

My mum, *Endlessly*, 1949–

My heart was broken for the first time in 1971. Her name was Heather, the same as my first ever inamorata. Botany must be so ingrained. This Heather was blonde and Australian and she worked in the alpine and herbaceous department at Kew. I even told her I loved her. It was the first time I'd said that to anyone. She didn't tell me she loved me, but then I thought I might grow on her. She had the loveliest smile. We went out for several months until, at a party, I went to look for her and found her sitting on a bed, kissing a Canadian.

I ambled around aimlessly for weeks. Then there was Nita, small and pretty with long dark hair. I caught her on the rebound, and it only lasted a fortnight before she went back to him, leaving me a note in which she quoted the rhyme:

> A wise old owl sat in an oak
> The more he saw the less he spoke.
> The less he spoke, the more he heard.
> Why can't we be like that wise old bird?

Try as I might, I failed to see the connection.

But then came Calluna (which, with a twist of irony, happens to be the Latin name for Heather). She was a tall, blonde laboratory technician who asked what I saw in her. I told her that I saw the same in her as she did in me. At last there were passionate intimacies, but it was over within a month, and that was that.

I was beginning to get used to a life on my own, but what I also had to get used to was the fact that the student course would soon be over. And I still had no idea whether I had gained my diploma. Those last weeks of waiting were agonising. I had managed to get through my first two sets of yearly exams, acquitting myself reasonably well. I had even been awarded a cup for 'The Best Academic Student in the Second Year', and again my dried and pressed flower collection had impressed the judges. But the third year was exceptionally tough.

We were taught landscape construction by a fat architect with a wonderfully filthy sense of humour. Alan Blanc would explain the intricacies of tarmac and reinforced concrete, and point out the differences between bollards that were described as 'circumcised' or 'uncircumcised', depending on the presence or lack of the 'ring' on the end. He would ring up the Supervisor of Studies and announce himself as Dr Merulius Lachrymans (the Latin name for dry rot).

John Brookes was our landscape design tutor, charged with lighting our creative fires and refining our artistic sensibilities. Men from the Met Office lectured us in meteorology; there were the rules of genetics to master, and the intricacies of plant physiology.

My thesis: 'The Asymbiotic Germination of Orchid Seeds', couched in suitably scientific terms, was based on a relatively straightforward comparison of various nutrient solutions available for the raising of orchids from their dust-fine seeds without the benefit of their usual mycorrhizal association. Does that sound impressive enough? It involved autoclaves and agar jelly, and sterility was of prime importance. Its comparison with the current state of my love life was not lost on me.

But I put that out of my mind. And worked in the arboretum with the avuncular George Brown, an accomplished arborist and a fine man. In his rolling Devon burr he would assure me: 'Oh, I'm sure it will be fine, Alan. Don't you worry, heh-heh-heh,' before getting on to his bike and pedalling off into the sunset.

And he was right. It was fine. I landed a Diploma with Credit. Not Honours – I missed that by a couple of marks. A disappointment, but hey, I had my diploma, and real letters after my name. Now I was Alan Titchmarsh, Dip. Hort (Kew). All I lacked was a job.

I mused on all kinds of things. I wrote to a specialist alpine nursery which said that there was a good chance of employment, but when I saw the rate of pay I quickly realised that all would be well, provided that I could avoid eating.

I looked at jobs in Parks Departments, but none inspired, and I didn't really want to be stuck behind a desk and given the unglamorous title of 'Technical Assistant'. What I would have really liked was to stay on at Kew. I enquired if there was any chance. There was. How would I like to be Gardens Supervisor in charge of the Queen's Garden, the seventeenth-century garden behind Kew Palace?

I would like it very much, I said. So that was that. And that was where I was headed, until John Simmons, the newly appointed Curator, called me into his office. He asked what I thought about education. I said that, on the whole, I thought it was a good thing, and that I had toyed with teaching when I was at college, even sending off for a prospectus with a view to becoming a rural studies teacher. The combination of showing off (those school plays had a lot to answer for) and working in horticulture seemed the perfect combination. But then Kew and its matchless range of plants had seemed a more attractive proposition.

'How would you like to set up some staff-training courses here?' he asked. I think I gulped a bit, and blustered a bit and then said 'yes'.

So that's what I did. Within a month I had been interviewed in Whitehall, signed the Official Secrets Act, been given a black briefcase with EIIR embossed on it in gold, and a large key engraved with the words 'Royal Gardens, Kew'. An office was found for me in a third-floor garret in Descanso House, tucked away in a corner of the gardens, and I signed a chit in triplicate for my new bike.

For the second time in my life I thought I had died and gone to heaven.

The staff-training courses would need to be started from scratch, and cover all the basic horticultural skills. I would have to teach practical garden craft from digging to taking cuttings, as well as things like pest control and basic botany. The classes would be organised on a day-release basis, and at the end of the course staff would come away with a certificate stating that they had undergone a course of practical instruction at the Royal Botanic Gardens, Kew.

I enjoyed putting the whole thing together, under the watchful eye and the wise counsel of Leo Pemberton, and for the first year I enjoyed the teaching and the instructing. But by year two the gloss was wearing off. What had been a stimulating challenge to set up was turning into a repetitive round of lecturing and demonstrating to a group of people who were not always totally committed.

I would sometimes be given the job of showing prospective employees around the gardens. Some of them were clearly from aristocratic backgrounds and imagined that working at Kew would give them some kind of earthy social cachet. I took around one such lady of uncertain years and, at the end of our little tour, I asked her if there were any questions. 'Just the one,' she said. 'Do you get a good screw?' There was a brief moment of confusion, until I realised that in her efforts to appear like 'one of us' she was asking about the wages.

The gardens staff at Kew, like the workforce in any other situation, comprises folk of varying keenness, from the avid to the terminally reluctant. I found it hard to understand why my own boyish enthusiasm was not always matched by those whom I was teaching.

Things came to a head one day when I found myself leaning against the wall in my office, gently banging my skull against the plasterwork. I didn't even know I was doing it until I felt the pain. This was stupid. It was time I moved on.

In the weeks that followed there were moments when I thought I must be mad. I had a fine job, the key to Kew Gardens, and a bike. I could stay here for life, if I wanted to. Just like a lot of others. Kew was great at looking after its own – there were botanists in the herbarium who had started as teenagers and who were carried out as corpses in their nineties. It was clearly a recipe for longevity. And, in my case, boredom.

Teaching, however much it had appealed, was clearly not my bag. The repetition and the marking out of my future into academic terms filled me with horror. I would have to move on.

Leo came into the office one day, reading a horticultural journal.

'Whom do we know with a literary bent?' he asked, thinking

of his current batch of students who were on the look-out for jobs.

'Me,' I said.

'Oh.' For a moment he looked surprised. Then he smiled. Perhaps he knew already. 'You'd better apply for this then.'

'Assistant Editor, Gardening Books,' it said. 'For the Hamlyn Publishing Group. Applicants should be literate and preferably possess a qualification in horticulture. Salary by negotiation.'

I got the job.

I handed over the trappings of office – my bike, my briefcase and my key – and moved from the Royal Botanic Gardens, Kew, Surrey, to Astronaut House, Feltham, Middlesex. Not exactly an improvement in address but, I hoped, a job that would lead somewhere.

But where? And to what? I don't think I really knew, except that it seemed right at the time, and I've always been unable to do anything except follow my nose, and my instincts.

When set down like this it seems like a rash and foolish move – to leave behind a good job in the country's most famous and revered botanic garden to become a desk-bound pen-pusher, poring over somebody else's words. All I can say in my defence, your honour, is that I must have had some vague idea that it was a step in the right direction. Boredom can never be alleviated by prestige, security and a decent wage packet. Stimulation is everything. And somewhere in the back of my mind that dream of being the next Percy Thrower was refusing to go away. Funnily enough, Hamlyn happened to be his publisher. It crossed my mind that I might get to meet him. It never occurred to me that I was about to become his editor.

24

The Other Mr T

'Avoid using punctuation marks for dramatic effect. The narrative should create its own excitement.'

Mary Weatherall, marking Alan Titchmarsh essays, 1964

The editorial office of the Gardening Department at the Hamlyn Publishing Group was presided over by the tall, diffident and white-haired Robert Pearson, gardening correspondent of the *Sunday Telegraph*. Working to him were two ladies – the kindly Susanne Mitchell, who went on to edit the Royal Horticultural Society's journal, *The Garden*, and Moyna Kitchin, a small, busy, bird-like woman with a passion for cats. Between the two of them they taught me everything I needed to know about editing. And cats. My spelling was sharpened, my grammar honed, and my hyphenating skills put into place by these two over the next couple of years.

On the surface of things, editing is a dreary desk-bound job; in reality it was anything but. Yes, there were galley proofs to pore over and correct – those long strips of typesetting to check for errors and omissions – and page layouts to put together with the art department. But there were also photo shoots of gardens and house plants to arrange, transparencies to commission and select, and authors to meet and learn from.

I worked with Arthur Hellyer – A.G.L. Hellyer – who, many

years earlier, had been responsible for putting together *The Gardeners' Golden Treasury*, the fat red book that had been my bible in the Parks Department. It contained *Sanders' Encyclopaedia of Gardening, The Encyclopaedia of Garden Work and Terms*, and *Plant Portraits*, the three books combining to make a tome as weighty and worthy as *Who's Who*. Arthur had been editor of *Amateur Gardening* magazine for many years and was accepted as the greatest all-round gardening writer of his generation.

He was avuncular and gentle, with a lovely, embarrassed sort of laugh during which his whole body shook, and a prodigious memory for plants and people. Slightly stooping, with grey hair and a grey, bristly moustache, he would recount, in rather patrician tones, stories of great gardeners like Ellen Willmott of Warley Place – 'all black bombazine, draggling along in the gutter after having her gin at the RHS show' – and A.J. Macself, his predecessor on *Amateur Gardening* who had a loathing of what he would call 'copyists', people who could not produce their own original material. I took the warning.

With Will Ingwersen, Britain's leading alpine expert, I worked on *Classic Garden Plants*, and managed to meet people whose names had been legends to me in the preceding years – Jack Harkness and Alan Bloom, Geoffrey Smith and Percy Thrower.

My very first gardening book – if you don't count Beatrix Potter's *The Tale of Peter Rabbit* – was *Percy Thrower's Encyclopaedia of Gardening*, bought for me at Broadbents on The Grove, by my mother one Christmas. I was asked to help Percy revise it, which involved nothing more than sending correspondence and pages to and fro between Astronaut House and The Magnolias, Percy's home near Shrewsbury.

But Bob Pearson had planned a new book, Percy's bible on

fruit and vegetables. Would I work on that one with him? Over
the next few years I travelled up and down between Feltham and
Shrewsbury, meeting the great man and discussing his books,
sitting down to lunches – always a roast that Percy would carve
– and talking with Connie, his wife, who always seemed to me
to be the perfect celebrity wife, nicely turned out, gracious and
welcoming with a slightly regal bearing. But then she was the
wife of the King of Gardening.

It's funny the things that stick in my mind about these visits.
A soap-on-a-rope in the shape of a carrot, hung from Percy's
bath tap. Changing a plug on an electric heater for Connie. (Percy
was a skilled practical gardener but useless at DIY. My plumbing
may not be up to scratch but I can change a plug.) I remember
Percy being photographed harvesting vegetables, and holding a
large carrot between two swollen onions with a friendly wink to
camera.

At that time Percy was a gardening god. He reigned supreme on
television – had done for years. He was accompanied on *Gardeners'
World* for a time by Arthur Billitt, formerly head of the gardens at
Boots' research grounds at Lenton in Nottinghamshire, and later
the owner of Clacks Farm, which also became a TV garden, but
for much of the time Percy performed alone, with a matchless sense
of timing. Not only was his richly accented delivery beautifully
paced, but he could also come out to the second, without the need
of a stopwatch.

'Three minutes, Percy, please,' Barrie Edgar, Percy's *Gardeners'
World* producer of the time, would say, and Percy would oblige
with a perfectly formed piece to camera – with a beginning, a
middle and an end – coming out within a second or two of the
appointed duration. I watched, and learned.

Percy had grown up at Little Horwood in Buckinghamshire,
where his father Harry was also a gardener. He started in private

service, including a stint in the gardens at Windsor Castle where he met his future wife Connie Cook, the head gardener's daughter. He moved on through Leeds and Derby Parks Departments, ending up as Parks Superintendent of Shrewsbury, where he was instrumental in raising the profile not only of The Dingle – one of Shrewsbury's open spaces – but also of the town's flower show.

Percy started broadcasting on radio, moving into television on *Picture Page* and *Gardening Club*, the programme I watched with Mickey Hudson when I was a lad. *Gardeners' World* followed, and his association with the BBC ended only when he took part in a series of TV adverts for ICI Garden Products.

'PERCY THROWER TO GET THE BIG WELLY BOOT', ran the headlines. But Percy knew exactly what he was doing. He had been the mainstay of BBC gardening for around thirty years and had clearly had enough. He continued to write his gardening columns in *Amateur Gardening* and the *Daily Mail*, and there was still a large market for his books. He had left Shrewsbury Parks Department some years earlier, and now ran his own garden centre on the outskirts of the town.

His garden at The Magnolias was a pleasing mixture of traditional features – a rockery and a pool, trees planted in grass, a lean-to greenhouse with a grape vine and a larger greenhouse for tomatoes and pot plants. There was a decent-sized vegetable plot, roses, shrub and flower borders, and at the centre of it all a modern house with wood-panelled dining and sitting rooms, Royal Worcester porcelain on the shelves and a Volvo estate in the garage.

At Chelsea Flower Show each year, he would stand in his corner of the *Amateur Gardening* stand and sign books, magazines and calendars from morning till night, always with a polite word for everyone, and usually with his pipeful of Tom Long clamped into his mouth. He wore a suit with a waistcoat, though in later years allowed himself to broadcast in a casual shirt rather than the waistcoat and tie that were his early trademarks.

Percy was not the easiest person to get to know. In the early days of our acquaintanceship it was difficult to see where the performer ended and the real man began. His delivery was always beautifully measured, rich and deep in tone, thanks to years of pipe smoking, and it seemed to me that he had been broadcasting for so long that he couldn't stop. Queen Victoria complained that when Gladstone talked to her, she felt that she was being addressed as a public meeting. When Percy talked to to you, you felt as though he were talking to his TV audience. Until you got to know him.

Over the years he became more relaxed, and then his eyes would twinkle as he dropped in a cutting aside, or his face would become grave as he condemned some recently developed piece of horticultural equipment with his most damning of verdicts: 'Gimmick'.

It's not that Percy was a stick-in-the-mud, rather that he would want plants and gadgets to prove themselves before he would give them his seal of approval. But somehow, if he were alive today, I'm not sure that he would find it easy to embrace organic gardening, having grown up in a world where chemicals seemed to provide all the answers in the short term at least.

For several months I beavered away at the editing, wondering if I would ever get a chance to write something of my own. I did. A paperback for a magazine called *Wedding Day and First Home*. It was all about house plants. Not exactly a proper book, but it was a start. An overworked author had let Bob Pearson down. He was due to be delivering the manuscript that week and confessed that he had not even started. He would not be able to make Bob's deadline.

Bob looked worried, and paced up and down the office in that distracted way he had, muttering to himself and scratching his head. Finally he asked, in desperation I suppose, did I fancy having a go? I tried not to bite his hand off.

By 1979 I was legitimately in print. Between hard covers. A proper book. It was called *Gardening Under Cover* and there's a picture of me on the back of the jacket, wearing a red sweater, looking about fifteen, tending the plants in the new greenhouse behind a little terraced house in Sunningdale. The photograph was taken by my wife.

25

Her Indoors

'When a man says "My wife doesn't understand me," one thing is
clear: his wife understands him only too well.'

Felix Hanbury, *Staying the Course*, 1982

'We never see your wife, do we?' said a taxi driver a few weeks
ago.

'Er . . . no.'

'Why's that then?'

'Well, she's just not that keen to be on television.'

He sighed. 'Couldn't we just see the back of her, bringing in a
tray of coffee or something?'

It was a kind thought. But it probably won't happen. It's not
that my wife is pathologically shy. It's just that she's refreshingly
normal, and that's why she'd rather stay off the screen. She's even
a bit funny about having her photo taken at home, but then I
think most women are.

I've already said that you're unlikely to see us relaxing in an
'At Home' feature in *Hello!* or *OK!*, though the eagle-eyed may
have spotted us pictured together once or twice within the pages
of those magazines when we get snapped at the odd posh do.
We do get out, but not solely to events that are due to be covered
by cameras and featured in the pages of glossy magazines.

It sounds a bit snooty, I suppose. A bit grand. But it's not meant to. It's just that we both like our home life and that of our kids to be as normal as possible, and that means trying to have as much privacy as the next man. We have friends round all the time, and a TV crew in the garden once a week – because the garden is my workshop – but we don't want them in the house. I mean, have you seen the mess they make?

So how much do I tell you, and how much do I keep to myself? Well, her name is Alison, and we met at the Barnes and Richmond Operatic Society in 1972 during my last year as a student at Kew. After enjoying the Operatic at home in Ilkley, I thought I might have a bash at improving my social life by joining one down south. So I did, and landed my first decent-sized part. The show was *Half a Sixpence* at Richmond Theatre, in which I played a miserable apprentice draper called Buggins and Alison was a dancer. I admired her long neck, her shiny hair, her grace, her ability not to take herself too seriously – and her laugh. We went out at first with a group of friends, who are still our closest, and our first proper date was on New Year's Eve 1972 when her father and mother had to turn out in dense fog at half past one in the morning because I couldn't find a cab. They wore overcoats and frowns over their pyjamas and nightie and didn't say a lot.

There were no thunderclaps when I first met Alison. I just enjoyed being in her company. There was and is a naturalness about her; a sort of spiritual generosity. I remember being on a train journey on my own when we had been going out for about a year. I was staring out of the window thinking about her. It was quite a calm realisation – I knew I did not want to be without her.

She's a bit younger than me and she was a teacher of dance and games at a school in Brighton when we started going out. When I cashed in my pension on leaving Kew I had a lump sum which I could either spend on an Augustus John drawing, or a car. I bought a blue Mini, being ever practical. It is difficult to

take your girlfriend up and down to Brighton every weekend on
an Augustus John drawing.

She loves sport and I can take it or leave it. We don't row, but just
occasionally there are brooding silences. Both of us swear when we
drop things. I had to propose twice before I was accepted. We were
married in the summer of 1975 at St Mary's Church, Barnes. Her dad
was an Alderman and one-time Deputy Mayor of Richmond-upon-
Thames and was also chairman of the operatic society. Her mother
was the wardrobe mistress, but in spite of raising her eyebrows at
my measurements (height: five foot nine inches; waist twenty eight
inches; weight eight and a half stone) she did not object to the union.

If I list Alison's attributes it will sound like a character reference.
She is patient to a fault, kind and funny. She makes me smile a lot.
She's a hugely inventive choreographer, capable of teaching the most
unmusical person to dance. She is tolerant of my own spending
excesses (books are a particular vice), and is the most unmaterial-
istic person I know. All of which makes her sound like Mary Poppins
– practically perfect in every way. But she has her faults – she only
ever drinks a couple of glasses of wine, and she is no gardener.

Mind you, even these qualities can be turned to her advantage:
I can garden happily without interference, and she is usually
prepared to drive us home. In case that sounds like an especially
chauvinistic remark (which it is), let me confess that recently, after
a drinks party given for me in a rooftop wine bar by the BBC
(don't ask – it has worried me ever since), we were being driven
home in a chauffeured car, yet my wife still retained her equilib-
rium. Now most of the time at parties I will drink enough to put
me over the limit, but not enough to make me fall over. Merry,
not plastered. On this particular occasion the wine had flowed
freely from six thirty onwards and I and many of my fellow presenters were still knocking it back at eleven o'clock – two hours
later than the advertised finishing time. (BBC executives are

generous but ever conscious of the licence fee.) The only trouble was that by then the modest supply of dainty canapés was long since finished, in spite of the fact that the wine was still flowing. Neither was any more food available from the bar at that late hour, so we got in the car to come home.

Alas, the large amount of wine I'd put away began to wreak its revenge in the absence of any food which might otherwise have soaked it up. I had to ask for the car to be stopped three times on the way home to be sick, once falling headlong into a thicket of brambles somewhere along the M3. As I lurched into the back seat of the Mercedes for the last time – just a couple of hundred yards from our front door – my wife, to her eternal credit, turned to the driver, smiled wanly and said, 'I'm dreadfully sorry, but he gets car sick.'

It was a kind thought, but somehow I think he knew the truth.

We have been married now for twenty-seven years.

I stayed with Mr and Mrs Bell in Kew until the day I married. Ali and I looked all over Barnes and Richmond for somewhere of our own, but at the price we could afford found only basement flats where rising damp and sinking damp met in an aromatic fungal tidemark.

A couple of friends who lived in Windlesham asked if we had looked at property down their way. They clearly assumed we had more money than we did. But one Sunday afternoon, with nothing better to do, we looked, and we found a tiny terraced house in Sunningdale – a sort of artisan's cottage in dusky red brick with stone quoins at the corners and a Welsh slate roof – three up and three down and just one room wide. The fifteen-foot by forty-foot garden was on sandy soil and wonderfully easy to cultivate. Alison did mutter something about priorities when I had demolished the old chicken coop, made a pond and a plank bridge near the Comice pear tree, sculpted two tiny borders and planted old roses before so much as a roll of wallpaper had been unwrapped. But we did decorate some of the house before we moved in, and I built cupboards and put up shelves, tiled the bathroom and, with the help of my dad, put up my greenhouse.

No room in the house was more than ten feet square, and we needed all the space we could get – two bedrooms and a bathroom upstairs, a sitting room, dining room and scullery downstairs, with an ancient lean-to that the estate agent was pleased to call a 'conservatory' on the back. At the end of this was the coal house and another loo. We painted the sitting room green, the dining room chocolate brown, and I put louvred doors on every cupboard.

The winter of 1975 was bitterly cold and we were relieved that we'd ordered a gas fire. But it failed to arrive, in spite of daily phone calls to the gas board, so the week before Christmas I took a sledgehammer to the chimney breast in the sitting room and we put in a coal fire. So good was the draught under the floor that the carpet would rise in the middle of the room like a balloon. But we were warm.

There was an old wisteria growing up the front of the house, and I trained it around the side wall as well. On a warm May day we could throw up the sash windows and breathe in the sweet scent of those long, lilac flower tresses.

The front garden was tiny – barely six feet by twelve feet – and in early spring was perforated by the amethyst spears of *Crocus tomasinianus*. I had already begun my love affair with old-fashioned roses and planted four of them in that small patch of sandy earth – pale pink 'Maiden's Blush', slate purple 'Belle de Crécy', deep crimson 'Tuscany Superb', and the candy-striped 'Rosa Mundi'. Hardy geraniums were used to make a summer rug underneath them.

We'd sat down some months previously and discussed which

of us would give up our job when we got married. We were both prepared to move to be with the other, but in the end it was Alison who left her teaching post in Brighton and I commuted to Feltham daily.

We'd hoped that she'd be able to find another position locally, but it proved impossible. Teaching jobs were thin on the ground in the 1970s, especially in dance. As a result, over the next five years until our first child came along, my wife became a shop assistant in an ironmonger's (she is still unnervingly knowledgeable about grades of screws) and a hairdresser's receptionist in a hotel at Heathrow airport (which means that she's quite capable of cutting my hair in an emergency). Alison's powers of observation have often got me out of a tight spot in both DIY and personal grooming. I'm not being patronising. Just grateful.

After two years of editing books my feet began to itch again. I wanted to spread my wings; find something a little faster. Bob Pearson suggested magazines. I took his advice and became assistant editor and eventually deputy editor of *Amateur Gardening* magazine, then based at King's Reach Tower in Stamford Street, London SE1. I didn't relish commuting to the smoke, even though the train journey from Sunningdale was a straightforward one, and the offices of IPC could be reached by a ten-minute walk from Waterloo.

But I enjoyed the job, working with the mercurial Peter Wood as editor, and writing at least three pages of the magazine each week myself. I'd begun contributing to *AG* when I was at Hamlyn, and the extra funds came in handy for doing up the house. Mr Bell had carried out the survey as a wedding present and said that the floors needed treating for woodworm, and that some kind of damp-proofing repairs would be necessary. I scribbled away in the front bedroom most evenings, clacking away on a black and chrome typewriter, and then on an electric one which at first I thought would run away with me. A simple dash would become a rat-tat-tat of machine-gun fire if I pressed the key as hard as I had done on my pre-war 'Continental' model with its cotton-reels of ribbon. I typed with two fingers – still do – but can manage around sixty-five words per minute, about as fast as my brain can think. It seems pointless bothering to use any more of them and struggling to keep up mentally.

I began tackling more books, such as the *Boots' Guide to Greenhouse Gardening*. With this came my first experience of a signing session. I wasn't very well known, but found myself sitting in Boots in Manchester from 10 a.m. until 5 p.m. one Saturday in May. It turned out to be Cup Final day. And Manchester United were playing. In seven hours I sold three books. I still shudder at the memory. But it did give me time to work on my autograph. It's fairly flowery. Sometimes people ask how long I took to perfect it. When I say 'seven hours in Boots the chemist' they look at me strangely.

My name must have been getting about. People started asking me to write more. At the request of *The Times* gardening correspondent Roy Hay I wrote a book on climbers and wall plants, and another in the same series on windowboxes and tubs. This one had been drafted by another writer, rejected by Roy, as the series editor, and needed completing and knocking into shape.

Understanding Roy Hay on the telephone was not easy. He was a basso-profundo mumbler, and working out where one word ended and another began in his sub-volcanic rumblings was never simple. But I gathered that he wanted me to write the windowbox book under an assumed name. We settled on Robert Hardisty, the name of an uncle of my mother who had died in the First World War. It seemed a fitting way of giving him a longer life.

* * *

It was during my time at *AG* that I first met Geoff Hamilton, who was then the editor of a rival publication, *Practical Gardening*. We'd encounter one another regularly on press trips, when gardening journalists would be taken by coach to look at seed trials of new plant varieties, and newly formulated composts and garden products.

'All right then, boy?' he'd ask. He always did. Every time we met. He was fun to be with and always down to earth, but I did use to be amazed at his capacity to get annoyed. Each week on the back pages of *Garden News* he would kick up stink about his latest *bête noir* – the over-packaging of garden products, the lunacy of destroying limestone pavements, the shortsightedness of government. His grouses were almost always legitimate.

Geoff had a jacket and tie in those days. He dressed quite smartly. It always made me smile in later years when he presented *Gardeners' World* and boasted that he did not own a suit. Perhaps he'd grown out of it. Or used it to cover his compost heap.

We fell to talking about my lack of funds on one of these coach trips. 'Well, why don't you write for me?' he ventured.

'Don't be daft. I'm assistant editor of *Amateur Gardening*. Peter would have my guts for garters.'

He turned round, to see Peter Wood a few seats back, deep in conversation with the person next to him, then he leaned towards me and whispered, 'Write for me under a pew-sod-o-nym.'

So I did. I had several pew-sod-o-nyms over the next few years. Richard Arncliffe and Tom Derwent were the favourites, and I did once threaten to use the name Diggory Delve. It was rejected.

Geoff unnerved Alison once when he rang up and asked to speak to Tom Derwent. She was convinced it was the tax man who thought we were on the fiddle.

26

Hello, Auntie

'He's got a very good face for radio.'
Anonymous producer

It's only now, when I come to write it down, that the course of my life seems to have been carefully mapped out. But not by me. Not consciously, at any rate. I always claim that I have never had a career plan. But maybe it was so deeply ingrained that I was not conscious of it. When I worked in the nursery I was told I would go to college and then to Kew. I never thought to argue. It seemed the most natural thing to do.

When I tired of teaching at Kew, I knew that I wanted to write, and to broadcast. I am not very good at making myself go in directions that offer little challenge. It's not selfishness, it's just that it seems such a waste. If a passion for something points you one way it seems to me that it is morally wrong to go in another just because it is the easier or the steadier option.

I once asked Dame Judi Dench why she was attracted to the roles she took on. 'I only take on a part that I don't think I can do,' she said. Well, I suppose I'm a bit like that. In an earthy sort of way.

Twelve or thirteen years on from those dreamy days in Mum and Dad's back garden where I would pretend to be Percy Thrower, my life was undeniably moving in that direction. I could now claim to be a gardening writer.

But there is a world of difference between being a writer and being a broadcaster. Not all writers can communicate verbally. Some of our greatest literary figures can bore the pants off you when they open their mouths. Some of our most accomplished gardeners become the human equivalent of Mogadon when they endeavour to pass on their skills.

Wary of these pitfalls, I made tentative enquiries at *Amateur Gardening* just after my arrival. Had anybody any idea how you got into television?

'Funny, that,' said Graham Clarke, the sub-editor. 'We had a letter last week asking us if we could recommend anyone for a radio programme. Hang on. It's here somewhere.' He ploughed through the mountain of paper on his desk and pulled out a crumpled letter. It was from the producer of *You and Yours* on BBC Radio 4; a woman with the suitably horticultural-sounding name of Marlene Pease.

I laid out the letter on my desk and smoothed away the creases. It explained that from time to time the programme had need of a gardening expert. Was anyone on the staff of the magazine prepared to help? I stared at it. Supposing I was sent away with a flea in my ear? Pathetic. Stop being so sensitive. But was I an expert? Remember what they said at college about experts: 'X is an unknown quantity and spurt is a drip under pressure.' Both sentiments seemed true.

I drafted a reply and sent it off, then spent the next fortnight examining the post every morning for the letter that never came.

About a month later, quite out of the blue, I took a phone call at work. It was Marlene Pease. She seemed very pleasant. Kept asking me questions. The conversation lasted half an hour, and I seemed to do all the talking. Naïvely I wondered why. At the end of our one-sided chat she said, 'Well, I think you'll do.

Would you like to come in and record a piece for us?'

'Er . . . yes. Of course. When?'

'Tomorrow?'

'Yes. Fine.'

'On turf.'

I forget what happened that afternoon. It is lost in a blur. But I did find myself, the next day, sitting in a studio in Broadcasting House with Derek Cooper, whose gravy-browning voice was famed for its lustrous timbre.

I had done my homework, formulated the sort of things I wanted to say, and Derek Cooper, looking at me over the top of his half-moon glasses like some beady-eyed colonel, was courteous and encouraging in his interview.

I went home to Sunningdale full of it, telling Alison all about the studio, the red and green lights, the faces behind the window, Derek Cooper's generosity. The programme was due to be broadcast on Sunday lunchtime. It was Thursday. I had to wait nervously for my debut.

The great day dawned. We tuned in. We sat down and listened. And then came the introduction. Derek set the scene, about the verdant lawn being one of the most important parts of the garden, 'but if you want to make one, how do you go about it? Well, to find out, here's our expert, Alan Titchfield.'

We sat in silence. My first broadcast, and they had got my name wrong. As if to add insult to injury, I listened to myself warbling on in my high-pitched, reedy tones – like a stork with sinus trouble – interrupted from time to time by Derek Cooper's Bisto bass. We came to the end of the piece and I sat, crestfallen, staring apologetically at my wife, who smiled encouragingly and squeezed my hand.

Derek Cooper sailed skilfully into the back-announcement. 'Well, I must apologise to Alan Titchmarsh for calling him Alan

Titchfield. Dynamic he may be, but no thunderbolt. I'm sure we'll be hearing more of him.'

It's funny how sometimes fate takes a hand. Sends you a white dove. Or in my case, a greenfly. It was the summer of 1979, and European aphids swarmed across the English Channel in their millions. In Margate and Dover they filled the air, great clouds of them, sticking to fresh paintwork and blocking air conditioning systems.

The phone rang at home. It was the *Today* programme. Would I come and do a piece on greenfly? Tell the folk of Kent what to do? Of course I would. Half an hour later, *You and Yours* rang. Would I come and do a piece on greenfly? Tell the folk of Kent what to do?

Ah. Yes. I explained that *Today* had just rung and I'd already said I would do a piece for them. But I was sure that I could also do *You and Yours*. Make it different. *You and Yours* were not convinced. They put the phone down rather grumpily. I thought I had lost my job.

The following morning, having been picked up at 5.30 a.m. by a chauffeured car, I turned up at the *Today* studio and was shown into the Green Room. For the first time, I felt the buzz of a live news programme. Battling through the mêlée were Brian Redhead – all beard and horn rims – and John Timpson – bumbling and florid – filleting the newspapers, tucking into toast and about to earn their daily bread. I felt slightly sick. The programme began, shrill and important, packed with gravitas, the political agenda of the day. I watched as politicians were wheeled in and grilled, then wheeled out again. There were newsreaders – the dark-haired and mellifluous Laurie Macmillan, thunderous Peter Donaldson and Brian Perkins, whose vowels seemed to move the furniture – the maverick young sports reporters who appeared to speak in a foreign language, and then me. Trundled in for a bit of light relief. A nod in the direction of benign bucolia.

Timpson and Redhead interviewed me with mounting incredulity and not a little humour, grateful, it seemed, to have a break from the heavier items of state, but also a little sceptical that this was a story worth covering.

My bit was the humorous tailpiece of the morning, and after a tongue-in-cheek goodbye to the nation, they downed their headphones, shouted 'Well done', and led me back to the Green Room. I had never seen whisky drunk so early in the morning. But then to these guys it was the end of their working day.

'See you again, Titchmarsh!' said Redhead. 'Yes, yes. Wonderful!' chuntered Timpson, his cheeks even redder than before.

And they did see me again. On high days and holidays – Good Friday and Christmas Eve, Spring Bank Holiday and St George's Day – I would be hauled in to advise the nation on such weighty matters as planting potatoes, sowing parsley, making cut flowers last in water, and caring for festive pot plants. And I loved it.

But what of *You and Yours*? For the rest of the morning, behind my desk, I worried that I had unwittingly put myself out of a job. Then the phone rang. It was the BBC. But not the radio. My interlocutor was a producer from the early evening television current affairs programme, *Nationwide*. He had heard my piece about the greenfly invasion of Margate on the *Today* programme, and would I care to repeat it that evening on live TV?

Now if you say the word *Nationwide* to people today you will get one of two answers. The younger half will think it's a building society, and the older half will say, 'Ah, yes. The skate-boarding duck.'

For a good number of years during the Seventies and Eighties,

Nationwide was the country's most popular current affairs programme. It went out in the early evening and consisted of a mixture of national news and local stories, with many of the regional presenters appearing in the nationally broadcast segments. Watching the programme gave you a feel of the mood over the entire country, and allowed you to get to know its natives. Viewers in London would know Mike Neville who presided over the North East, and Bruce Parker who was king of the South. Now, in our quest to be global and pan-European we've forgotten about Norfolk and Newcastle, Scotland and the West Country. Unless there's a riot. Or a murder.

Nationwide had its frivolous items – the skate-boarding duck is the most famous – but it also addressed the harder issues of the day. And through it all came a feeling of family, within its body of presenters, and within the country. It wasn't old-fashioned, it just celebrated Britain, something we're not encouraged to do today. It also showed kids just where Norfolk was. Yes; *Nationwide* was a good geography lesson.

Among the presenters were Frank Bough and Sue Lawley, Hugh Scully and James Hogg, Sue Cook and Michael Barratt, and the man who became my first television interviewer, Bob Wellings.

I left the *Amateur Gardening* office late in the afternoon wearing my blue and white striped shirt and dark blue tie, having spoken to the programme's researcher about the sort of things they might need in the studio – rose bushes and sprayers and the like. I arrived and was taken to the studio floor for a walk-through. I felt like a child in toyland. There was Frank Bough, booming to camera as he rehearsed his autocue, and here were my props to be put in order. In a nervous daze, I tried to unscramble my thoughts and sort out my props.

The cameras, about five of them – great lumbering beasts on wheels – finally deserted Mr Bough and glided towards me like

Daleks. I felt as though I were being sized up by a pack of hungry predators. My heart beat faster. Maybe this wasn't such a good idea after all. Maybe I was out of my depth.

'Alan!' It was a voice I knew. A friendly voice. Of course I knew it, I heard it every evening.

Bob Wellings squeezed my hand and smiled. 'Good to see you. Thanks for coming in. Know what we're doing?'

The question came as a surprise. So did my answer. 'Yes. I thought if we started here, with the greenfly, and worked our way down there, through the sprayers . . .' I carried on. Bob looked at me with his eyebrows raised, smiling indulgently.

'Fine. Well, yes. I'll just drop my questions in then.'

We blocked the camera moves and I was shepherded out of the studio as Sue Lawley rehearsed her side of things. And before I knew where I was, the programme had started, I had been made-up, miked up, stood behind my rose bush and we were away.

I could actually feel my heart thumping my chest, almost see my shirt moving. And I could see Bob Wellings' hand shaking – the one that was holding his script. Was he nervous for himself or for me? A bit of both, I suppose. I mean, I must have been a risk. But we did it. And then I was thanked, and then the cameras slid away to cover the sports results and I went home.

'It was fine. Well done!' Alison was encouraging. 'What did they say?'

I was dazed. Drunk with power. Live television. It was like tasting blood. 'They said I was great. And would I go back again and do some more.'

'Wow! You've made it then!' She gave me a hug.

And I thought that perhaps I had. My first bit of live TV – any TV – had gone well, and I had been asked back.

They were true to their word. I did go back. But it took a year.

Twelve months later somebody's rooftop garden collapsed into the flat below. Would I go along and tell the nation how to garden on a rooftop without inconveniencing the neighbours?

I did. They seemed to like it. 'Wonderful!' they said. Would I like to do some more?

'Yes,' I said, and went home to tell Alison that in another year's time I'd probably be asked again.

From the following Friday I had a weekly spot.

27

Now We Are Three

'Relying on your instincts is all very well, but instincts are not renowned for paying bills.'

Henry Foord, *Pocket Economy*, 1988

It all came to a head in 1979. There I was, married for four years, with a child on the way, living in Sunningdale, commuting to London for the day job, and fitting in weekly radio spots as well. I'd come home in the evening, have my tea, watch *Coronation Street* and then go upstairs to write, either an article or a book. By the weekend I was knackered. Something had to give.

IPC decided to move the *Amateur Gardening* offices to Poole in Dorset. I decided not to go with them. There were sharp intakes of breath all round. Was this wise? With a baby on the way? The job of deputy editor was a secure one, and one day, on Peter Wood's retirement, I would more than likely become editor. That would mean an increase in salary and an entry in *Who's Who*. Ah. I see.

I was flattered at the persuasive techniques that were used, and a little disbelieving. The management gave a dinner for the AG staff down in Poole, to show us all how friendly they were, and how lovely life would be in Dorset. The managing director of the leisure section was seated between Alison and myself, the significance of which completely passed me by until afterwards. He endeavoured to work his charm on her, perhaps assuming that 'the little woman' was the fly in the ointment. But the die was cast when we were all shepherded on to a coach by a local firm of estate agents and given a tour of the sort of properties we would be able to afford in Dorset, most of them on housing estates. My life was about to be managed for me. When I watch Tom Cruise in *The Firm* – where his life is managed by the Mafia – it takes me back, and makes me shudder. And so I left, with good wishes, and a request to continue writing for the magazine.

There was one slight problem. With a baby on the way the front bedroom would be needed for the cot. Where would I write? This was a watershed in my life. Here began my lifelong love affair with the shed.

I tucked it underneath a conifer hedge on the right-hand side of the garden. It was eight feet long and four feet wide, lagged with loft insulation and hardboard and lined with books. A narrow worktop was fixed under the window, and there was just enough room for a chair. It was not so much a shed, more a corridor. I had an intercom link with the house (a cheap baby alarm from Mothercare) and Alison made patchwork curtains for the windows. Just as now when I'm sitting in my shed writing, looking out over the garden, I was the happiest man on earth. During the day I wrote and broadcast and gardened, and during the evening we could live a life.

Apart from Alison, the only person to encourage me in this foolhardy freelance exercise was my mother-in-law, Daphne, the friendly dragon. Everyone else shook their heads and asked me if I had not been a touch hasty. Daphne just said, 'Well done, dear!' I warned Alison that in a year's time we would probably be living in straitened circumstances. She said not to worry. As long as I was happy. Bless her.

The reverse happened. Things took off. The *Nationwide* slot became a weekly event, as did a five-minute radio programme called *Down to Earth*, first as part of *You and Yours* and then standing on its own every Saturday morning at five minutes to eight on Radio 4.

After an opening chorus of native birdsong recorded in my garden, Mike Gilliam would interview me about some topical item for the weekend, always beginning with the words 'Morning, Alan!' People would shout it across the street at me. Not many of them. I wasn't that well known then. But it was a catch-phrase that was recognised; a bit like the old radio gardener Fred Streeter's, 'The answer lies in the soil'.

Even Prince Charles once confessed that he listened to us, and enquired, 'Are those birds real?' As opposed to what, I wondered?

Sometimes people would vaguely recognise me and try to remember the name. In a shop one day a man approached me. 'I know that voice, don't I?'

'Do you?'

'Yes. On the radio.'

'Yes.'

'Saturday morning.'

'Yes.'

'Gardening.'

'Yes.'

'It's Arthur Negus, isn't it?'

It was my first real taste of fame. I'm not at all sure about it. I don't know anyone who has been improved by it, and I can think of a few who have let it go to their heads. I do wonder, when I hear kids on TV saying they want to be famous, if they really know what they are asking for. Don't get me wrong; fame has considerable advantages. It allows you to write books like this; it can get you a table in a restaurant. But it also has its obligations. As well as *Noblesse Oblige* there is *Célèbre Oblige*. And in public there is no time off. When you are outside your front door you are fair game. Anonymity is like virginity – once you've lost it you can't get it back.

To be fair, most people are very polite, very encouraging and very kind. How can I complain when people say 'Thank you for the programmes', or 'Nice to see you'? I even manage to smile sweetly when workmen shout across the road, 'Where's Charlie?' And so does Alison, though sometimes through gritted teeth.

I have a handful of kind and devoted fans who send birthday cards and occasional letters, like Gwen in Brighton and Audrey in Maidstone. They've become friends over the years – special kinds of friends. They are not intimates, but neither are they weirdos. Audrey gives me a designer handkerchief every birthday (I've never been a fan of tissues), and comes to see my one-man shows, bringing her scrap books to be signed. Her husband drives her, she never outstays her welcome, and her parting greeting is always 'Go on then, give us a blaster'. And after the blaster – the peck on the cheek – she waves merrily and says, 'See you next time.'

Another fan stitches all my book covers in needlepoint; I gasp at her talent and her kindness, and worry that her children might not be getting their tea. And then there are the folk who just come up and say 'hello' at events like the Chelsea Flower Show and BBC Gardeners' World Live.

Interviewers always ask what strange things I get sent through the post, half expecting, I guess, that I will say 'frilly knickers' and give them a bit of copy. I can't oblige. I did once have a bra thrown at me on stage, but I think that was probably for Charlie. Most of my post is full of rotting vegetation to be identified, or simply requests for signed photos.

The nicest things that happen are the most ordinary. At Gardeners' World Live in Birmingham a couple of years ago I was signing books. The queue was a long one, snaking right across the hall at the NEC. I try to have a word with everyone who comes – enough to make them happy, not too long to keep others waiting – and I genuinely enjoy saying hello. It really is not an effort.

On this particular occasion, two thirty-something mums finally made it to the front of the queue. I had never seen them before, but I could imagine that they had left the kids at home and were on a girls' day out. They were well spoken. Ordinary. Normal. And as the first one of them took back her book after I had signed it she just burst into tears. 'I'm so sorry,' said her friend. 'It's all too much for her.'

Weird? No. Odd? No. Just nice, and natural and pleased to be there. A friend of mine says that we all need to touch the coat-tails of the famous. Thanks to working in television I've met a lot of my own heroes over the years, and the ones who have not disappointed me have been the ones who have lived up to my expectations. People like Alan Bennett and Laurie Lee, Harry Secombe and Stephen Sondheim. They were not grand but good humoured and gracious, and careful not to burst the bubble. I have met others – a few Hollywood stars, rather more young 'soap' actors – who have been brittle, rude and prickly, for no reason that I could fathom. Some celebrities just enjoy being like that. Presumably.

Only once have I come close to being unpleasant, and that was when Alison and I went out for dinner one evening. Just the two of us. In a restaurant. I had my fork halfway to my mouth when a man clamped his hand around my arm and said, 'Now I've got you. You'll have to answer my question before you can get away'

I smiled and waited for my arm to be released. But it was a close call.

*   *   *

As my workload grew, so did Alison, and on the morning of 27 May 1980 Polly Alexandra Titchmarsh entered this world, making even more noise than her father. Polly was born in Ascot, for which she has always been grateful, teasing her younger sister, Camilla, that Ascot sounds better than Basingstoke, the place on Camilla's birth certificate.

It was a fairly rapid delivery, though not without colour, and both father and mother were present.

The midwife asked if we'd mind if a few students came to watch. We were both past caring. Let them come in. The more the merrier, we just wanted it to be over. And so, Polly arrived to a full house. She's never been an especially noisy child, but as she emerged, she cleared her throat, as if to address the nation. Then she thought the better of it and began to wail heartily. I noticed her fingers. They were perfect miniature versions of my own. They are more like her mother's now, but they were mine then.

It's not easy to control yourself at the birth of your child, but then there is no reason why you should. They wrapped Polly in a length of white muslin and gave her first to Alison and then to me. I just stared at her. Stared and stared. And cried – silent, heaving sobs of pleasure, and of relief. Then I looked up at the semi-circle of medics grouped around the bed. I noticed that behind their surgical masks, every last one of them had tears running down their cheeks. It was the first birth I had ever attended, and it was theirs, too.

28

Daddy's Sauce

'Ruddy kids. They take up the best years of your life and then they bugger off. I'd tell them they were ungrateful if they stuck around long enough to listen.'

Ted Watson, *Down and Out in Suburbia*, 1985

If you ask any dad with daughters to choose his favourite bit of fatherhood I reckon he will say that period when his children were in single figures – slightly older than a toddler, but not so old as to be entering adolescence. At this stage they love you openly and without a second thought and will charge down the stairs to greet you with an excited 'Daddee!', their arms flung wide. You will lift them high in the air and whirl them round to shrieks of delight, and then you will bury their head in your neck and kiss them and kiss them and kiss them.

Then they grow up, and you have to be more circumspect. It's a wistful memory, rather than a sad one.

I have two daughters. Camilla was born two years after Polly, just after we'd moved from Sunningdale to Hampshire. Do they get on? They do. Do we get on? We do. I've been lucky. I know it doesn't always work that way, but nothing in my life has given me greater pleasure or caused me greater pride than these two girls. (It's okay. There's little chance that they will see this. They love me, but not enough to read my books.) They have always spoken to me and always loved me. I know that. It's just that now they are older they love me in a different way. Teasingly. Indulgently. Exasperatedly.

For years now, Polly has been known as 'Pops', and Camilla as 'Min'. They call their mum 'Mum' but they call me 'Poos', short for 'Daddy-poos'. There is no dignity for the man in our house. They don't want mauling any more. Most of the time a peck on the cheek and a brief hug will do nicely. But thankfully there are also the days – just occasionally – when I still have to wipe away a tear for them, and when a longer hug is needed. It's a funny thing growing up. For them, and for me.

Nobody tells you how to be a dad. You just have to find out for yourself. By trial and error. Fathers of sons have expectations. Fathers of daughters have worries. That's not chauvinism; it's basic paternal reality. You worry that you love them too much. You worry that they won't come home. You worry about the boys they might meet: 'Oh, Dad! I know what I'm doing.'

Yes. But so does he.

When they start to drive your worry turns into paranoia, until you hear, once more, the sound of the car returning.

'Dad! I am a careful driver.'

Yes. But what about the others?

Why can't they see that? Why can't they understand why you worry? Why, when they go out and you say 'Be careful', can't they just say 'I will', instead of 'Oh, Dad!'

Because they are daughters, I suppose, and that's what daughters are for – to worry fathers.

But I've never pined for a son. I've happily watched my youngest daughter in plays, and my eldest in swimming competitions, but I've never had to stand on a freezing touchline. I'm grateful for that (even if Alison would have died and gone to heaven if she had managed to produce a rugby international). To be fair, so would I. You get what you get, and you love them regardless. It's not difficult. But then, perhaps I'm stating the obvious.

The halcyon years were those in the Eighties when we would go up to Yorkshire with them and stay with their grandma and grandad. We'd pick up Mum from Uncle Bert's shop on Skipton Road. It was a grocer's and a sub-post office, rich with the smell of sides of smoked bacon hanging from the ceiling, and Mum would break off from serving and come home with us in her nylon overall, making a fuss of the kids and cooking us supper.

When Dad came home from work, his old tweed jacket smelling of putty and copper pipe, he would wash and change, then play motor bikes using Camilla's pigtails as handlebars. She still remembers.

In the evening the grown-ups would go out for a drink, first in Ilkley, and then, at half past ten, to Addingham, the village up the road, where the pubs stayed open for another half-hour – The Sailor, or The Swan, or The Fleece. And then it would be back home with Mum and Dad and their friends, Tommy and Vera, and with my sister Kath and her husband Richard, who was my father's apprentice way back in the Sixties. I was best man at their wedding; Richard was best man at ours. We'd put away beef sandwiches and another beer. We didn't drink a lot, but we talked for Britain.

My dad's relationship with Alison was wonderful to watch. She called him 'Fil' (father-in-law) and he called her 'Dil'. The naming bit is always tricky with in-laws. John Betjeman once became engaged to a Brigadier-General's daughter, and went to see her father to ask for her hand. The old man acquiesced and then moved on to the tricky subject of how Betjeman should address him. 'I think "father-in-law" is too formal,' he said, 'and Jack is rather too familiar. Perhaps you'd better just call me Brigadier-General.'

It's great when your dad likes your wife. A sort of seal of approval. My dad was not a great flirt, but I used to watch him talking to Alison and his eyes would have a sparkle that I saw at no other time. Except with my mum, of course. But that was different.

We'd return home after a few days up north, with great lumps of gammon and rashers of smoked bacon from Uncle Bert, fresh eggs and freshly ground coffee. A sort of Red Cross parcel. There were times, during our first few years of marriage, when we had to duck below the window when the milkman came for his dues. He got paid the following week – we never owed anything for long – but sometimes it was touch-and-go. I took on an allotment, down by the church, so that we could grow our own vegetables. We saved twenty-five pence a week with the local butcher for our Christmas joint, and eked out the bacon, the gammon and the eggs from our visit to Skipton Road post office.

I was reminding my mum of this a few weeks ago. 'Yes,' she said. 'And now you could buy the shop.' I felt slightly ashamed.

When the house at Sunningdale became too small for a growing family we moved to Hampshire, a bit further down the M3. We left our little house with many happy memories, bar one. It makes my blood run cold to recall it. The staircase was very steep. It ran straight up from the front door. There was no 'hall', as such, just a square yard of carpet at the foot of the stairs with the dining room door to the right and the sitting room door to the left. I was in the kitchen when I heard the shout, and the sound of a falling body.

I rushed to the foot of the stairs and found Alison lying on her side, squashed into the space between the two doors, cradling a five-month-old Polly in her arms. The baby was frowning and grizzling. Alison was sobbing and crying with pain. She'd fallen from the top of the stairs to the bottom with the baby in her arms. I tried to get her to stand up. She cried out. She could not move.

'It's all right, you're safe now, I'm here.' Pathetic really. I hoped it would make a difference. That she would get up. She did not. I called the ambulance, and after shots of painkillers they managed to get her on to a stretcher, along with the baby.

They rushed them both to hospital where they were X-rayed. Polly had fractured her skull and Alison had a shattered elbow. They hoped that these were the only injuries.

That night was the darkest of my life. I sat by the bed where Alison lay with her arm held up in a sling supported on a metal stand. She seemed to be sleeping, but her face kept contorting in pain. Then I went to look at Polly in the ward next door. She was lying in a cot with a drip going into her arm. Sleeping. There was a musical mobile fastened to the bars. I wound it up and read the words that were printed on it:

> When at night I go to sleep,
> Fourteen angels watch do keep,
> Two to whom 'tis given
> To guide my steps to heaven.

I sang it softly to her, and prayed harder than I had ever prayed in my life. The following morning she cut her first tooth and, thank God, she has never looked back.

Her mum had no injuries other than the shattered elbow which, said the surgeon, looked as though someone had put a bomb inside it. She never got back its full movement, and there are days when she will say a loud 'Ow!' as it reminds her of the

Blush pink with a delicate scent. And the 'Alan Titchmarsh' sweet pea isn't bad either. It's still winning prizes 17 years on.

Below: Breakfast Time in 1985. Nick Ross tries to look interested but gradually loses the will to live.

New Sweet Pea
Alan Titchmarsh

Daytime Live from Pebble Mill – the very first show in 1987. With Kate O'Mara, Peter Skellern, Roy Castle and Pamela Armstrong. Roy taught me a tap-dancing routine, and it took ages! The programme eventually became *Pebble Mill* and my lunchtime date in Birmingham lasted 10 years.

An entire *Pebble Mill* programme with Dudley Moore in 1995. Already ill, he had lost none of his ability to reduce an audience to fits of helpless laughter, and his playing of jazz lifted them out of their seats.

Sir Dirk Bogarde, interviewed at the National Theatre in 1994. A bit of a hero, and not a disappointment. We swapped occasional letters – he was a keen gardener, now reduced to a balcony 'which, after years of gardening in ACRES, is a bloody bore.'

With Siân Phillips and Dame Judi Dench after a programme devoted to Stephen Sondheim's National Theatre Production of *A Little Night Music*. Keep a dry eye after Dame Judi has sent in the clowns and you're a tougher man than I am.

Showing the Queen around my Gold-Medal winning Chelsea Garden in 1985. 'I like your onions,' she said. 'They are nice and small. When they are large they taste of nothing at all.'

Queen Elizabeth, the Queen Mother, politely smiles at a risqué story and looks around for a means of escape at a Gardeners' Royal Benevolent Society bash.

'Just tucking your shirt in, Sir!' Fitting a radio mike on the Prince of Wales at Chelsea Flower Show 2002.

With Alison, Polly and Camilla in 1986.

Introducing them to water –
Polly on the river.

Left: Polly practices her ballet, aged 9.

Right: Camilla, aged 5, shows every sign
of becoming an intellectual . . .

Below: . . . but fails, at the age of 3,
to recognise her dad, dressed as
Father Christmas, at the playgroup
Christmas party.

Barleywood – home for 20 years. A north-west facing slope on chalk, clay and flint. You'd be mad to tackle anything like this. Fun though.

At home with Grace (*top*) and Favour (*bottom*). We lost Favour last year, but Grace battles on, aged 14.

On top of Crough Patrick, Ireland, for *Titchmarsh's Travels*, which followed the routes of ancient pilgrimages.

past, but she manages to play tennis pretty passably. Better than me, anyway.

And I still worry about staircases.

In Hampshire we found a detached house whose core dated from the turn of the nineteenth and twentieth centuries and which had been built around in dusky orange brick during the 1970s, and roofed with deep red concrete tiles.

Originally it had been what was called a 'colonial', a corrugated iron shack with a verandah and two acres of land. The village was at one time full of these colonials, built for soldiers returning from the Boer War, so that they could earn their living on a smallholding. A few years before we bought it, two-thirds of an acre of land had been sold off and another house had been built, but it was slightly further up the hill and at a safe distance.

The house, when we found it, was pleasant but nothing special. It was the location – the genius of the place – that appealed to us. The vibes were right. The house itself was at the bottom of a hill, a one-in-four slope of chalk, clay and flint. The plot was ninety feet wide and a furlong from bottom to top – an eighth of a mile. It sloped to the north-west and was about 600 feet above sea level. It still is. We bought it, standing under the oak tree at the top of the slope and looking out over the farmer's field.

We moved in during November 1981 and Camilla arrived the following August.

Over the last twenty years we have built on in just about every direction: three dormer windows in the roof, another bedroom over my study at the front, a conservatory at one end and a large room at the other which we call 'The Orangery'. It has a wooden floor, mirrors and a barre down one side (serve me right for marrying a dancer), and the girls and their mum practised ballet there when they were little. Now we've turned it into a little theatre. Like you do. It has a small, raised stage, crimson curtains with red tassels, and a plywood proscenium arch painted with cherubs, known as the 'Botticelli botties'. An artist friend in the next village painted them for us, refusing to charge us the going rate, saying she needed to get back into practice after having children.

At Christmas we put on silly home-spun entertainments for the village – the latest was 'Larry Botter and the Chamber Pot of Secrets' – and sing carols and have wine and mince pies. At other times of year I can sometimes manage to persuade friends in 'the business' to come and put on a one-man or one-woman show. We don't pay them anything. Not even expenses. But everything they raise goes to a charity of their choice.

I'm amazed at who we've managed to haul in over the years. The cast of *The Archers*, Kit and the Widow and Patricia Routledge have all trodden our boards. Alan Bennett has been twice. The villagers can't believe their luck, and neither can we.

As the years have gone by we've also acquired more land from the farmer at the top of the hill. It's not that I'm trying to buy up Hampshire, it's just that I enjoy doing my bit for nature conservation. And privacy, if I'm honest. We've bought it bit by bit, a little at a time, and now have thirty-five acres of meadow and woodland, including four acres known as 'The New Wood', which we planted in a day.

It's wonderful what you can achieve with a little press-ganging. We sent out a flier to all our friends in the village. 'Come and Plant a Wood in a Day', it said. I'd mown the rides in this vacant patch of field, spot-weedkillered where all the trees would go, pushed a label in each spot saying what sort of tree should be planted there, and on a Sunday in December 1992 between 10 a.m. and 4 p.m. we planted more than a thousand six-inch-high trees in cylindrical shelters to protect them from deer.

There were families with dogs, and families with unruly toddlers. We served them soup and bacon sandwiches, and I gave demonstrations on tree planting. We planted oak and beech, field maple and birch, wild cherry and blackthorn, whitebeam and hawthorn. At the end of the day the field had become a forest of pale green plastic tubes.

But now, ten years on, the trees are more than ten feet tall. The field has become a young wood. I knew that planting a tree was fun, but planting a wood is mind blowing. I'm planning a celebration right now, when all those who signed the visitors book in 1992 can come back ten years on and see how their trees have grown. We've lost a few to field voles, who have chewed away the bark at the base, and a few more to deer, who fray the bark when they rub the felt off their new antlers in spring, but those that remain are strong and vigorous and we've done our bit for posterity.

Polly and Camilla joined in. I'm often asked if they are keen on gardening. The reply is always the same. 'They are girls of twenty and twenty-two. Were you keen on gardening at that age?'

But I hope. I do hope. And one of them threw me an olive branch a few weeks ago. 'Dad?' she said.

'Yes?'

'When I get married, will you design my garden?'

I felt a glow of pride. 'Of course I will.'

And then I worried. 'Who is he?'

29

Branching Out

'Most people can gain a certain pleasure from being critical, but journalists must learn to make a living out of it.'

Katharine Weston, *Pen and Sword*, 1966

Until I was thirty-seven I made my living solely from being a gardener. Well, that and writing and broadcasting about it, which is not so dirty but still connected. From *Nationwide*, and a plastic lawn on the roof of Lime Grove studios, I moved indoors to *Breakfast Time*. In the days of the red sofa the programme was more relaxed, more magazine-like. Now it's called *Breakfast News*. It's very sound, but not quite so popular. Or so much fun.

I was given two weekly slots – still of the regulation four minutes – one, a filmed piece from a famous garden, or in the countryside, and one a 'phone-in' from my own garden (I was the first person to use a cordless phone on air – a rather pathetic boast) or sometimes live in the studio.

For the first time I found myself sitting next to famous people, advising Elton John on the care of his maidenhair fern, talking to Kiri te Kanawa about her roses, and being sandwiched between Russell Harty, Jonathan Miller and David Puttnam at Easter and talking about daffodils being sold as cut flowers in spiked bunches (which means that they come with leaves).

At the end of the programme Frank Bough and Selina Scott said goodbye. 'And goodbye,' said Jonathan Miller, looking at the folk sitting on either side of him, 'from the spiked bunch.' I thought it was hugely witty.

All kinds of people watched *Breakfast Time*. During my second year there a well-dressed gentleman walked into the Lime Grove reception area during the course of the programme and said that he had an appointment to see Selina Scott. He identified himself, and the uniformed security man telephoned up to the Green Room to check that this would be in order.

'I've got . . . just a minute . . .' The security man put his hand over the mouthpiece and addressed the gentleman. 'Excuse me, sir. Which country did you say you was King of?'

'Greece,' came the measured reply.

During one programme I had been talking about roses and extolling the virtues of well-rotted horse manure as a mulch. I had a bucket of the stuff in front of me on the sofa. You know what it's like with crumbly brown manure – you just can't keep your hands out of it. I was stuck in up to the elbows, even if Selina Scott was a bit taken aback by my enthusiasm. She leaned away from me.

As the closing signature tune swelled in volume and the credits rolled I began to scrape the brown enrichment from my hands. Out of the corner of my eye, I noticed the bodies on the studio floor parting like the Red Sea. Ridiculous, I thought. It doesn't smell that much.

And then I heard a voice. The editor's. 'Don't shake hands with him,' he said. 'You've seen where they've been.'

I looked up in time to see the Princess of Wales walking towards me, smiling. Her hand was outstretched in front of her. So was mine. They met with an audible squelch, and as she gazed at me from under those long lashes, the only thing I could think of to say was, 'I'll never wash again.'

I found her a wet wipe in the make-up room, and apologised for the mess. 'Not to worry,' she said. 'I don't see much of that; it's my husband who does the gardening.'

We met again a few months later. I was signing books at a Red Cross Christmas Fair in the Guildhall. I wasn't scheduled to meet her, but she saw me, signing away, and came across, wearing a smart black-and-white dog-tooth checked suit and seamed stockings with little bows at the heel. Funny what you remember.

I'd been on the programme that day, outdoors, doing something or other. 'You looked frozen this morning,' she said. 'Weren't you wearing your thermals?'

So it is that I can boast to my intimates that the Princess of Wales once enquired about my underwear. And, yes, her charisma took your breath away. It was one heck of a smile.

I decided, now that I was working as a freelancer and doing quite a bit of television, that I really needed an agent. It wasn't just that I wanted to hit the big time – to do something more than a slot in a current affairs programme – it was also that I hated talking about money. I would never have made a door-to-door salesman. I'd have ended up giving the stuff away. I'm useless at haggling in markets on foreign holidays. I always give them more than they want because I can't see how they can survive on such a pittance. This was clearly not the way to proceed with my career. Better to get an agent to do the negotiating for me. I made enquiries of others in 'the business', and after a recommendation arranged an appointment with Annie Sweetbaum.

Annie is known to the kids as 'Annie Darling'. Since they were little she has always rung up and said, 'It's Annie Darling!' She is everyone's idea of what an agent should look and sound like.

She is larger than life, with a carefully coiffed meringue of blonde hair, and she wears power-dressing suits that are immaculately cut. She has some very showy jewellery.

What she thought of me on that day in 1984 when I turned up wearing green wellies and a rugby shirt and carrying a birch broom I have no idea. I'd been at a photo shoot for my latest book. She sat quietly (which is not like her) while I explained that I wanted an agent who could 'put me about a bit'.

'All right, darling, we'll give it a go.' She smiled, shook my hand, and stepped over the pile of mud I'd left on her polished floor. I've been with her ever since.

Along with Lili, her right-hand woman who deals with me on a daily basis, and Caroline, my PA-cum-secretary, they keep me in my place. But then, as everyone knows, behind every successful man there's a woman telling him he's wrong. Or, in my case, half a dozen of them.

Daytime television began in 1986. Until then we were blessed either with schools programmes or the test card – the one with the girl, the clown, the chalks and the blackboard.

Roger Laughton was the man charged with bringing entertainment to the sick, the unemployed, the retired, the truant and the nursing mother – for that was the accepted wisdom about any broadcast made between 9 a.m. and 5 p.m. We'd met when he was involved with *Breakfast Time*. Newly appointed as Head of Daytime Television, he asked if I had ever thought of doing television that was not related to gardening. I said I had not. He said that I should. He asked if I would like to audition for a live programme called *Open Air*, which was to be an hour and a half of viewers' feedback each weekday – a sort of extended *Points of View* with teeth. It was to be broadcast from Manchester.

I said I would think about it. I did. I auditioned. My competitor was a man called Peter Bazalgette. I got the job. Peter Bazalgette was very pleasant about it and said that actually he thought production, rather than performing, was more his sort of thing. He went on to found his own company, Bazal Productions. They've done quite well. They produce *Big Brother*, *Ready Steady Cook*, *Food and Drink*, *Changing Rooms* and *Ground Force*.

'Five days a week suit you?' asked Roger.

'Oh, no. I couldn't do that. I'm a gardener. I've all my writing to do. I'll do one day a week, if that's all right.'

Sometimes my nerve astounds me. But Roger agreed. I would do one day a week, and they would use an Irish reporter they were trying out on the other days, along with my co-presenter Pattie Coldwell. He hadn't done any network television to date, just local stuff in Belfast. But he was a nice lad. We got on well together. We used to have supper in the pizza house across the road on our cross-over evening. His name was Eamonn Holmes.

Open Air was a baptism by fire. I might have been there only one day a week, but I had to learn a new craft quickly. This was live television with autocue, to be read naturally while listening to producer talk-back and timings that were fed into one ear. At the same time I had to interview guests, appearing to give them my full attention. It was one step on from walking and talking at the same time. And several on from walking and chewing gum. The guests might be people in the street, or they might be the stars of a programme broadcast the night before – those who were prepared to travel up to Manchester.

I would field questions on behalf of the viewing public, and I would lob in my own questions as well, losing myself in a conversation that often turned out to be heated, and almost always interesting. Almost. There were exceptions. There is nothing more daunting than hearing a voice in your ear saying, 'Seventeen minutes left on this item,' when you know it's a bummer.

BBC bigwigs would be called to defend themselves in the face of vituperative criticism, sometimes successfully, sometimes not. I tried not to think of it as crawling, and at the same time tried to avoid losing my job – occasionally a difficult balance to strike. Over the course of the year we encountered most of the BBC hierarchy, including the then Director General, Sir Michael Checkland, and the Chairman of the Governors, Marmaduke (now Lord) Hussey. I talked to them both quite happily, if a touch respectfully, and could never quite bring myself to adopt Pattie's more familiar affectation of calling them Mikey and Dukey.

The skills needed in presenting live studio broadcasts are often underestimated. Take the use of the teleprompter or 'autocue'. 'Oh, he's only reading autocue' is a criticism often levelled at presenters and newsreaders who appear to be breezing along. It is the most uninformed of remarks. If anyone is reading autocue well you will hardly notice. If they are reading it badly you most certainly will.

The words come up on a piece of sloping glass directly in front of the camera lens, so you appear to be speaking right into camera. Keep your head too high and you appear to be talking down your nose to the viewer – instant arrogance. Get the camera too close and the audience will see your eyes move from side to side. If it is too far away you will start to screw up your eyes as though you are short-sighted (which you probably are).

Position the camera at the correct distance from you, and gently move your head as you speak and all will be well. It will look natural. Provided you don't move your head too much. If you do you will get 'the nods' and drive your viewer barmy. Oh, and try not to look like a rabbit caught in headlights. The way to do that is to kid yourself that you are talking to an invisible person. Child's play.

Then there are your hands. If you are sitting down they are less of a problem. You can arrange them on the desk or the arms of the chair or in your lap. But if you are standing up it gets a bit more complicated. Keep them rigidly by your side and you will assume the appearance of a foot soldier addressing a sergeant-major. Move them too much and they will distract the viewer from what you are saying. (On occasion this can be used to advantage, but most of the time it is to be resisted.) Put one of your hands in your pocket and you will look relaxed, but keep it there too long and you can look slovenly. Fold your hands in front of you and you will look like a centre-forward protecting his privates in the face of a penalty kick.

So how can you look natural? Easy. Put a coin in one hand. Don't fiddle with it too much, just hold it. It really helps. Alternatively, if you are outdoors, put one hand on a fence or railing, but don't lean on it too much. If you're a gardener you can hold a trowel, or a plant. But then not every television presenter is a gardener.

On a multi-camera shoot the moment will come where you must change from looking at one camera to another. (In a live programme the one with the red light on the top is the one whose picture is being transmitted.)

When the director in the gallery asks the vision mixer to cut from one camera shot to another, you will have to change as well. Do not attempt to synchronise your turn with the vision mixer's finger which is punching the button. You will never succeed. Instead, turn from the first camera and look at something else – a script, a person, a prop or a piece of scenery – and then turn to the new camera. It looks the most natural thing in the world.

What no one can teach you is how to get used to the voices in your ear, the 'talk-back' that presenters of live programmes must listen to at the same time as they are speaking. Their content will vary from the vital, 'Two minutes left on this item', to the personal, 'Ask about the divorce'. You will be counted into video inserts while you are speaking your introduction – 'Ten, nine, eight, seven, six, RUN VT, four, three, two, one . . .', and you must have stopped speaking by the time the film begins or you will crash into it.

You may be on 'switched talk-back', in which case you will hear nothing except your own instructions, or 'open talk-back' when you will hear all the conversation that goes on in the director's gallery, from other presenters' instructions and counts to swearing and witty asides.

Your earpiece might fall out. If it does, put it back in again. Nonchalantly. If you can't find it, or if talk-back breaks down and you can hear nothing, you will have to rely on your floor manager. He will be standing somewhere near the camera and he will occasionally hold up fingers. They are not intended to be insulting. They are your counts; firstly they will be minutes, and then he will count down the seconds to your next move or piece of film. But you can't look directly at him or you will lose eye-contact with your viewer; you must just catch him out of the corner of your eye.

Trying to get an interviewee to stop talking is not always easy. I once did resort to putting my hand over Su Pollard's mouth to stop the interminable flow of words, but there are few guests with whom such treatment is either necessary or acceptable. Always one tries to let the interviewee get to the end of a partic-ular answer. If this is an involved story it can be time-consuming. One director, having given me verbal warnings in my earpiece from his microphone in the gallery, 'One minute now . . . wrap up, please . . . have to hurry you . . .' finally said, exasperatedly, 'Alan, we're going to have to be rude in a moment.'

I have waffled my way through studio links with the wrong

piece of autocue script on the screen, and with script that has refused to move. I have gazed steadfastly at the wrong camera for fully half a minute, and I have broadcast with my flies undone. I once thanked a guest and called her the name of a close friend (which was similar, but not the same), and I still get no pleasure from seeing myself on the screen. Most broadcasters are just the same. You get used to yourself, but you never really learn to admire your performance. Just as well, I suppose.

Of course, when you're learning how to be a television presenter, they don't tell you all this. That would make it too easy. You have to work it out for yourself. But then, it's only reading autocue, isn't it?

30

The Old Feller

'Just make sure you've got a trade to fall back on.'
Alan Titchmarsh Senior to Alan Titchmarsh Junior

My dad was a classic Yorkshireman, but never in that brusque 'professional northerner' sort of way. That wasn't Dad at all. He wore a flat cap, and he liked plain food, but his style was altogether quieter. Never, in my entire life, did he tell me he loved me. I would have been embarrassed if he had. He made it obvious in other ways.

Before I got married, whenever I came home to Yorkshire, every evening as I went to bed, he would tap on the neighbouring wall from his and Mum's bedroom; 'rat-ta-ta-tat-tat', and I would respond with 'tat-tat'. Always he did it. Without fail.

Sometimes he would turn up the radio when I came home, if 'Welcome Home' – very popular at the time – was playing on Radio 2. A really soppy, folksy tune. 'Welcome home, we-e-el-come; close the door and come on in.' Dad would turn up the volume and sing along, throwing me an ostentatious wink and a beaming smile. A northern man, yes, but not a cold one.

He would dress conservatively when he wasn't at work, a sweater and trousers, the classic cream-coloured shorty-raincoat when he went out, maybe a dab of Old Spice in the evening when he took Mum to the pub. Every now and again he would come downstairs from having a bath and boast that he had had so much water in it that no links were visible on the plug chain. One Christmas he declared, as he came into the sitting room in a cloud of perfume, 'I've got everything on!' and those who had given him deodorant, bath foam and aftershave laughed at his outrageousness.

My sister cornered me once when I was on my own about the fact that when Dad and I met we would always shake hands, rather than kiss. He had always kissed me goodnight when I was little, but when I reached my teens it stopped. I don't remember a particular date. It just sort of didn't happen any more. I took it as a sign that now I was a man, and a handshake was a manly sort of greeting.

Kath said, 'It's really odd. You look like two businessmen.'

I remembered the occasion with the umbrella and wondered if it was something to do with not turning into a nancy-boy – you know, if your dad kisses you you might go the other way. It was stupid. Kath was quite right.

The next time Mum and Dad came to stay with us down in Hampshire, I hugged them and kissed them both on the cheek as they came in through the front door. From then on that was what we did, and my father never once demurred. I'd grown up, I'd got married, I had kids. I suppose it was all right now.

I'd often sit at his feet when he was in his armchair watching telly. I'd lean back against the front of his chair. Sometimes he would lower his hand and ruffle the hair on the top of my head. It happened even when I was in my thirties. He didn't need to do anything else. Explain anything. This, and the knocking on the wall, were enough.

He never told me about the facts of life. Instead, my mum gave me a little book from the Mother's Union. I was probably about eleven. There was nothing in it I didn't know. She promised me the second volume when I had read the first. To date it has not arrived.

My dad never called me 'Alan'. To my mother I was, and am, 'Sparrow', but to my father I was always 'Digby' or 'Dig', after Dan Dare's sidekick in *The Eagle*.

There are those who assume that the relationship between a northern father and his son is based on suppressed emotions and a rod of iron. In my case nothing could have been further from the truth. My father, though a quiet man and unostentatious in his affection, was not unhealthily repressed. He was just the way he was.

Mum and Dad were quite inseparable. They had a few close friends but mainly did things on their own. Mum had her 'hens' – Daisy and Kathleen and Muriel – three friends who met one evening a week to knit and sew and gossip, visiting each other's houses in rotation, and Dad had his night out at the pub or the British Legion, but mostly they went out together, or with Tommy Leighton, the Station Officer for Ilkley Fire Brigade, and his wife Vera. After the pub they would always go to one or other of their houses for the late night sandwich, but I don't think my parents ever had anyone round to dinner. It just wasn't the custom.

My dad's favourite wine – discovered relatively late in life – was Crown of Crowns, – sort of one leg up from Blue Nun. But for most of the time he drank Double Diamond, until you couldn't get it any more. My mum was a whisky drinker, at least until her arthritis took hold. The only thing that ever made her completely legless was one glass of Cherry B, but that was when I was too young to remember.

By the time I was married and living in Hampshire they would come to visit us two or three times a year in an old Ford Capri, behind the wheel of which my father resembled a bespectacled mole peering out at the traffic. He would always spend the first half-hour after their arrival discussing the road works and the route they had taken in Proustian detail. I learned to sit quietly and nod, though on occasions I would forget myself.

'You know that turning at Northampton, the one by the Esso filling station?'

'No.'

'You do, you do! It's the one with that big white house next to it – the one with the "Beware of the dog" sign.'

'I don't, Dad.'

'You do!'

It was all quite pointless. I should just have nodded.

It was the same when he was talking about someone in Ilkley who had just died.

'You know Harry Thwaites's brother-in-law – the one who used to sell the coke at the gasworks?'

'No.'

'You do, you do! He was Elsie Featherstone's husband – the one with the limp.'

'I don't remember.'

'You do. YOU DO!'

'Dad, I left home fifteen years ago . . .'

It became a family tradition I suppose. Like dad's 'Doh!' Every time something went wrong – a tap washer he was fixing, or a ballcock, or a piece of glass he was trying to cut – you would hear the tell-tale 'Doh!' and you would know Dad had had a disaster.

His pride at my unexpected achievements was quietly under-stated. He was not given to extravagant praise, but he would listen eagerly to my explanations of what I was doing, and his eyes would glow with excitement. Just occasionally I would catch him telling one of his friends some story that I had related to him. He would look embarrassed at being found out, and change the subject with an airy 'All right, Digby?'

In 1986 I was in Stoke-on-Trent, filming for the Stoke Garden Festival. There were no mobile phones back then, and after two days' filming I got in the car and drove home. Alison met me at the front door, and told me that my dad had died. A heart attack. It was very quick.

I walked up the garden and stood under the oak trees at the top, just looking out over the fields. I stayed there for half an hour, then came back down to the house, packed a bag and drove up to Yorkshire to be with my mum and sister.

I returned to Hampshire after a few days, and went back to Yorkshire with Alison for the funeral the following week. I made him a wreath of sweet peas. 'Alan Titchmarsh' sweet peas. They'd been named after me a couple of years previously. But my dad was called Alan, so they are also named after him.

Sixteen years on I still miss him. He might have been a quiet soul, but he left his mark on me. I can still feel his hand in mine when we shook hands. I can still feel the touch of his whiskery cheek against mine. He's not really gone, because as long as I live he will be a part of me. Maybe that's what's really meant by 'eternal life'. Living on in the hearts of those you leave behind.

But I wish he'd not died at sixty-two. I wish he'd seen me when I bowled to Colin Cowdrey, and I wish he'd seen me get my MBE. I wish he'd seen the girls grow up.

But above all, I wish there was still somebody who called me Digby.

31

Through the Mill

'The funny thing about television interviewing is that everybody
else thinks they can do it better than you.'

Russell Flaherty, *On Air*, 1994

'Did you ever see yourself as a chat-show host when you were
an apprentice gardener in Ilkley Parks Department?' Sometimes
this was asked with a wry grin, sometimes with a raised eyebrow.
In truth, it had never crossed my mind. It all boils down to 'having
a go', I suppose.

After a year of *Open Air* I was contacted by the editor of a
proposed new lunchtime magazine programme which would deal
with everything from star interviews to issues of the day. There
would be occasional 'strands' on subjects as varied as tranquil-
liser addiction and crop circles. There would be fashion reports
and film previews, all leavened with live theatrical performances
and music. It sounded exactly like *Nationwide* at lunchtime.
Daytime Live, as it was to be called, would be transmitted every
weekday from Pebble Mill in Birmingham. It predated ITV's *This
Morning* with Richard and Judy by a couple of years. From the
moment the series was mooted I knew it was what I wanted to
do. It would give me more freedom than *Open Air* where the
interviews dealt simply with the previous night's TV
programmes.

My interview for the job was not conducted over a power-lunch. Instead it took place over afternoon tea at Browns Hotel in London, all chintz and cucumber sandwiches. Steve Weddle, the editor, and producer Mark Kershaw, whom I'd worked with for a few years on the BBC's Chelsea Flower Show programmes, did not so much grill me as give me the gentlest of toastings. I remember leaving them to muse over their Earl Grey, wondering if I'd ever hear from them again.

Within three months I was sitting in the anchor man's chair in the Pebble Mill foyer five days a week, with Pamela Armstrong and Judi Spiers, then Sue Cook and Floella Benjamin and finally Gloria Hunniford.

The programme which really had become a legend in its own lunchtime, *Pebble Mill at One*, had ceased transmission two years previously after umpteen years on air and been replaced by the *Pamela Armstrong Show*. But Pam, having been wooed over from ITV's *News at Ten*, was not settled in her new post. She was ready for another change. In what would be her final year with the BBC extra presenters were brought in to continue *Daytime Live*, once she had left.

The programme evolved over the ten years I spent in Birmingham, becoming, after a few years, *Scene Today* and, finally, as if giving in to the public who had always loyally hung on to the title, *Pebble Mill*, though it was now at ten past twelve instead of one o'clock, and transmitted from a large studio rather than the glass-fronted foyer.

For the last few years the 'magazine' items disappeared and it was a talk-show proper with 'live' music, and in the sole charge of one presenter, rather than two or three. After the first year of presenting five *Daytime Live* shows a week, I was able to cut down to three a week which suited me better in terms of the rest of my work, though it still meant that I spent half the week away from home.

The compensation was that I lived every 'Miss World' contestant's dream – I got to travel and to meet people. During the off season, between May and September, there would be trips to the States to interview 'big names', and during the rest of the year they would show up at the studio.

Yes; I can hear you. 'Just a minute. You're a gardener. I thought all you ever wanted to do was to be Percy Thrower.'

True.

'So why were you wooed by all this presenting lark, and interviewing stars?'

Wouldn't you be? Be honest, if you're the sort of person who is a born nosy parker, what would be your reaction if somebody offered you a chance to sit down and interview just about anybody you liked for an hour or so at lunchtime, wouldn't you quite like to have a go? Well, I did.

Not that I was prepared to give up my 'proper job'. I continued to write my gardening books and my weekly column for the *Daily Mail,* and still presented the Chelsea Flower Show programme, but after eight years of four-minute gardening slots with never a sign of anything longer, I saw the chance to present my own chat show as adding another string to my bow. It was a way of gaining additional expertise, being able to handle a studio audience, and holding together a live one-hour programme. It was not a view shared by all. There were those who thought that I had sold out, given up being a gardener and become 'just another chat-show host'. There were mutterings in the gardening world. I tried to ignore them.

Daytime television also became an easy target for the critics – wallpaper television they called it. Well, there's wallpaper and wallpaper. There's Colefax and Fowler and there's Decor 8. I'd pitch myself somewhere between the two. Sort of Sanderson. Hopefully.

Not everyone agreed. My two favourite criticisms (though at the time they were deeply wounding) came from Victor Lewis Smith in the *Evening Standard*. 'If you have half a mind to watch Pebble Mill,' he wrote, 'you will have made ample intellectual provision.' Unfair. But beautifully phrased.

His second was even more wounding: 'The five most debilitating words in the English language are: "Ladies and gentlemen, Alan Titchmarsh."'

Oh, I can laugh now, but my kids had their letters of protest written out ready to post. I thanked them and put them in the bin.

Like all performers I have little time for critics, unless they happen to like what I do. When they admire my work they are discerning, perceptive and astute. If they don't like me they are misguided, jealous, bitter and untalented. But like all performers and writers, deep down I know that the reverse is true. If they like me, I have managed to pull the wool over their eyes. If they dislike me, I've been rumbled.

Whatever the case I like to think I made a decent fist of things on *Pebble Mill*, in spite of being a soft target. Interviewing is about more than being just a good listener. It's about being a conduit between your guest and the audience, showing them off to the best and most entertaining effect. It is not always easy. I learned pretty quickly that just because someone plays the part of an interesting character in a drama on the box that does not necessarily mean that they are interesting in themselves. They are sometimes. But not always. I never asked a question I did not want to know the answer to, and although not exactly challenging in the Paxman mode, my conversations were always intended to be stimulating rather than fawning and obsequious.

And I did manage to gain interviews with people who were not so omnipresent that they would turn up for the opening of an envelope – Sir George Solti, Dame Judi Dench, Placido Domingo, George Shearing, Sir Dirk Bogarde, Alan Bennett and Stephen Sondheim. In the States I met Jack Lemmon and Al Pacino, Tony Bennett and Artie Shaw, Donald Trump and Cindy Crawford, and over here, Glenn Close and Dustin Hoffman, Mickey Rooney and Julia Roberts.

Ah, Julia Roberts. Well, there has to be one, doesn't there? I interviewed her first in London and then in Rome. In London, at the Dorchester, she had been dressed in a long floral-print frock in muddy brown, with black Doc Martens. She took a while to warm up, but seemed quite smiley by the end. She signed my press release for *The Pelican Brief,* 'For Alan, Love and Peace, Julia Roberts.' I was pretty bowled over. But I covered it well.

When we met in Rome a few years later it was to promote *Mary Reilly* – not her best film, but then after *Pretty Woman* she can do what the hell she likes as far as I'm concerned.

These film-related 'star' interviews are conducted at what's know as a 'press junket'. The star sits in a lavish hotel suite, and two cameras are set up, plus studio lighting and sound, to cover the interview. A queue of reporters lines up outside, and they take it in turns to sit in the interviewer's chair. As a rule they are allowed between ten and fifteen minutes of chat before they are politely asked to leave and given two video cassettes – one of themselves asking the questions, and another of the star answering. If you've seen *Notting Hill* you will know exactly what it's like. I played Hugh Grant. Julia Roberts played Julia Roberts.

She was dressed in black this time – a neatly cut jacket and trousers – her shiny dark brown hair tumbling over her shoulders. She flashed me a smile as I walked into the room. 'Hi! How are you? Nice to see you again!'

I stood there, hopefully not too open-mouthed. 'You remember?'

'I have a perfect recollection,' she beamed.

I don't think she was fibbing. Frankly, I don't care. I gave her a copy of *Alan Titchmarsh's Favourite Gardens* and answered questions about her bulbs. When I left she gave me a peck on the cheek. I am a man of simple pleasures. I can now die happy.

Meg Ryan and Claudia Schiffer, Elle MacPherson and Debra Winger, Sir Anthony Hopkins and Morgan Freeman, José Carreras and Sir Anthony Dowell. They all passed through. Hundreds of them.

It sounds like a boastful CV. After all, they are everyday names to any watcher of television. But it is different, somehow, when you are the person meeting them. There is no need to be star struck – that would be awkward and counter-productive – but it would be a waste not to savour the moment.

There were occasional embarrassments – the pretty young actress who was more concerned about her split ends than her interview, and spent the entire rehearsal time teasing them out rather than meeting my eye. She left the studio floor with a sigh and went back to the Green Room to snog her unknown actor boyfriend. They were lying full length on the sofa. I left them to it. She was Elizabeth Hurley. He was, and is, Hugh Grant.

Fay Weldon managed to conduct an entire interview with her back to me. Maybe she was having an off day. Joan Collins was brittle and tricky the first time we met; better the second. And whatever they say about her, close up her complexion is pretty unbelievable for a sexagenarian. I think that's what she is.

But more often than not I had a ball, and discovered that if interviewees found that you were not there to undermine them or let them down they would have a ball, too. It was lunchtime entertainment, for goodness' sake, not a frontal lobotomy. Life needs confetti as well as brain surgery.

Through it all, I pictured the viewer, scrambled egg on toast on his or her knee. If I could stop the fork half way on its journey to the mouth while the viewer was engaged in our conversation that was enough.

The powers that be must have thought that I got away with it, because I was asked to take on the late night Radio 2 *Arts Programme* when it came from Birmingham, and to stand in for John Dunn when he was on holiday. It was fun. Except for the once.

I had to go to London. To the Grosvenor House Hotel. To interview Bette Davis. I knew I would have to do my homework. I'd seen *Whatever Happened to Baby Jane?* And so I read her book from cover to cover. I had forty-two questions prepared and was determined not to turn the interview into some sycophantic 'What was your favourite film?' sort of affair.

We hovered in reception for a good half-hour, during which time the publisher's publicist (it was a volume of memoirs that Miss Davis was here to plug) encouraged me to ask questions about face lifts. I decided not to play that card. Not at first, anyway. Not until she warmed up.

I was eventually ushered up to Miss Davis's suite with my producer and sound recordist in tow. The door was opened by her secretary, a woman called Kathryn Sermak. She was young and attractive, wore a tight-fitting black woollen dress and had a deliberately firm handshake. (I'd read in the book that Miss D was keen on firm handshakes. No problem. So am I.)

As Miss Sermak pulled me into the hallway with her octopus grasp, Miss D stepped neatly out of a side door. It was all perfectly choreographed.

'Good morning,' she said, and gave me a handshake for which I almost needed whiplash treatment. 'Come this way.'

She turned on her heel and walked down the corridor towards

her sitting room. She was minute. Bird-like. Four feet something. I could have closed my fingers around her ankles. The air was filled with floral perfume. The contrast between her steely demeanour and the herbaceous fragrance was unnerving.

'You sit there.' She pointed to a sofa on one side of a low, glass-topped coffee table. She sat opposite me on another sofa, her mouth set in a lopsided scowl, her black bob of a wig shining in the winter sunshine that slanted through the window. Like her secretary, she, too, was dressed in black. It was like a convention of crows. On the table in front of her stood a wine glass filled with filter-tip cigarettes; alongside it a silver goblet whose line of condensation showed that it contained something cold. There was nothing in front of me, except my forty-two questions.

We made desultory conversation while the sound man rigged up the tape recorder and the microphones. Or rather, I did. Miss Davis responded to most of my vapid small-talk with grunts or one-word answers. Heigh-ho. What fun. I girded my loins.

Finally we were ready for the off. I noted that, in her memoirs, she had stated that she was not 'a woman', but 'a broad'. 'What,' I asked, 'is "a broad"?'

'A broad is a woman who does not use feminine wiles.'

I had hoped that the interview would be sparky, and that Miss Davis would take pleasure in putting me down as a whipper-snapper of an interviewee in a sort of Yankee Lady Bracknell way. I was quite prepared for it. It would make for an entertaining interview. So I posed my next question:

'Miss Davis, do you mean to tell me that you have never used feminine wiles?'

I waited for the put down. But it was not the one I had expected.

'You shouldn't talk to me like that,' was all she said.

I felt a sinking feeling in the pit of my stomach, the sort that comes when you know you've misjudged a situation. I apologised, and noticed the secretary beginning to pace up and down, staring at the floor, her arms folded.

I changed tack. 'You say in the book that you were offered the part of Scarlett O'Hara in *Gone With the Wind*, and yet you turned it down.'

'Yes. I was and I did.'

'Why was that?'

'Because at that time they wanted Errol Flynn to play Rhett Butler and I said that there was only one man who could play Rhett Butler and that was Clark Gable.'

She had been scathing about several Hollywood leading men in her memoirs, including Ronald Reagan. He might be the current President of the United States but his acting talent cut no ice with her. I should have had more sense, but with the grim inevitability of a rolling avalanche I motored on. I asked if she thought Ronald Reagan would have made a good Rhett Butler. She got up. She walked out. I never saw her again.

Her secretary ran after her, then returned a few minutes later, incandescent with rage. How dare I not show Miss Davis enough respect? How dare I ask such impertinent questions? My producer's face turned a whiter shade of pale. I listened for a few minutes and then put my side of things calmly but firmly, explaining that I did, indeed, have a lot of respect for Miss Davis, and that I had simply been anxious to have a robust rather than a servile interview. It was all to no avail. We had seven minutes of interview on the tape which the secretary insisted that we hand over to her. We did so. We left. And instead, for that night's programme, I recorded an interview with the Reverend Roger Royle. Not earth-shattering, but less threatening.

I shared the experience, some months later, with Sir Peter Ustinov. 'Ah, Bette Davis!' He nodded slowly. 'I remember working with her in *Death on the Nile*. Terrifying. Quite terrifying. David Niven and I had a scene with her on the deck of the riverboat. We used to bolster each other up every time we encountered her. Very nerve-racking. She had to smoke a cigarette in a long tortoise-shell holder, and she wore a white hat with a black veil.'

He leaned forward conspiratorially and said, in his Hercule Poirot voice, 'When she exhaled, the smoke came out in little squares.'

32

The Greatest Show on Earth

'Nah, you don't want to go there, guv'nor; the traffic's a nightmare at this time of year.'

London taxi driver, on being asked to drive to Chelsea, May 2001

Remembering what my dad had told me, about always having a trade to fall back on, I never gave up the day job. It still says 'gardener' on my passport. Well, it did until I had to have one of those new maroon jobs. It's stretching a point, I know, but I still consider myself to be a gardener first and foremost, a writer second and a broadcaster third. It helps me to keep things in perspective.

Pebble Mill took up a fair amount of my time in the Eighties and Nineties, but the powers that be decided the programme had run its course and transmission ended in 1996. My future seemed unsure. I was not certain which way to turn. I never stopped writing about gardening, and I had kept my hand in on television by presenting the BBC's coverage of the Chelsea Flower Show.

I love Chelsea. No other flower show has an atmosphere like it. Oh, it's good to have newcomers like Hampton Court Palace Flower Show and Malvern and Tatton Park – there are now so many of them as to make your average gardener dizzy – but nothing matches Chelsea's sense of occasion.

For a start there is the timing – the third week in May – late spring, a wonderful moment in the year. Everything fulfilling its promise; nothing tired and worn. Chelsea is optimism under canvas, or it was until they replaced the Great Marquee with a sort of pavilion. But we soldier on, those of us who enjoyed the *fête champêtre* that was Chelsea until they brought in the new building. And it is much better for the exhibitors, just not quite so romantic.

People dress up for Chelsea: posh frocks, jackets and ties. They picnic on the grass of the Royal Hospital, and the scarlet-coated pensioners weave among them. A military band plays selections from *The Yeomen of the Guard* and *Me and My Girl*. A cup of tea costs far too much. It's lovely.

My first appearance presenting the show on television came about in 1983 because I was making a Chelsea garden for *Woman's Own* magazine. I was writing for them at the time. I designed the garden and, with the help of a great landscaper called Mike Chewter, built it on site in the space of three weeks. Totally knackering, but fun.

Mike came recommended by a regular Chelsea exhibitor who would not be needing his services that year. Sturdily built, with hands of leather, a walrus moustache and weatherbeaten complexion, he coaxed me through the process, always keeping cool in the face of seemingly insurmountable odds, and always solicitous ('Cup of tea, Alan?'), and encouraging ('Doesn't that look lovely!'), when I'd planted something, or we'd completed a bit of paving.

At that time the BBC's Chelsea coverage was presented by Peter Seabrook, with another television personality as his sidekick – often a female, and usually someone with presenting rather than horticultural experience – a newsreader or a travel show reporter. In the few years prior to 1983 they had co-opted one of the exhibitors at the show to be a co-presenter as well, and it was this role that I was asked to fulfil.

With a touch of envy, I had watched Peter Seabrook doing the job for as long as I could remember. It was, after all, the plum job, apart from *Gardeners' World*, which was now firmly under the belt of Geoff Hamilton. But only just. I'd tried for it, and failed.

I'd been for a chat with the producer of *Gardeners' World*, John Kenyon, in 1980 when Peter Seabrook left the programme. John was looking for a replacement, but he decided, in the end, to go with Geoff Hamilton because his garden, Barnsdale, was in the Midlands – Rutland – and far more typically placed for the viewership, he reckoned, than mine in Hampshire. He probably also thought that Geoff would be a better presenter. Whatever his reasons, his judgment was sound and the programme was a great success, though it did delay my mainstream appearance in a gardening programme by seventeen years.

I was disappointed at the time, but sanguine, I think. Fatalistic. No point brooding on it. Not for more than a day or two, anyway. But now I was asked to chip in at Chelsea for a year. I was pleased. Delighted. But I had no idea how hard it was to be.

Making one of the outside gardens at the Chelsea Flower Show is one of the most arduous, stressful and challenging undertakings for any gardener. Standards of plant cultivation and finish are high, and the work is labour intensive. From a football pitch, a perfect garden is made in just three weeks.

I sweated and slaved, dug and paved, planted and positioned things, with Mike and his mate Ray doing most of the hard landscaping, and keeping me on an even keel. Plants would be late arriving, rain would lash down and hold up the work, the paving took an age to lay. I fretted. Mike Chewter pacified. During the last two or three days, as well as finishing off the garden I had to begin filming the stories for the programme. I hardly knew which way to turn. I was asleep each evening before my head hit the pillow, and up again at the crack of dawn.

On the last day, the turf that had been promised a day previously finally arrived, and with sleeves rolled up and sweat dripping off my chin, I rolled it out and patted it into place, then stood back to take a look. It had the appearance of a chequerboard rather than a lawn.

Peter Seabrook stood at my elbow. 'What shall I do?' I asked.

'Just leave it. It'll freshen up on its own.'

'Should I brush it?'

'No. Just leave it.'

I did. And it was fine.

Peter had been there at my interview for the programme. He had not been easy to impress. The editor, Neil Eccles, who was in charge of outside broadcasts, gave me an easy ride and was warm and welcoming. Mr Seabrook less so.

When Neil had asked all his questions he turned to Peter. 'Anything else?'

Peter leaned forward in his chair. 'Supposing you have to do a piece on a little viola called "Jackanapes". It's on one of the stands at the show. What would you say?'

I was nonplussed. 'Well, I don't know yet. I'd have to find out about it.'

'Really? Wouldn't you say, "This is a lovely yellow and purple viola called 'Jackanapes', named by that famous lady gardener Gertrude Jekyll after her pet monkey which used to clamber all over her as she walked round her garden. Just look at those bright little flowers. A really good garden plant."'

I sat open mouthed. 'Probably.' It was the best response I could manage. I went home depressed.

I need not have worried. When it came to being a workmate, Peter Seabrook was the most generous and helpful co-presenter I have ever met. He saw me battling with my show garden and trying to do my programme research in between. When I was faced with an exhibit of plants about which I knew little, he would flip up the pages of his shorthand notebook and give me chapter and verse on the plants, their grower, the age of his grandmother and the marital status of his children. Free, gratis and for nothing. He would not make a great show of it. Quite the reverse. He personified quiet generosity. I hope I've learned from him.

The programme went down well, and my garden won a Silver Gilt medal. Not bad for a first timer. But it was not the 'coveted Gold Medal'. The Gold Medal is always described as 'coveted'. But then it is. It's what every single exhibitor aims for. Chelsea is the gardening Olympics, and no one wants silver.

Our double act continued for several years, the repartee becoming more robust with age. One newspaper dubbed us 'the Morecambe and Wise of the gardening world'. I don't think we were that funny. It's just that Peter loves hybrid tea and floribunda roses; I'm more of a shrub rose man. He hates them. He loves chunky dwarf French marigolds. Strange. But then he's from Essex. I prefer graceful penstemons. I live in Hampshire.

In 1985 I was to make another garden at Chelsea, again for *Woman's Own*. This time it was to be a 'Country Kitchen Garden' with knapped flint walls, succulent vegetables and fresh herbs. There were pretty cottage garden flowers, red campions in long grass underneath apple trees, Chinese Chippendale benches and a gurgling rill. I was still presenting the programme. It almost killed me. But Mike and Ray and I finally won a 'coveted Gold Medal' and I got to meet the Queen. I dressed up for the occasion in an outfit that now makes me blush, a maroon and black striped blazer with white cricket flannels, white shirt and primrose bow tie. The Queen didn't seem to mind. I walked her around the garden and she admired my onions. 'They are nice and small,' she said. 'I don't like those large ones; they taste of nothing at all.'

I've not made a Chelsea garden since. I thought I might as well quit while I was ahead.

If I were to pick one moment that ranks above all others at the Chelsea Flower Show it would date from the time of the Great Marquee. The show runs from Tuesday to Friday, with a press and royal preview day on Monday. I would be called to be on camera at six o'clock on Tuesday morning, having also filmed over the weekend and until quite late on the Monday. I would stay in London, usually with a friend, and make sure I was in the show ground by 5.30 a.m. Only the gatekeeper would be up at that early hour. I would show my pass, give him a nod, and walk down the deserted avenues towards the Great Marquee. There I would unpick the rope that held closed the canvas flap, and walk into its three and a half acres. No one else was there. Nobody saw me. The exhibitors had finished their work and were having a brief lie-in. The plants would be at their pristine best, fresh and, as yet, unseen by all except regal eyes. I would stand, and stare, and try to take it all in, breathing deeply and inhaling the scent of a million flowers. Then I would saunter between towering banks of delphiniums and roses, strawberries and tropical flowers, smelling the crushed grass beneath my feet and listening to the early morning song of the blackbird.

Every year I would do this, and every year I would be alone for a few minutes in the Garden of Eden. And when I left the marquee and went back outside, I would always have trouble seeing through the tears.

Nowadays the programmes are transmitted every day, but then, in the days of only one programme, filming was usually finished by the end of Tuesday. I would have the rest of the week to myself, but I spent a fair proportion of it, in those early years, on the

Amateur Gardening stand, signing magazines and books, answering questions, and lunching with the editor, Peter Wood, and Percy Thrower.

Percy had his own corner on the *Amateur Gardening* stand in Eastern Avenue, and his public would queue as he signed his calendars and books and offered a tip here, a handshake there. He was a true pro; a pleasure to watch. Courtly and gracious, a giant among gardeners.

He fell ill during my first year at Pebble Mill. They took him to Wolverhampton Hospital, about ten miles away from Birmingham. I planned to go and see him, but it turned into an exhausting week, researching guests at night, rehearsing in the morning, doing a live show, then planning the following day's programme in the afternoon. I would put off my visit till the following week. I went back to my hotel. I couldn't settle. I really should go and see him. I got in the car and drove to Wolverhampton.

The nurse told me which ward to go to. I walked through it but I couldn't see him. Then I heard a voice: 'Hello; look who's here!' I turned round to see Connie Thrower. She was wearing her coat, and sitting by the bed of a thin, pale, elderly man, who was lying back on the pillow and breathing slowly. It was Percy. Beside his bed, on the cabinet, was a card from the presenters of *Blue Peter*. His arms lay still on the blanket that covered him.

We chatted for a while. Or, rather, I did. Percy had little energy to spare. He was very tired, and after about half an hour I stood to take my leave and shook his hand. He held on to it, for around half a minute. Then he whispered, 'Thank you for coming,' and gently let it go.

The following day, driving home in the car, they announced his death on the radio. I pulled in and sat for a while.

33

Messing About in Boats

'The first time you shout I'm outa here.'
Alison Titchmarsh to Alan Titchmarsh, on a boat, 1994

Apart from the image of the sun shining on my garden, there's a picture that I see in my mind's eye whenever I'm stuck in a place I'd rather not be. It is the view of the wake behind my boat – the varnished wooden handrails gleaming in the sun, the white mast standing out against a forget-me-not blue sky, the blue ensign flapping in the breeze, and white water rolling over like a liquid ploughed field behind them. Most of my time is spent on dry land; some of my time is spent digging it, but when I need a change of air I head for the water.

It's eight years now since I learned the wisdom of Ratty's advice in *The Wind in the Willows* that 'there is *nothing* – absolutely nothing – half so much worth doing as simply messing about in boats.'

Of course, I'd heard all those horror stories about the cost of such a hobby, that it was not a lot different from standing fully clothed in a cold shower poking ten-pound notes down the plug-hole with your big toe. But I reasoned that I would not need to go out on such days. I would be a fair-weather sailor and nobody on my boat would be seasick.

For around twenty years I'd crewed for sailing friends on an irregular basis, perhaps once or twice a year. I remember being quietly pleased when one of them remarked that I seemed to have a natural ability on the water. It came as a bit of a surprise, especially since I have no ability *in* the water. Oh, I can swim sufficiently well to stay afloat, but the prospect of me completing a cross-Channel passage with the breast stroke is about as likely as my becoming a member of a boy band.

For several years I kept coming home with *Yachting Monthly* and *Classic Boat*. They grew into quite a pile by my bed. I dreamed of having a boat by the sea, just forty-five minutes away. But one thing bothered me: to go sailing you need wind. If you have no wind, you have to rely on your motor, and I have sat in quite a few sailing boats when there is no wind, while a throbbing but underpowered engine just about manages to keep pace with the tide, enabling you to remain, quite comfortably for an hour or two, in exactly the same place.

I have watched sailors on bright, sunny days looking forlornly at a floppy ensign before heading down to the sailing club for a few more pints, simply because there is hardly enough breeze to allow a feather to become airborne. A good day wasted.

Then there were all those complicated names that sailors use. They never call a rope a rope – it's a warp, or a painter, or a sheet or a shroud. A bit like calling a spade a non-mechanical earth moving facilitator, though at least in this case the description does give you some idea as to what the thing is meant to do. But what do you do with a shroud, except use it to bury people at sea?

Oh, I could have knuckled down and learned the terminology, but I found myself being drawn more and more towards a motor boat. Under power I could go out whether the day was breezy or calm, and the family would not have to worry about reefing or gybing, tacking and going about. Added to which we occasionally sail in the company of a friend called Leo. The prospect of my wife being clouted over the head by the boom every time I called 'lee-ho' to tack, in the belief that I was calling him over, would, I thought, render regular crewing unlikely.

No. A motor boat it was to be. But which? I have always hankered after a boat with character, but the prospect of owning something with teeth also appealed. Must have been my age. Mid-life crisis Ferrari equivalent. We went to look at a smart speed-boat: all-white plastic, aquamarine go-faster stripes, glass sliding patio doors, microwave oven, burr-walnut dash and a capacity to travel at thirty knots. That's quite fast in sailing terms.

We had a test drive. Thrilling! Skimming across the water like a flat pebble hurled by a discus thrower. We reached the Isle of Wight within minutes of leaving the South Coast marina. And then we came back. We'd all held on tight as the boat slapped through the waves, and the only disaster was the Pyrex dish that shot through the glass door of the oven because the people who were selling the boat had forgotten to take it out.

But there was nowhere to go. Oh, there were plenty of places to go *in* the boat, but nowhere to go *on* it. We all sat in the cockpit, hanging on, until we arrived at our destination, and with a slightly lumpy sea the journey could be distinctly uncomfortable.

We decided that the kids would be bored rigid if all they could do was hang on for grim life until the passage was over and they could explore the fleshpots of whatever resort we arrived at. No. We needed a larger boat, and one that travelled at a more sedate pace which allowed everyone on board to do their own thing as we voyaged.

We found our dream machine eight years ago in a second-hand boat sale in Lymington. She is a thirty-eight-foot trawler yacht, a description which conjures up images of fishing nets and oilskins.

She is known, in the trade, as a Eurobanker, which makes her sound like a Brussels executive or a gnome from Zurich. She is neither of these things. To us she is a fine lady, now in her twenty-second year, who has become a part of the family. She has twin 80 horsepower diesel engines capable of achieving a steady eight knots. She has spacious teak decks on three levels and a lot of varnished woodwork, a white mast which can be fitted with a steadying sail, a flybridge which offers a fine view of the water, and accommodation which to me ranks with the Orient Express.

The saloon is lined with teak. We have a modern galley (kitchen), two heads (loos), a hip bath and a shower, plus a large double stateroom (lovely word for a cabin) and one containing two bunks for the girls or visiting friends. She is our cottage by the sea. She is the great escape. She is a means of changing the scenery without ever leaving home, and we all love her to death.

This is a great help. Buy a boat that you yourself like, but which your family only suffer, and you are destined for lonely week-ends. If the family like it and are happy to crew for you (in my case, on the understanding that at the first order which is shouted they will mutiny and go home) then you are a happy man.

When I am not on the boat I daydream about her, which is half the fun of owning her. We manage to get down to her perhaps every other weekend between April and October, and spend most of August aboard, sometimes sailing down to the West Country.

We've not been abroad. I'm not really bothered about crossing the Channel, to tell you the truth. Do that and you have to get involved with paperwork and certificates of competence which sound a bit too bureaucratic for my liking. In the UK, boating has always been self-regulating, which some regard as folly, but which most regard as a practical solution. In theory, anyone can take any boat on to the water, even if they have never handled one before. On the continent that is not the case, but in spite of the difference in regulations, there are no more boating accidents in this country than anywhere else.

Anyone with half a brain learns the ins and outs of boat handling anyway, from skilled friends, or on a Royal Yachting Association approved course. I'm a qualified Day Skipper, with the intention of one day becoming a Yachtmaster. I have a certificate which allows me to operate my VHF radio, and have been on a diesel engine maintenance course. But the best way to learn how to handle a boat is by doing just that, remembering that when you are out in open water it is relatively easy; it is when you start to come close to things like pontoons, jetties and other boats that things start to get tricky. Boats don't have brakes, and as one skipper of a large fibreglass bathtub which was bearing down on my bows exclaimed, 'I can cope with wind, and I can cope with tide, but I can't cope with them both at once.' In my experience, there is rarely a time when they don't both occur simultaneously.

But the secret, in among all the knowledge gained and experience accrued, is not to let the first thrill of being on the water slip away. I still get excited when I turn on the engines and motor out into the Solent. I love spending the night at anchor in a calm bay, being rocked to sleep by the water, and I dream of, one day, sailing right around the coast of Britain.

I hope I never have to forgo the pleasures of spending a week tied to a buoy in Salcombe harbour, or of putting into Cowes and opening a bottle of chilled Sauvignon Blanc up on the flybridge, watching the world sail by. No fish and chips taste like those brought aboard from the fish shop in Lymington, and no mackerel can ever have the flavour of the ones I catch from the fishing line tossed over the back as we troll across the Solent at three knots, intent on being self-sufficient for supper. I have watched the sun set on the water, and the moon casting its silver light on crystal ripples, and these images are the ones that stay with you, rather than the tricky moments, the foul weather and the cost of it all.

Make no mistake; boating can be very expensive. You can spend £25 million on a Superyacht if you have the funds, but you can also spend £250 on a sailing dinghy which will get you afloat and let you experience for yourself the last great escape. The smaller the boat, the greater the fun, they say, and I reckon I have thirty eight feet of the best fun afloat.

I have bent a lamppost on the end of a jetty, I have occasionally come into contact with another vessel unintentionally (but fortunately at very low speed), and yes, I have been caught out by the weather. A couple of summers ago we journeyed back from the West Country across Lyme Bay in a sea which the Brixham Coastguard called 'slight to moderate'. There was little wind, and the forecast was good. We set off on the forty-mile journey where for most of the time we would be out of sight of land, on a moderate swell. By the time we were half way across the bay this had built up to about five metres. The boat lifted up and crashed down again every few seconds on a voyage that lasted nine and a half hours. It was impossible to stand up without hanging on to something. Eating and drinking were out of the question. My wife and daughters lay flat on the cabin floor, while I stood up and helmed. I could not do so from the flybridge because of the spray.

When we eventually cruised into Weymouth harbour, picking strands of seaweed off the flybridge, they politely asked if they could complete the journey by car. I hadn't the heart to say 'no'.

Even closer to home things do not always go according to plan. In our first season we had decided to show the boat off to friends. We would take them out one Sunday from Chichester Harbour

into the Solent for a leisurely cruise. A simple pootle. We set off
at 11 a.m. (sorry; 1100 hours) in, according to my log book, 'Brisk
breeze – cloudy, some sun.'

We motored through the lock on free flow – always a bit like
white water rafting – and wove our way through a couple of
yacht races in the harbour, managing to make contact, albeit brief
and glancing, with only one of them. We then proceeded towards
Chichester Bar Beacon. The wind was noticeably fresher now –
Force 5 – and the water choppy. We started to bounce, and furniture began to move.

Several small children shrieked. One of them shouted 'Stop
the boat!' and another had a nose bleed down one of our new
life jackets. An oil lamp glass was smashed and the television
leaped off its shelf and on to the floor. (Yes, I know it's supposed
to be a boat, not a caravan, but if you want to get small children
to sit quietly for hours in a rain-sodden harbour you have to
provide them with a telly. It's a fact of life.)

One of our friends fell down in a corner. Alison was quiet, but
clearly braced by the quality of the air on the flybridge. The
mother of the shrieking children bellowed 'Sit down' to anyone
who showed signs of stretching their legs.

I turned the boat round and cruised back to anchor near to a
beach called East Head in Chichester Harbour. It's a great place
for children to play, and the beach can be reached by dinghy once
you have dropped the hook. After a certain amount of fiddling
it did drop, and then we lowered the dinghy and fitted the
outboard. It refused to work. One hour later I took it off, stowed
it in the lazarette and got out the oars. I rowed parties of children to the shore. Twice. I returned for tea. It was now 1510 hours.

Tea was just being served when the small children on the beach
shouted that they were ready to be picked up. They were hungry.
The children's father (not an especially strong swimmer) put to

sea in the dinghy, in a strong ebb current. Having rowed just far enough to be out of reach he broke a rowlock and began a) going round in circles and b) drifting away. He had to be rescued by a man in a dinghy with an outboard that *did* work.

Our friend's wife, having already cast aspersions on her spouse's swimming prowess, now became scathing about his oarsmanship. They live in Henley.

The man in the dinghy with the working outboard motor very kindly agreed to ferry the shoreside passengers back on board. We thanked him profusely and gave him two cans of lager for his trouble.

Another of our friends, an accomplished yachtsman, then hauled up our dinghy with the boathook. The rubber end came off the boathook, which then fell into the water and drifted off. The Harbourmaster, in his boat, with a very large outboard, rescued it and brought it back. We thanked him even more profusely. The dinghy and the boathook were firmly secured to the deck.

It was now two hours since the child's nose bleed and one hour since Alison retired to bed feeling 'drained'.

We sat down for drinks. My friend – the poor rower and weak swimmer from Henley – discovered that the sell-by date on his lager (the same as we gave to the man who rescued us) is May 1994 (one year previous). I radioed the boat of our rescuer – appropriately called *Cloud Nine* – to apologise. He did not say much.

We pulled up the hook at 1900 hours, and motored slowly back up the harbour. The races were over now. It was a quiet, calm evening. Geese cut an arc across Hayling Island, and everyone sat quietly, gasping at the copper ribbons of cloud on the delphinium-blue sky. It's lovely, boating. Isn't it?

* * *

In winter my old girl sits in the harbour, or comes out to have her bottom scraped. I go down each week to check that she's okay, that her bilges are dry and her warps secure. We'll potter out for the day if the weather is fair, and plans are already being made for future trips when, hopefully, the family will have forgotten about the voyage from hell and the day everything went wrong. I won't ask them to do Lyme Bay for a bit. A spot of gentle Solent cruising will ease them back in. I've had the outboard serviced. And the rowlocks fixed. Even the lager is new.

And when I'm up to me knees in muck and manure, the rain running down my neck as I try to get the garden in shape, I remember voyages past and plan for the future, secure in the knowledge that I'm one of a select band of folk who know the magic of being afloat and the independence that comes of having your own transport around the island on which you live. Mr Prescott can have as many Jags as he likes, and rattle on about the folly of clogging up the roads. All I ask is a small ship and a satellite to sail her by. That will do me nicely.

34

Dumb Friends

'I am always distrustful of people who prefer animals to humans. Give me humans every time; they are not nearly so intellectually threatening.'

Lenny Duval, *Autobiography*, 1980

A man may be master of his own house, but only if he does not have animals. Our household timetable is completely dictated by them. I have friends who don't want 'ties', so they don't have pets, and there are days when I envy them. When the rain is lashing down at half past seven in the morning, and the dog decides to roll in a pile of fox shit; when the cats have caught a nestling bluetit as it tried to make its maiden flight; and when the chickens are off lay and paddling about in a sea of mud, then the prospect of a lie-in is tantalising. But the rest of the time? No contest.

My morning walk, each day, looks like a scene from the Pied Piper. Behind me, as I stroll through our fields, is Grace, a yellow Labrador. Her sister, Favour, died a year ago now, and Grace is fourteen. She is turning into a deaf old lady. Conveniently deaf. She can hear the rustle of her food sack at half a mile, but not the call to leave alone any deer, fox or badger droppings even if it is bellowed a foot from her ear.

The cats, Spud and Hector, follow on behind. Hector is white and buff, and called after my Parks Superintendent boss. Spud is black with a white bib and paws and is called after – a potato. Inspiration went. They were called Tilly and Floss until we discovered they were chaps. Alison gave them to me as a birthday present four years ago, and I used to tuck them into my jacket when I walked the dogs, so that they could come, too. They caught the habit, and now all three animals come on the walk each day, strung out in a loose crocodile. They are one of life's greatest pleasures. Until you lose one of them.

Our first dog, Lulu, was another yellow Lab. We got her when she was two years old. She was owned by someone who worked in the Foreign Office and who was called overseas. At that time we lived in the tiny house in Sunningdale. It was madness really. A Labrador is not a small dog. But we were prepared to exercise her, and we had the loosely named 'conservatory' for her to sleep in.

For two months she drove us mad. One evening we went round to friends to say that we were at the end of our tether. She was just too boisterous. We could no longer cope. They said to give it another week, and that if she had not calmed down by then we ought to take her back. The next day she was a changed dog. Telepathy? Who knows. But it was as quick as that.

Loo, as we called her, was my dog. I trained her, walked her and generally was her right-hand man. I used to wrestle with her, and she'd do a passable imitation of a lion, opening her mouth and pretending to eat me, which had the kids shrieking with laughter. I filmed a series of walks for *Breakfast Time* and she came with me. She could do eight or ten 'takes' without getting bored, always taking the same route, always performing perfectly in front of the camera.

And then I went to work at Pebble Mill and spent half the week away from home. Loo never forgave me. She would lie still in her basket when I came home and never raise her head. After a few hours she'd sidle up to me with her tail gently wagging, having firmly put me in my place and let me know that I was no longer in total charge of her emotions. She died, eventually, at fifteen. I don't remember ever being so heartbroken at the loss of an animal.

I performed in a music hall from time to time – still do occasionally. With friends. I do a number called 'Leanin', which is the song of a West Country yokel all about sowin' and reapin', and leanin' on gate watching' the world go by. The last verse is about his dog, how it is his best friend and a bit of a poacher. Then he tells how it passed away and is now sleeping under the hedge over yonder, where the sunlight is glinting. I had to perform it within a month of losing Loo. It just about finished me off.

Then, last year, we lost Favour, Grace's sister. Grace and Favour have always been Alison's dogs. She's done all the walking and training this time. But we had a bonus with Favour. She fell ill and the vet had to remove her spleen. He said that he doubted she would last more than a few weeks. We had two years of fun from her after that. Bright as a button she was, until one Sunday, after a great morning walk, she collapsed in the middle of the vegetable patch and the vet had to be called to put her to sleep.

I feel sorry for vets. They never see you when you are having fun or your pet is doing well. They just pick up the pieces when things are going wrong. I keep meaning to ring Martin, our young vet, just so that we can have a normal chat. He's been round to despatch two of our dogs now, and must feel a right heel. Every time he walks out of our back door, nobody is in a fit state to speak.

Both dogs are buried in the garden; both are still very much a part of us. You swear, every time you lose one, that you'll never go through it again, but you do. It's not just masochism. It's pure

pleasure when things are going well. Even when the rest of the
world is sitting in judgment on you, your dog won't, and neither
will your cat. No. Your cat will be a law unto itself.

I know that being keen on nature I should not have cats. They
are blamed for the loss of much of the bird population. But I
reason that my two have a large enough territory – plenty of
fields and woods – to hopefully make that less of a problem, and
they are very good at keeping down the field voles that try to
destroy my trees, nibbling away and ring barking them at ground
level. If only they would stick to these. The trouble is, you can't
make them selective. If I thought it would do any good I'd stand
in front of them with a wildlife identification chart and a pointer,
showing them what they could and could not kill. Mice, voles,
shrews, rats and squirrels have all fallen prey to them. So have
moles. A couple of weeks ago, Spud caught a weasel. Very neatly.
There was a small bite on its neck, no other sign of injury. I felt
desperate.

But the worst thing of all was the long-eared bat I found on
the floor of the potting shed. I can only hope that it was injured
when they found it. They must, after all, be almost impossible to
catch. It was a *Gardeners' World* filming day. I showed the corpse
to the sound recordist. 'They are very rare,' I informed him.

'They are even rarer now,' he said.

I felt the sting of guilt.

At other times the cats are charming. On *Gardeners' World*
filming days they are guaranteed to perform. Just as Loo did.
When the camera is laid on the ground, Hector walks up to it
and gazes down the lens. Both he and Spud are the masters of
slow and sexy walks in the background when I am trying to
explain, with due gravity, the way to prune a shrub or take a
cutting.

Once, when I was crouching down planting potatoes, Spud

leaped on my back. We left him there while I finished my piece to camera, though I doubt if anyone heard what I was saying – they'd be too intent on watching him wash his paws.

'Do you think a cat might walk past?' ask visiting camera crews, anxious for a bit of action.

'Try and stop them,' is my only reply. 'The only way you'll get rid them is by locking them in the potting shed with a plate of fish.'

Even the bloody chickens get in on the act, clucking and cock-a-doodling when we are trying to record sound, until they are nobbled by the fox. In spite of a high wire fence one or two of them usually manage to get run off with each spring when the cubs are desperate for food. Brenda, a large, black bird with gleaming plumage, lasted until she was about six, the veteran of several attacks. After one particularly vicious midnight sortie I was ready to wring her neck but Sue, who helps me in the garden, and who is even softer than me when it comes to living creatures, took her down to the vet. Poor old Brenda was in a terrible state. Bits were hanging off her. But she was still alive.

The vet stitched her back together, but she was never the same shape again. She looked as though the parts he had been able to locate had been put back in a slightly different order. Her under-carriage now was low and lopsided, but she still produced the odd egg, bless her, even if it was a very odd egg, and took a deal of popping out. She finally fell off her perch one night, rather like an old soldier who just faded away. We buried her in the garden, too. The person who takes on this place after us is going to have to be given a map.

Being an organic gardener I am fairly tolerant of wildlife, but Sue really takes the biscuit. She won't even kill a snail. She has to take them on a long walk. I have warned her that they have a homing instinct, and that they can probably travel a couple of miles back to their original domicile, but she remains unrepentant. Trust me to get saddled with the Mahatma Gandhi of the gardening world.

I ask her to set mouse traps in the cold frame where we grow our pots of bulbs. She does. But they are humane traps that catch them alive, and then Sue is committed to another long walk because mice can come home even faster and further than snails.

It serves me right for running these thirty-odd acres as a nature reserve. I mean, you can't be a naturalist and like only certain forms of wildlife. Well, you can, but you have to at least tolerate the rest. I love the badgers, but I don't like their digging and their dung pits. I love the moles (because of *Wind in the Willows*) but I don't like the molehills they make on my lawn. I love the foxes but hate the carnage they inflict in my chicken run, and I like the deer but wish they wouldn't browse my trees and fray the bark with their antlers.

Butterflies are, perhaps, the safest bet, but even there I am faced with a crisis of conscience. I was growing some cabbages to feature on *Gardeners' World*. I like to think I can show the way when it comes to brassica conservation. I also happen to be a Vice President of Butterfly Conservation. I watched, one afternoon, as a large white butterfly was flitting over my cabbages. The gardener in me wanted to bump it off and see my young plants grow to maturity. The butterfly lover was quite happy watching the insect as it lowered itself on to the leaf and carefully deposited its minute, ivory-coloured cylindrical eggs individually on the surface of each blue-green leaf.

I thought very carefully. Which did I most enjoy: eating cabbage or watching butterflies? It was not a long thought process. When the cabbages grew, their leaves turned into lace curtains as the black and grey and gold caterpillars devoured them greedily. I then watched the caterpillars walk up the wall and fasten themselves to the brickwork where they pupated. And I watched the next generation of butterflies emerge and flit away on the warm summer breeze. I dug up the remains of the cabbages and put them on the compost heap.

I know. 'Call yourself a gardener?'

35

Hearts and Minds and Hands and Voices

'I can't be doing with all this "happy-clappy" stuff in church. I feel a bit sorry for God. I mean 'e 'ad quite enough with the Sally Army bashin' their tambourines, and then this lot came along. No. I likes my religion nice and quiet. *Songs of Praise* on a Sunday evening. That'll do nicely.'

Ron Kemp, *Bradford Nights*, 1992

I parked my car, checked that my tie was straight, and walked up to the great west door of Lincoln Cathedral. Tentatively I pushed open the smaller, studded oak door at its centre and as I did so the cymbals crashed, the orchestra notes swelled, and a congregation of several hundred launched into 'All things bright and beautiful'. It was a handsome way to arrive at my first ever *Songs of Praise*. An usher came up to greet me.

'Where were you sitting yesterday?' he asked.

'I wasn't here yesterday.'

'Oh well, don't worry. Just sit in the back row and nobody will notice you.'

It was another chance encounter. It seems they always are. Roger Hutchings was in charge of religious programmes in Birmingham while I was working on *Pebble Mill*. I bumped into him in the corridor one day. 'You go to church, don't you?'

'Yes.'

'Do you fancy presenting *Songs of Praise*?'

It can't have been as glib as that, but that's the essence of it. The nub.

I was a bit wary, I'll admit. Of being boxed. Classed as a 'God-botherer'. A bit pathetic really. But I genuinely like the programme, and I do feel that a church service should be a part of Sunday evening viewing. And, dammit, I like a good sing, especially when people can't hear me too much.

'The God Slot' has its detractors, but I am not one of them. To many viewers this is their only way of participating in a church service. We are, at heart, a Christian country, and we should not be ashamed to celebrate our faith without worrying about being 'uncool'. Having one set of beliefs does not make you a religious fanatic, or close you off to the belief of others. Not unless you are unbalanced. Most of us are not.

During the course of five years I travelled all over Britain and all over the world with *Songs of Praise*: Good Friday in Jerusalem – the best chicken pie I have ever eaten is served there in the YMCA. St Patrick's Day in New York, where, in St Patrick's Cathedral, an enormous black lady pinched my seat when I stood up to announce the next hymn. She refused to budge and I had to stand from then on. Wearing a bullet-proof vest in Bosnia, and watching lines of refugees queue for soup. These were doctors and surgeons and lawyers and builders whose possessions now fitted quite easily into two plastic carrier bags. And visiting an orphanage in Rumania. That was the most harrowing of all.

On arrival I was taken on one side by an English doctor. 'Look,' he said. 'I know you will think this is silly, but I have to warn you.'

'I'm sorry?'

'The children. You might find it a bit disturbing.'

'I'm sure.'

'Only . . . there's something that happens.'

'What do you mean?'

'It might not strike you until later, but there's always one child above all others. It happens. And you might be a bit emotional.'

I toured the wards, the little rooms where the metal cots were lined up – crudely painted pictures on the walls, the sound of wailing babies. Women in plastic aprons were feeding them, and changing them. It was a bit like a farm, except that it smelled of disinfectant. And babies.

I had taken a small teddy bear in my luggage. I gave it to one small scrap of a child. Her name was Cosmina, and she stared at me with deep brown eyes. She had a knowing look. But she could not have known anything. She was just a few months old.

I picked her up and gave her a cuddle. She cuddled me back, then pushed me away and stretched out her arm in the direction of her cot. I put her back and left her looking out between the bars. The teddy bear lay in the far corner, abandoned.

That night in my room, having changed my clothes for dinner, I found myself sitting on the bed sobbing. It wasn't until I tried to go to sleep, with the image of Cosmina refusing to leave my mind, that the words of the doctor came back to me.

But most of the time *Songs of Praise* was a much happier experience. Nobody talks much about goodness today. If newsreaders dare to bemoan the lack of 'happy stories' they get the sack. Television, radio and newspapers bombard us on a daily basis with troubles – our own and other people's. We are expected, each one of us, to take on a sort of global responsibility. It was never like this when we lived in small tribes. Life stopped at the riverbank, or the edge of the cliff. It might not have been so intellectually stimulating, but it was emotionally less demanding. Today, each one of us must worry about famine and war, civil unrest and terrorism. We must worry about it because it affects us, directly or indirectly, but the fact remains that it is only a small part of world affairs. There is more good out there than bad. It's just that we never hear about it. It passes by unsung – except on *Songs of Praise.*

I'm not talking about saccharine goodness, or cloying senti-mentality, just honest, straightforward endeavour. Triumph over the odds. Or attempted triumph, at least. Through *Songs of Praise* there shines not some triumphantly glib claim that 'Jesus Christ has solved all my troubles', but a ray of hope derived from a sound faith. Over the years I interviewed all kinds of people, from a father who had lost his son in the troubles in Northern Ireland, to a woman who was in prison for murdering her daughter.

I met those who could have been forgiven for having no belief in a God who could let such atrocities happen in His world. I talked to people who had overcome devastating injuries, to young people who knew they were dying, and to those whose lives were dedicated to helping the sick or disadvantaged. You can't help but be touched by encounters like these. They leave you feeling inadequate, moved and sometimes angry but, above all, they remind you of the strength and basic goodness of the human spirit.

There is a lot of good out there. *Songs of Praise* helps to cele-brate it.

Religion has its perks, too. I got to play cricket for the Archbishop of Canterbury's Eleven. I wasn't very good. But I did console myself with the fact that:

When that one great scorer comes,
To mark against your name,
It matters not who won or lost,
But if you were on the Archbishop of Canterbury's side it
 can't do you any harm.

We were playing against the Governor of the Bank of England's Eleven. Sort of God versus Mammon.

I also got to drive a Morgan. Wonderful car. It was in series called *Titchmarsh's Travels*, in which I took the routes of the old pilgrimages to Canterbury and Walsingham, Knock and Loch Deargh – otherwise known as St Patrick's Purgatory. The last is not for the faint-hearted. The shrine is on an island in the middle of the lough. It is only for Catholics of a robust disposition.

We were taken over in a small, open boat, powered by an outboard. The weather was not kind – cold with squally showers. On arrival the crew separated from me. They would film events. I was taken to a changing room, to remove my shoes and socks. From now on, until the following day, I would walk barefoot, and I would not speak, except for the Lord's Prayer and the Hail Marys.

The purgatory began. Hour upon hour of repeated 'Our Fathers' and 'Hail Marys' in the ice-cold basilica, followed by walks, outdoors, barefoot, around the various Stations of the Cross. We also fasted. This continued through the night, with twenty-minute breaks between services.

My feet were frozen. My hair was wet. I stood, and sat, and walked, and murmured along with the rest of the pilgrims. It was a strange experience, at times mind-numbingly tedious, at others deeply fatiguing and, right at the end, triumphant. I have never been so grateful to put on my shoes and socks. And chips have never tasted so good as they did at my first meal in twenty-four hours.

On our way over to the island in the boat we had been filming my arrival. Another pilgrim, a small woman, sat in the corner of the boat, turning her face away from the camera. When the camera stopped running she turned to me and said, with a soft Irish lilt, 'You shouldn't be filming this. It's not right. It's private.'

I apologised for the intrusion and tried to assure her that we would be as unobtrusive as possible. We did not intend to film her if she wanted privacy. She nodded, but looked unconvinced.

After several hours of worship in the freezing cold she came up to me on one of the walks around the shrine. She slipped something into my hand. 'You might need this,' she whispered. Then she smiled shyly and walked on. It was a rosary. I have it still.

There are great injustices in life. I was given a decent treble when I was a boy. Soaring, it was. Hugely satisfying. What I have now is a rather average tenor, but it does not stop me enjoying an occasional foray into vocalisation. During my years in the Barnes and Richmond Operatic Society I tackled the character baritone roles of Sir Joseph Porter in *HMS Pinafore* and Ko-Ko in *The Mikado*, and I've even performed the Lord Chancellor's Nightmare Song from *Iolanthe* at the Barbican. For money. But I can't help thinking that I was booked for novelty value rather than vocal quality.

During a further series for BBC Religious Programmes, rather optimistically entitled *Titchmarsh on Song*, I toured the country listening to 'all kinds of music' and joining in. Standing in the middle of the Huddersfield Choral Society and singing 'Fling Wide the Gates' is, on the one hand, supremely exhilarating and, on the other, absolutely terrifying. You'd think that in the middle of all that lot you'd be reasonably well hidden. Don't you believe it. You are as exposed as a wart on the face of Kate Moss.

But the best part of the series, for me, came in Wales. I was talking to the Morriston Orpheus Choir. We filmed our chats and recorded our music. They were a great bunch of guys. Wonderful fun. I told them about my dad. About how his favourite hymn had been '*Cwm Rhondda*' – 'Guide Me O Thou Great Redeemer'.

Something made me ask the question. I couldn't stop myself.

'Look. You wouldn't let me conduct you singing it, would you?'

The conductor handed over his baton. 'All yours,' he said, and smiled.

My heart beat like a drum. My stomach churned. Serve me right for asking.

The organ began the introduction. I stood on the podium and faced the towering ranks of men, all of them in white shirts, ties and navy blue blazers. A proper Welsh male voice choir, all watching my stick. I brought them in, almost on the right beat, and then got into my stride.

'Guide me, O thou great Redeemer,/ Pilgrim through this barren land,' they sang, in that tight, brooding, close harmony that is unique to Wales.

> I am weak, but thou art mighty,
> Hold me with thy powerful hand.

And then it came, in a great soaring chorus that made the hairs on the back of my neck stand on end:

> Bread of Heaven,
> Bread of Heaven,
> Feed me now and evermore . . . evermore . . .
> Feed me now and evermore.

Oh, I hope my dad enjoyed it as much as I did.

36

Forty Years On

'I do not hold with the sentiment that it is better to travel hopefully than to arrive. Give me arrival every time. At least then I
know where I am.'

Paul Laroux, *Sentimental Journey*, 1980

They say that the worst thing that can happen to you is that your
dreams come true. I know what they mean. Dreaming is a harmless pursuit if kept in perspective. Reality can be scary. And sad.

In my forty-eighth year Geoff Hamilton died suddenly, and
I inherited *Gardeners' World*. The pleasure of taking on a
programme I had idly dreamed of presenting as a child was totally
overshadowed by the loss of a good friend.

We'd talked about my take-over for the best part of a year.
I'd made occasional guest appearances in the programme
during 1995 and 1996, and Geoff, having held the reins for
seventeen years, wanted to concentrate more on writing, his
nursery, and other television projects. *Gardeners' World*, being
the BBC's flagship gardening programme, is broadcast thirty-
six weeks a year, from February through to November, and it
swallows up ideas and projects with an unrelenting hunger. It
is also, traditionally, broadcast from the garden of its main
presenter.

Geoff and I talked things over at BBC Gardeners' World Live

in June 1996. 'When do you want to start?' he asked.

'I don't mind. It's up to you. Tell me when you want to go.'

'You realise you can say goodbye to summer holidays?' he said ruefully.

We decided that I would take over at Easter 1997, after which Geoff would make guest appearances in the programme and I would become the main presenter. But tragedy struck, and in autumn 1996 Geoff died of a heart attack on a charity cycle ride.

It came like a bolt from the blue. I was in South Africa, leading a tour looking at the flowers of the Cape. I was telephoned in the early evening, and off and on until midnight I talked to British newspapers, furnishing them with quotes for Geoff's obituary. The rest of the time passed in a blur. I remember the following morning telling everyone on the coach that he had died. They were understanding when I had to leave the tour early and return home to present the programme.

I was nervous about taking over the reins under such circumstances, and saddened at the loss of a long-term friend. What would the reaction of the viewers be? My style was different to Geoff's; should I try to be more like him so that they didn't feel short changed? But I knew I couldn't do that. I had to be me, and hope that I fitted the bill.

With a week's notice the film crew turned up at my garden. It was a testing day. A bit nerve-racking. Items were hastily cobbled together. I tried to appear pleasant and personable, though it was a difficult balance to strike – somewhere between quiet respect and an enthusiasm for the subject. But you can't treat a gardening programme like a funeral.

As the weeks wore on I began to find my niche, but I worried that Geoff's loyal followers might desert the programme now that he had gone. It seemed that every newspaper I opened contained a panegyric about him and said how much he would be missed. I know. I missed him myself. It began to get me down. How could I hope to fill the gap? But I underestimated the British public. They are no fools; they will not be deceived, and they are more astute than they are often given credit for. You can't make them like you, but what they will always do is give you a chance to prove yourself.

I received letters. To my surprise they did not say 'clear off'. One woman wrote to say that she was worried about me. I feared the worst. She went on to explain that she had just lost her favourite television gardening presenter, but that I had lost a friend. She said that I must give myself time to grieve. Sometimes folk can take your breath away.

A few months on, amid more letters, I came across one which sounded like the missive I had dreaded: 'I was a great fan of Geoff Hamilton,' it began. 'When I heard that you were about to take over *Gardeners' World* my heart sank.'

I feared that at last I had been found out. The letter continued: 'I have been watching you over the past few weeks. You'll do.'

It was enough. I began to look forward, rather than back, and tried to make the programme I had always dreamed of presenting, my own.

We film *Gardeners' World* exactly one week ahead of transmission, so you can see precisely what the weather was doing in my garden seven days earlier. The programme is a sort of club sandwich: my chunks of practical gardening fit in between other features, garden visits, interviews with nurserymen and items about a particular group of plants.

The content of my lumps is arrived at in discussion with my producer, Colette Foster. I've always wanted to keep my garden as a real garden, rather than turning it into a stage set, a series of little 'model gardens' bounded by interwoven fencing.

Pretending that it is smaller than it is. My reasoning is that I want the garden to work as a whole. This might lay me open to the 'It's all right for you with your rolling acres' criticism, but as the Duchess of Devonshire once said, 'You can only leave your spectacles in one room.' In other words, the whole thing might be big, but it is composed of lots of little bits that are the same as anybody else's. Even if my garden is not quite Chatsworth.

The garden needed a name. I did not want to use the name of the house, simply to retain a bit of privacy. We toyed with 'Hilltop', but the producer thought it sounded too windy. Then came 'Larkhill'. I was told it was the name of a prison. We finally decided on 'Barleywood', because the garden is surrounded by woodland, and the field at the top, over which we gazed when we bought the house, was, at that time, filled with barley.

The acre of paddock above the third of an acre of garden was taken into cultivation, and during the course of the last seven years it has become a garden in its own right. There are wild flower slopes, a large pond, a long greenhouse, Mediterranean garden, beds and borders, all of them presided over not only by me but also by Bill and Sue.

Sue has been with me for fifteen years or more. She was one of the mums at playgroup when the kids were little. She's part time, but it's a big part. Bill was our decorator. He's become what is laughingly known as the 'Estate Manager'. He deals with every-thing that is not green. Unless he's tackling it with a chainsaw. He usually spends one day a month in casualty. Both he and Sue are totally indispensable.

We try to develop one or two new areas of garden each year, or rejuvenate a bed or border that has gone past its best. Much of Bill's winter is spent in the fifteen acres of woodland, planting trees, coppicing hazel, generally managing it as a nature reserve. We've fenced the deer out of the newly planted woodland, and we enjoy the increasing activity of badgers, look up at the circling, mewing buzzards, and watch the airy flight of butterflies in summer with great pleasure.

From time to time we'll feature the butterfly meadow, or the bluebells on *Gardeners' World*, but I am anxious above all that that the basic craft of gardening – the sowing of seeds, the taking of cuttings and the general cultivation of plants – is passed on to a new generation. If it sounds like missionary zeal, fair enough. That's exactly what it is. *Gardeners' World* has that responsibility to its viewers.

We get it in the neck every now and then, mainly over programme style. But no programme can stand still, and modern production techniques are constantly evolving. While not slavishly striving for the shock of the new, even an old horticultural war horse has to move with the times. We all thought the original *Forsyte Saga* was the best television ever. If you look at it now, it creaks. If *Gardeners' World* had not evolved it would appear similarly old-fashioned.

Oh, there are times when I think that the music is a bit too intrusive, or that too much emphasis is placed on tricksy camera work. But mostly, provided the true intent of the feature shines through, I'm happy.

In Percy's day *Gardeners' World* involved a crew of forty-two people and two large outside broadcast vans. Today there are just five of us: a producer/director, cameraman, sound recordist, production assistant and me. They leave their cars in the village hall car park.

For me, shooting begins at eight on a Friday morning and ends between five and six in the evening. Lunch is taken on the hoof. Well, in the potting shed to be exact.

There is no script. I make it up as I go along, but each item is constructed in my head before we start. Roughly. Each item is shot in wide angle, medium close-up and tight close-up, and I have to try to remember which hand I used to put the compost in the pot, and which finger I used to point at the flower, so that I can repeat it on a different-sized shot. If I get it wrong, the production assistant, with an eagle eye for continuity, will, apologetically, but firmly, tell me so. At the end of the day the videotapes are taken away for editing with the other filmed inserts that are shot on location.

Gardeners' World has always had more than one presenter. In Percy's day there was Arthur Billitt and Geoffrey Smith; today I am in the company of Pippa Greenwood, Chris Beardshaw, Rachel de Thame and Joe Swift. They are all very young. It's a bit worrying.

Back in the 1970s, when I was already broadcasting on radio, I did write a letter to Radio 4's *Gardeners' Question Time* offering myself for the panel. I was twenty-seven at the time. I had a reply from the then producer and chairman Ken Ford explaining that he could not possibly entertain using anyone under the age of thirty-five, simply because they would lack the all-round experience needed.

I look, now, at Chris Beardshaw, *The Flying Gardener*, in his twenties, and wonder why it took me so long.

From time to time I'm allowed out of my garden, to present *Gardeners' World* from other locations. Last year we made a programme about islands. Joe went to the Hebrides, Rachel to Anglesey and Chris to the Shetlands. I started on the Isle of Wight, then flew by helicopter to the Isle of Man – interviewing gardeners in both places – and finished up in the early evening on St Michael's Mount in Cornwall, having a gin and tonic with Lord St Levan. Then I got a car home. It was all a bit surreal.

But not so surreal as an interview I conducted in a garden in

Wiltshire. I arrived to find the production team trying to stifle a fit of the giggles. I asked why.

'No. Nothing. You'll see.'

'What do you mean?'

'It's just that . . . well . . . the interviewee.'

'What?'

'He doesn't wear much.'

'Oh.' Clearly the type who likes to garden with his shirt off.

'Where is he?'

'Round the back.'

'I'd better meet him before we start.'

'Yes. It might be a good idea.'

I found him. Standing in the middle of a rose bed, his long, flowing hair fastened back in a pony tail, his face adorned with a grizzled beard. He wore a pair of knee-length boots, and a pink silk jockstrap. Nothing else.

It's difficult. You try not to look, but your eyes are drawn magnetically to it. I made pleasant conversation, trying to maintain eye contact.

It was the sound recordist who got us out of a spot. 'I need something to fasten the microphone to,' he said. We managed to persuade the interviewee to put on a vest and a pair of Lycra shorts for the interview. He felt overdressed, he said. He wore the jockstrap all the time in summer, and the shorts only went on in winter. His wife wore hot pants. They were a lovely couple. Very keen.

It's not fair, I came second to Sebastian Faulks, but he didn't turn up. Still, Auberon Waugh was very sympathetic. I never worked out who the ladies with the knockers were.

The Garden God

Sex on legs will be here signing copies of his new novel

The Last Lighthouse Keeper

Friday 22nd October between 1 - 2 pm

If you are unable to attend reserve your copy by calling in or telephoning (01245) 268737

My gratitude to Ottakers in Chelmsford knows no bounds. As to the accuracy of their advertising campaign, there is considerable doubt.

Far Pavilion – a safe haven at the top of my garden and the perfect place to write.

Sailing and dogs – two passions. With Favour, and boat,
in the Far Pavilion.

Ah, if only the sea were always this calm. Evening drinks up top – chilled Sauvignon Blanc and the setting sun. A perfect combination.

The view from the stern of my boat, and a dream vision in my idle moments.

Chay Blyth, wisely keeping a hand on the wheel as we sail out of Brighton Marina at the end of a programme on English rivers.

Not a bad likeness – and he doesn't talk much either. Madame
Tussauds inflict me on unsuspecting Japanese tourists.

With my girls at Buckingham Palace. Invested as a Member of the Most Excellen
Order of the British Empire. 'Do we *have* to wear hats?' they asked. So we all di

With Mrs T at our Silver Wedding. How she's put up with me this long I'll never know.

Left: Polly (*top*) and Camilla now, aged 22 and 20. Lovely girls!

Just cut out to be a gardener.

37

Me Mum

'Old age comes at a very difficult time.'

Anon

I've talked a lot about my dad; less about my mum. It's only because she's still with us and I might get a thick ear if I say the wrong thing. And anyway, it's hard to be objective about your mum. Like most children, I went through that stage of thinking that everything she said was law. It never crossed my mind that some of her pronouncements may have been opinions. If Mum said that the ITV News was not as good as the BBC News then that was it. Try as I might to be objective, that suspicion still lurks there. Sir Trevor Macdonald might have been knighted, and he might have been voted the most trustworthy newsreader in Britain, but my mum is still not sure. I laugh about it. But at the back of my mind, in the compartment marked 'Upbringing', there is still this gnawing doubt.

I remember vividly the first time I answered back. I must have been about twelve. We were in the kitchen and she was trying to get me to do something that I didn't want to. 'It's not fair!' I said. 'Kath doesn't have to do that and I have to do it all the time.'

She stood still. And silent. I waited for the clip round the ear. It never came. 'Yes. I suppose you're right,' she said, then got on with the washing up. I felt sick with the thrill of it. I think she knew exactly what she was doing. I remember our relationship changing ever so slightly from that day on. For the better, I think.

She admitted to me, about five years after I'd left home, that it was a good job I'd gone. 'If you'd have stayed I'd have smothered you,' she said. And she would have. Her intentions were always of the best, but I wasn't given much latitude as a youth.

With the residue of my first week's wages (having given Mum her housekeeping) I went to Otley to buy myself some clothes. I looked in the army surplus store and came away with a khaki combat jacket. It had pockets everywhere. It wasn't new but it had been cleaned. I remember riding home on the bus with it, wrapped in a massive carrier bag. I showed it off when I got home.

My dad didn't seem bothered. It was more manly than an umbrella. My mum was horrified. 'You can't possibly wear that!'

'Why not?'

'Because it looks dreadful. You look like a soldier. And anyway it's second hand. Come on.' And she took me on the bus to Otley and made me change it for a new shirt. It makes me laugh when I think of it now. How on earth could I have been so pliant? So unquestioning? But that was just the way it was.

When Kath and I were growing up, Mum took her organisational skills to the Brownies. She became a Tawny Owl (not in a sort of Harry Potter transformation – it was the rank of the second in command of Ilkley Parish Church Brownie Pack). Miss Coffey was the Brown Owl (top dog), and when she retired, Mum became the supremo, and our house was suddenly full of things related to Pixies and Elves and Gnomes and Sprites. She was good with kids. They adored her – you could see that – and even Kath enjoyed being part of her pack. A disciplinarian she might have been, but she was also good fun.

She combined Brownies with bellringing, and being the

enrolling member of the Mothers' Union, but by the time I left home at the end of the 1960s, rheumatoid arthritis had begun to take hold and her hands began to suffer. Bellringing was no longer an option. She is no Amazon, my mum – she's about five foot three – but she could master the balance of a bell, at least until her grip went.

I think she rather enjoyed being a woman in a man's world. To be honest, she's always preferred the company of men to women. A man's woman. I remember asking her, when the arthritis started to bite, why she didn't join the WI or the Townswomen's Guild. 'Because I don't want to spend my life fighting over a teapot,' she said.

In her fifties and sixties, when Kath and I had both left home, Uncle Bert's shop – Skipton Road Post Office and Grocery Stores – became her daily place of work. In spite of the fact that they were twins, Bessie and Bert always had an uneasy relationship. The sibling rivalry was never far from the surface. Maybe it was because Uncle Bert was the only man she couldn't flirt with.

But they rubbed along, and we still had wonderful Christmas parties with silly games, even if the 'runs up the Dales' had become a thing of the past. When Uncle Bert died, Mum didn't say a lot about it, but there was an air of quiet desolation about her. It was the closing of a chapter. She was the last surviving member of her family now, Auntie Bee having died before Uncle Bert.

When my dad died, I wondered how she'd cope. He was the centre of her life. Oh, she led him a merry dance sometimes, but she was completely devoted to him. Relied on him. My dad wore the trousers, but he wore them quietly. 'Yes dear' was his stock phrase. Just occasionally he'd lose his cool, and we'd all keep a low profile for half an hour.

Once, when he came home a bit the worse for wear on Christmas Eve, having had a few jars with his mates after work had finished at lunchtime, she had a go at him. I watched him, though a crack in the door, sitting in the easy chair – on top of the newspapers that would stop his dirty overalls from leaving a mark – with his flat cap slightly askew and his eyes glazed.

He listened to her for a while, quietly ate his beef sandwich, and then got up and went out. I was terrified that he wouldn't come back. But he did. With her present. Like many working men, he'd leave it till the last moment.

Every year he'd raise an eyebrow to me on Christmas Eve. 'Got a minute, Digby?'

I'd nod and leave the room with him. Out on the stairs he'd pull a paper bag from under his jacket, and show me a manicure set he'd bought her, or a small piece of jewellery. 'Do you think she'll like it?'

'It's lovely!'

And then he'd grin and go away and wrap it, provided my sister could find him some paper and Sellotape.

On Christmas morning, sitting on Mum and Dad's bed, Kath and I would watch as Mum unwrapped her present from Dad. Always there would be tears – 'Oh, Alan! What have you done?!'

And Dad would hug her and smile beatifically at us. 'I think she likes it!'

Living alone, when you've lived as half of someone else for more than forty years is never going to be easy. Mum's solution is to be bloody minded about it. I wish, sometimes, that she would moan about her crippling illness, instead of being so cussed, but that's not her way. Instead, she fights back by being stubborn, infuriating, complaining that she can't find anyone to push her wheelchair and generally winding Kath up. She has a granny flat, built over the garage of her own house in which Kath and Richard now live. In spite of the fact that Kath has a teenage son and a daughter in her early twenties, and that she teaches full time, she still takes on the lion's share of Mum management. It is now my role to listen to both sides of the story. Mum still keeps us both on our toes.

At least she can keep an eye on me by watching my activities on television. I think she's quite pleased. Whenever I go to visit her she tells me of her latest encounter with a doctor or a nurse or a woman in a local shop. When someone new discovers her surname and asks 'Any relation?', she will beam up at them and put her head on one side: 'I'm his mum.' Then she basks for a bit in the reflected glory. She particularly enjoys the admiration of any new doctor: 'He thinks I'm wonderful.'

'Yes, Mum.'

'Says he can't understand why I'm so cheerful.'

'No, Mum.'

She was in hospital for a spell recently, and insisted that every nurse who came to her bedside, where I was sitting, should have a signed photograph. 'Now do you want one?' she asked a rather junior nurse.

'No, I don't think so, thanks,' said the girl brightly.

'Oh, I thought you did.'

'No. It's all right.'

I sat silently through all this, the photographs and the marker pen that I had been instructed to bring, lying idly in my lap. It does a child good to remember that a parent can still embarrass them, whatever their age.

But, like all children, I have always striven to make my parents proud of me, even if I sometimes fail. My mother has been given all four of my novels, now. I asked her, a while ago, if she had read any of them.

'Not yet, Sparrow.'

'Why? Is it because you've heard that there are sex scenes in them?'

'No.'

'Why, then?'

'They're a bit too heavy for my knees.'

'I'll get you a paperback version.'

'No. The print's too small.'

Finally, I managed to locate a large-print copy.

'How are you getting on?' I asked.

'I've started it,' she said.

That was a year ago now. An old envelope is still tucked between pages sixteen and seventeen. And the book is still on her bedside table. I think she likes other people to see it there. That's probably enough. She prefers Catherine Cookson really.

38

May the Force Be With You

'There is no such thing as an instant garden, and those who want one do not understand what a garden is. Gardens develop and grow – that is their nature. An instant garden is a contradiction in terms.'

Sarah Burgess, *The Educated Gardener*, 1982

They called it a vehicle. Very flattering. Something to utilise all my talents. Both of them. The interviewing and the gardening. They had this idea for a programme called *Over the Garden Wall*. It involved giving two neighbouring gardens a bit of a make-over. I would sit in a Wimbledon umpire's chair straddling the fence, using a lip-mike to give a commentary on progress. The two families would be in competition to see who could build the best deck or patio, and I'd keep hopping down from the chair every now and then and giving them a hand.

We did a pilot. It was all right. Nothing to write home about. It came to life when I got down off the chair and got stuck in, chatting with the families, laying slabs, planting plants. Otherwise it was a bit slow.

They thought about it for a while. 'What we need,' said the producer, John Thornicroft, 'is to do just one garden, not two, and we can forget about the umpire's chair. It's best when you're on the ground.'

I think I knew that.

'What we should do is get you to make the garden as a surprise for somebody, rather than having two families in competition. But you'll need help. You can't do it on your own. We'll get you a builder. And another gardener. Do you think it's possible? To make a garden in two days?'

'No.'

'Well, what could you do in two days?'

'I don't really know.'

'Are you prepared to give it a try?'

'Yes. I suppose so. But what about the builder and the gardener?'

'Don't worry about that. Leave them to me.'

And I did.

John called me up a week later. 'We've found them.'

'Who are they?'

'Well, the builder is a guy called Tommy Walsh. From Hackney. East Ender. He's been doing a bit of building for Carol Haslam, our executive producer. She says he's never short of an answer.'

'And the gardener?'

'Ah yes, now, well. I've been producing this series for Meridian called *Grass Roots*, and we've just used this great girl from a water garden nursery in Romsey.'

'What's her name?'

'Charlie.'

'Are you sure she's a girl?'

'Absolutely certain.'

'Any good?'

'She looks terrific.'

'But is she any good?'

'She's got amazing knockers.'

'Yes, but has she done it before? Presenting programmes.'

'She'll be under your instruction.'

'What does that mean?'

'She hasn't done a lot yet but I reckon she's got a great future. And she doesn't wear a bra.'

I had that sinking feeling you get when you know you're in for an uphill struggle. We had a lippy East-End builder who would probably turn out to be the Arthur Daley of the concrete mixer, and a good-looking girl with big knockers and no bra who had once made a water garden on telly. And the three of us would have two days to build a garden. It sounded like a recipe for disaster to me.

'Oh, and we've got a title.'

'Yes?'

'*Ground Force.*'

'Sounds like a military operation.'

'Well, it is, isn't it?'

Nobody expected the programme to do what it did. None of us. Second in the ratings to *EastEnders*. Beating *Who Wants to be a Millionaire* – and that in our sixth year of transmission. It can't all have been down to Charlie's lack of support. More than half our viewers are women.

It just worked. We got on like a house on fire from day one, and we all pulled our weight. There are times, I know, when it looks as though Charlie does all the work. Tommy gets very irritated when he spends a day and a half laying a patio, or a deck, or building a gazebo and the entire thing is covered in thirty seconds on screen, while Charlie's every move with every plant and pond liner and pump is closely followed. No. Not really. It only seems that way.

Are there tensions? Only of the sort you'd expect. They get irritated when I tell them the time too often, but then somebody has to manage the job. I get irritated when Tommy's sawdust flies all over my plants. Charlie gets irritated if I try to help with 'her' water feature, even if I did design the bloody thing.

But Willy, Tommy's right-hand man, always manages to put things in perspective. His Irish brogue took me a while to crack. For the first few programmes I could do nothing more than grin inanely when he talked to me, not having the benefit of an interpreter. But Willy's English and my Irish have improved since then. Now we understand one another perfectly. And when tensions are at their highest, Willy will often come out with a corker. We were soaked to the skin in Anglesey, and almost blown away. Tempers were fraying. 'Ach,' said Willy, 'I wouldn't put a milk bottle out in this.'

But my favourite remark remains the one he made when he saw a lorryload of turf being driven down the road. 'That's what I'm going to do when I gets a lot of money,' he said.

'What's that?' I asked.

'Send me lawn away to be cut.'

The programme's success is down to team spirit as much as anything else, and the magic of the transformation, and the reaction of the person we are surprising. Children love it. One mother of three said to me, 'They jump up and down on the sofa during *Top of the Pops*, and then when *Ground Force* comes on they sit absolutely still and silent for half an hour. Thank you so much!'

One young lad in Lancashire showed me around his own garden, next door to the one we were transforming. It was a wonderfully imaginative little landscape with water and plants and things that he'd made out of wood and stone. 'Where do you get your ideas?' I asked. He beamed. 'From *Ground Force*.'

There's a degree of grumpiness directed at *Ground Force* in some corners of the world of horticulture, a sort of resentment that gardening is being made available to the masses. There are dark mutterings about decking, shaken heads about the speed of things. I make no apology. We do a good and thorough job; we don't cut corners. And, anyway, crazy paving has reigned supreme for too long. Decking is just one alternative. And there is nothing wrong with water features and gazebos.

'But gardens develop over the years. They are not instant,' cry the detractors. Well, all I can say is that there are sixty families all over Britain who have been given a head start with a garden, and when we go back and revisit them we are heartened at the way the gardens have developed. The owners may not have given birth to the garden, but they have adopted it, and in my experience adoptive parents love their children every bit as much as natural parents.

There are moments when I admit to slight feelings of guilt about blue paint, but at one time all garden fencing was orange. I worry that my obituary will brand me as the man who planked Britain. In 1997, the year that *Ground Force* began, the DIY outlet B&Q sold £5,000 worth of decking nationwide. In 2000 that total had risen to £9 million.

'But wet decking is so slippery,' they say. 'So is wet York stone paving,' I reply, 'and when you fall over on that you break your hip. At least on a deck you bounce.'

The total annual spending on gardening, at the time of writing, is £3.2 billion. It has risen by a third over the last two years. That must be good for the horticultural industry, and it must be good for gardens and the environment. Not all the money is being spent on decking and paving. Much of it is being spent on plants – trees and shrubs, perennials and bulbs.

The problem, when you make a garden, is that you proceed in exactly the opposite way to painting a picture. When you paint, you create the picture first, and then find a frame. In the garden you must first make the frame – the hard landscaping –

to which you can add the picture – the plants. While it may appear that most of the programme is spent paving and decking and cobbling, and very little of it given over to planting, that is just the way things happen when you make a garden from scratch. And it becomes especially noticeable over a two-day time scale and a half-hour programme. In reality, once the garden is planted, there is little or no work needed in the future on the hard landscaping, and the plants then come to the fore. It becomes a garden.

We stay overnight wherever we are making the garden, and sometimes we will travel there the night before. This means staying in a hotel. With a dining room. And a bar. We work very hard during the day – manual labour can take it out of you – and by the evening we are ready for a little light refreshment. Well, it should be light. There are evenings, it must be confessed, when we do put away rather a lot of wine. But we all know what we have to do the following day.

Eagle-eyed viewers may notice the occasional hangover, but no quarter is given. You can stay up as late as you want. You can have a libation or two, or maybe three or four. But if you can't pull your weight the following day, expect no sympathy, only scowls and grunts.

We've all done it. Well, it's been a long run. My own Waterloo came with a plate of paella. We were in Bromley, making a garden for a fire station. In the evening the girls were drinking margaritas. Would I like to try one? No, thanks. Captain Sensible. I stuck to what I knew. White wine. And paella.

At five o'clock the following morning I was throwing up so hard that I burst a blood vessel in my eye. Mid-morning so red had it become that they took me to hospital.

The doctor said it would take a fortnight to get better. He was right. I spent the rest of the programme being filmed only from one side. I blame it all on a duff prawn. It's funny really, I always imagined that any injury to my eye would be caused by Charlie turning round a bit sharpish when I wasn't paying attention.

People's reaction to having their garden made over is wonderfully varied. There may be tears, or shrieks of surprise. One woman's legs went and we had to support her with an arm on each side. Sometimes the surprise is so profound that conversation dries up altogether, or is limited to 'I don't believe it! I don't believe it! I don't believe it!'

A lady wrote to me and said, 'Please can you stop people saying, "Oh God!"' I'm afraid I can't. I have no control over their emotions. If that's the way it takes them, that's the way it takes them.

Rita Radivan in Manchester could only say 'Oh!' repeatedly. Nothing else. She seemed to go into shock. Her ninety-year-old mother, who had accompanied her on a trip to Blackpool, returned home with her and was equally bemused. She came through the gate and made a beeline for me. 'Hello! What a surprise. How nice to see you!' She chatted cheerfully for ten minutes before turning round and saying, 'Oh! I didn't see the garden!' I think she thought I'd just popped in for tea.

There was the prison officer from Milton Keynes whose first words were, 'Who's knackered me gazebo?' and the irate neighbour in Sanderstead who threatened to call the council if we put up a pale blue shed in the garden next to his. He came round in the end. And anyway, his garden contained four sheds full of budgies.

There was the large black gospel singer in Luton who had to come home early from the health farm because she had food poisoning. She kept throwing up, and I hadn't the heart to say that she must stay there. When she saw Tommy her eyes widened like saucers. 'Ooh, aren't you big?' she said. And she wasn't small.

Norma in Croydon was our very first *Ground Force* victim. Her husband, Bill, had helped us build the garden. He was big, too, but unused to manual labour. He had a desk job. At the end of the first day he was shattered and rang Norma to say that he would not be joining her in her hotel that evening for supper, even though she was just seven miles away. He said he was just a bit tired. He didn't say why.

He did not tell us that it was his wedding anniversary. Norma was not amused. The following day, in the Whitgift Centre in Croydon, Norma's credit card went into meltdown. She returned home the following evening, loaded down with carrier bags and not a happy bunny.

We film *Ground Force* on one camera, except for the 'reveal' which is filmed on a smaller video camera carried, at that time, by our assistant producer Susan Bell. Susan is a twenty-some-thing blonde with an hour-glass figure. She positioned herself in a safe spot, to film Norma's return. That safe spot just happened to be behind the net curtains in Norma and Bill's bedroom, where she had a good view of the garden path.

Norma got out of the taxi and paid the driver. Her face looked like thunder, and her arms were loaded down with carrier bags. As she walked up the path to her front door, she glanced up at her bedroom window and saw, before the net curtain was smartly pulled to, a shapely blonde with a video camera. She came through the glazed front door like an Exocet missile.

'Hello, love,' said Bill.

'Don't you "Hello love" me!' she bellowed.

Before she could say any more, Bill had shepherded her through the house and out through the French windows into the back garden where she burst into tears and shrieked: 'Ooh! It's him off the telly!'

There are a handful of questions that I am always asked (apart from 'Where's Charlie?'). They are:

Whose idea was the programme?

Peter Bazalgette, the man behind *Changing Rooms* and *Ready Steady Cook.*

Do you really do it in two days?

Yes.

How much does it cost?

About £1,500. Sometimes it goes up to £2,000, but when we started in 1997 it was between £500 and £800.

Who pays?

The BBC.

Does it always rain?

Nearly always. In our first year we made sixteen programmes. Out of the thirty-two days it rained on twenty-nine of them.

Is it really just you, or is there a hidden army?

It's just us, along with any helpers we can rope in from the family we are surprising. Plus our secret weapon, Kirsty, who is our horticultural researcher, assistant producer and my prize possession.

What's the hardest garden you've ever had to make?

The next one.

Is it always as much of a rush as it seems?

More so.

How do you decide whose garden you do?

We make sure they are scattered all over the country, and we choose all types of people – old, young, married, single – and all types of gardens – long and thin, short and fat, sloping and flat.

How do you always manage to finish on time?

I have absolutely no idea.

What happens to the bits that go wrong?

They are always in the finished programme.

Why doesn't Charlie wear a bra?

She says she's more comfortable without one. As she can carry three paving slabs at a time, I do not feel inclined to argue.

Who designs the gardens?

I do.

Do you see them first?

No, I work from a video that Kirsty will shoot, along with a rough sketch plan. I don't see any garden until we turn up to do the job.

Who paints the watercolour?

Me.

Why don't you do gardens for disabled people?

We do. We've done four so far.

How many people are there on the waiting list?

Fifteen thousand.

How many 'special' programmes have you made?

At the time of writing, four. One for an old soldiers' home in Jamaica, one for a hospital in the Falklands, one for a children's home in India, and one in South Africa, for President Mandela. We have three days to make these gardens instead of two, and the budget is not so restricted.

What was it like making a garden for Nelson Mandela?

Ah, well that needs a chapter to itself.

39

Madeba

'Once in a lifetime you may meet a giant among men; someone who has a charisma so powerful that you feel you can reach out and touch it. What is charisma? It is the ability to inspire, and it is at its most powerful when it is founded on serenity.'

Robert Frazer, *Notes for My Son*, 1977

The odds against it ever happening were great. I still cannot really believe we pulled it off. I was asked to think about *Ground Force* 'special' – a garden for somebody important. I pondered for weeks. We'd need someone universally admired. The Queen Mother? Well, she has quite a few gardens already, including one new one gifted to her for her hundredth birthday. Mother Theresa is no longer with us so she was out. The Prime Minister? Too contentious. There was only one obvious person, the one they called 'The Man of the Millennium' – Nelson Mandela.

I told myself that it was unlikely we would ever get permission. But we had a production manager with South African contacts. He knew the right people to ask. We sent a tape of the programme to Mrs Mandela, Graca Machel, and with the help of Mr Mandela's one-time prison companion Ahmed Kathrada, who was known to a friend of the production manager, we did our best to persuade her. Finally, the faxed go-ahead came through, and after four months of preparation, we set off for South Africa to make a garden outside Nelson Mandela's new house at Qunu in the Transkei.

This part of Africa has extremes of climate – cold in winter and baking hot in summer. The plant material, from cacti to palms, would have to be able to cope with that. And my design would have to suit the man and his needs.

I sat down, during the weeks before we went there, and in between planning the garden I read Nelson Mandela's autobiography, *Long Walk to Freedom*. Even when we arrived in South Africa it was hard to believe it was all happening. But I kept a diary, and it seems that it really did.

Monday, 6 December 1999

Landed at Cape Town at 11 a.m. and driven straight to the President Hotel in Bantry Bay. It was opened by Mr Mandela about a year ago. A plaque in the cool, clean lobby says so. There are sensational views of waves crashing on to rocks on the coastline below us. No rest. Just a brief lunch – poolside – on a day with plenty of cloud before we head off to a nursery run by a white South African called 'Spoek' (Ghost), probably on account of his pallor. He is thin, elfin-like and good humoured. All kinds of wonderful plants growing out of black polythene pots nestle side by side in his ramshackle nursery. We plunder his nursery for bougainvillea and palms, herbs and pot-grown vegetables, an oak tree (a bit symbolic of home, I thought), an olive and all sorts of other goodies which we load into the back of an eight-ton truck. It will be driven to Qunu, near Umtata, by Jacob, an almost silent and extremely polite black South African who has religious texts pinned up in his cab. He smiles long-sufferingly as Tommy makes a lot of noise when he loses his hat by leaving it on the top of the cab as they drive off.

Back to the hotel and then out to eat at the Africa Café, where the 'African Feast' is plentiful and varied – rice, meat (assorted), cous-cous and vegetables – although it arrives in 'Africa time', about an hour after we sit down.

Return to the hotel at 11 p.m. and I sit up until 12.15 painting my watercolour of the Mandela garden.

Tuesday, 7 December

Woken by alarm call at 6 a.m. and set about finishing my painting. Bleary. It's hard to keep my eyes open at first, but the light is good and I take more care over the brushwork than I normally do. Quite pleased with it – a narrow rill of water with two upright jets, flanked by local blue-grey slate tiles and potted palms standing on gravel. A shady arbour with a bench seat where NM can sit in the cool. The old family millstone (on which his mother used to grind corn) will become a focal point at the end of the rill. I hope he doesn't mind.

I want to include locally thrown pots and painted poles as decoration. From the formal area with palms and rill there are paths leading between informal beds to make a circuitous walk where he can mooch around and think.

Breakfast at 7.15 – wonderful fresh fruit. Then out and off to a hotel in another part of town to meet Mrs Mandela, Graca Machel. I spoke to her briefly on the phone before leaving the UK and I tell everyone how lovely she was. But there are mutterings that she is a woman who knows what she likes and will always say if she doesn't. 'He will be happy with anything,' they say. 'She is the one you have to worry about.' Nervous that she may not like what I have planned. If she wants changes made, what do we do with the stuff that is now being shipped to Qunu?

The hotel is like a grand country house with wonderfully opulent gardens that include a vineyard and a rose garden. Coffee, tea and buns (lush creamy confections) are brought, and laid out on a table by silent waitresses in crisp, white linen.

Finally Mrs M arrives at 10.20 a.m. She is younger than I thought. She looks fiftyish but must be older? But then she is impossible to put an age on. She is dressed in a long black cotton shift, embroidered with gold. Her hair is intricately braided and styled so that it curves under into a short bob. She is animated and lively. I introduce her all round and she talks relaxedly to everyone. The sun shines, the plants are the richest of possible greens, and after a walking-in sequence, filmed coming down steps below a rose-covered pergola, we sit on a stone bench and I open the painting book to show her my plan.

She appears serious at first, and the crew later admitted to thinking that she did not like it. Then she smiles and pronounces it 'beautiful'. She talks of NM's love of the great outdoors. She calls him 'Madeba', the name used by his intimates. 'Madeba is a kind of person who is very rural. As he calls himself – a country boy. It beams out of him,' she says. 'It is completely out of his mind that someone from England would fly over and spend many days and hours doing this.'

I ask about his likely reaction. 'What I know for sure is that he'll be very, very happy. This is a very, very, very special present. It's completely different to all other sorts of presents he's had.'

We film two-shots and reverses (my questions – the single camera having been on her during the entire interview) and the whole time she remains interested in the conversation, with no hint of impatience or disquiet. An hour or so later she takes her leave, with promises to see us on Sunday, along with himself.

A general feeling of delight, both at her manner, and because in the interview she was so forthcoming about NM.

We drive to the botanic garden at Kirstenbosch where Charlie and Tommy film their bit about collecting 'bird of paradise' plants, while I walk around looking at this little bit of heaven that sits at the foot of Table Mountain. The sky is kingfisher blue.

While the others go up Table Mountain in the cable car I sit by the pool reading *Long Walk to Freedom*. One passage above all others strikes a chord. He talks about his time as a prisoner on Robben Island, the penal colony across the bay from Table Mountain, where he spent the majority of his twenty-seven years as a captive.

Almost from the beginning of my sentence on Robben Island, I asked the authorities for permission to start a garden in the courtyard. For years they refused, but eventually they relented, and we were able to cut out a small garden on a narrow patch of earth against the far wall.

A garden was one of the few things in prison that one could control. To plant a seed, watch it grow, to tend it and then harvest it offered a simple but enduring satisfaction. The sense of being the custodian of this small patch of earth offered a small taste of freedom.

In some ways, I saw the garden as a metaphor for certain aspects of my life. A leader must also tend his garden; he, too, sows seeds, and then watches, cultivates and harvests the result. Like the gardener, a leader must take responsibility for what he cultivates; he must mind his work, try to repel enemies, preserve what can be preserved and eliminate what cannot succeed.

I wrote Winnie two letters about a particularly beautiful tomato plant, how I coaxed it from a tender seedling to a robust plant that produced deep red fruit. But then, either through some mistake or lack of care, the plant began to wither and decline, and nothing I did would bring it back to health. When it finally died, I removed the roots from the soil, washed them and buried them in a corner of the garden.

I closed the book, showered and went to bed early.

Wednesday, 8 December

Up at 6 a.m. on a bright and sunny Cape morning and down to the waterfront to board a high-speed catamaran to Robben Island. We meet Ahmed Kathrada, a former 'political prisoner' who was incarcerated with NM on the island and is one of his closest friends and associates. Mr K, or 'Kathy', is very courteous and extremely articulate. He is a gentle, white-haired Indian gentleman in a white shirt with patches of embroidery. He spends a lot of time showing 'important international officials' around Robben Island which is now a museum and which, last week, was declared a 'World Heritage Site'. He takes me to the court-yard where they broke rocks for six months and where NM made his garden. The sun bakes down and the square, grey courtyard, with an old vine tumbling from a ramshackle concoction of rustic posts, heats up like a cauldron.

We look at a large, mounted photograph of prisoners crouching and sewing cloth on this very spot. He points out himself – centre, back row – and explains that after this photograph was taken and the media men departed, their needles and cloth were taken away and, once more, they were made to break rocks.

We go inside, to NM's cell. It is a small, grey cubicle about eight feet square, containing a bucket with a lid, three blankets and a mess tin and cup. The high, barred window looks out over the courtyard. I find it hard to speak.

Mr K explains how they were locked up at night, and hands me the large key. I hold it and think. The lights in this cell block – in Block B, political prisoners – burned all night.

Patiently and fully Mr K answers my many questions. We go on to look at the lime quarry where NM and his colleagues chipped away with pick and shovel for fourteen years. Here NM began to have problems with his sight, and the brilliant glare from the white, chalky sides of the quarry make it easy to see why.

Then to the beach where they harvested kelp for fertiliser, and where NM fell and damaged his knee. He still has difficulty walking.

I ask why Mr K seems to feel no bitterness and he explains that bitterness is unproductive and that the most important thing is that all races work together, not that power now simply shifts to blacks.

The nearness of this history is hard to take. Now, in 1999, it is just eight years since the prisoners were released, men who went from the bottom of society – shorts, no shoes, hard labour – to government. From prisoner to president.

Tourists tramp around. A Japanese film crew are here for a week to make a film. Today it is blazing hot. Like a holiday resort. Kathrada and Mandela arrived with their comrades in June 1964, the middle of winter, in wind and rain. I find it so remarkable that Mr K can come here now, so soon after his incarceration, and show people around with apparent equanimity.

As we boarded the catamaran, he has a bright conversation with a youngish man counting us on to the boat and ticking off our names. 'He was one of our warders,' he says, as though remarking that the man used to serve him on the cheese counter down at the local supermarket.

Afternoon – back to the hotel, then on to the airport to fly to East London (South Africa). A two-hour delay. Arrive at 8.45 p.m. Hasty dinner. To bed – shattered.

Thursday, 9 December

A lie-in until 8 a.m. Open the curtains and admire a view through palm trees and over low shrubs to a bay washed by Indian Ocean rollers. Breakfast, then pack for the road journey to Umtata. But first, jolly promo shots on the beach by the hotel. East London is rather like Douglas, Isle of Man, just out of season, but warm, humid and cloudy. I rewrite the trail, being unhappy about the leaden one provided by BBC Publicity, and we shoot both, just in case they object. Charlie and Tommy mess about in the waves, and I find myself becoming irritable.

We board the vans – people carriers they call 'combis' – and set off for Umtata. I drive the last half of the journey. Skies leaden. We listen to Richard E. Grant reading Ian Fleming's *The Man With the Golden Gun* and laugh at the creaky bits.

The terrain is like Wensleydale with straw huts and high temperatures. The combi in front radios us to point out NM's house, ahead on the right. We pass a smart, low, sprawling, two-storey villa with pan-tiled roof and terracotta walls, sitting grandly among the humble dwellings that surround it.

On to the Holiday Inn, Umtata, half an hour away. We lunch, then go to the pottery where Charlie is to interview the potter. I stay in the background and furtle around. The pots look good, if very hand-made. Like large egg-cups. I am worried about their ability to travel in one piece. One pot has already lost its bottom.

The potter, midway through the interview, says to Charlie, 'When do we do the kissing?' We buy pots – ridiculously cheap – and leave to take our first look at the garden.

On arrival, the security guards become nervous. 'Get back in your cars and wait.' We do as instructed, shooting nervous glances at one another. Then the all-clear is given, and I am introduced to a stocky black man with a shambling gait – Zet. His real name is Ophallus Zeekeleli. Can quite see why he prefers Zet.

We pass through a newly built security gate with spikes on the top, beside which sits a room filled with TV screens. The old house is in front of us, and we move around to the new one, a vast Spanish hacienda of a building. Past the pool, round the side, to the area I have picked as the bit we will turn into NM's private garden. Zet shows me around, while two security guards begin to look less nervous.

Our patch is about forty-five feet by forty feet (fifteen metres by thirteen metres). The turf is foul, like a rough cattle pasture. It is also soggy due to irrigation. And patchy. The soil is foul, too. Qunu has fifty inches of rain a year, and this is the rainy season. No change there, then.

I check the plants – they have arrived. But are there enough of them? Begin to worry. Suddenly this is all too real. Peep through the windows of the house. Builders still about, madly finishing it off for NM's arrival. The study and library – on the other side of the windows to our proposed garden – look sump-tuous. Like a top-class hotel. Very tastefully put together. The book must have done well.

We look, and look, and pace and leave, giving Zet a lift home on the way. We drop him off about a mile down the road. He points out a long, low building on the hillside. 'That's where Madeba went to school,' he says. 'And this is my house.' His finger rests on a shocking-pink shed built of concrete blocks. There is no glass in the windows. He goes now, to see his sister. His brother tried to take his own life in 1996, failed and had been unwell since. He was operated on at the weekend. He died on the operating table and his funeral is on Saturday. Zet will not go. He was not close. His wife and sister will go. He will help us with Madeba's garden. I do not know what to say.

During supper it starts to rain. Heavy, torrential rain. My boggy turf will be even more boggy tomorrow. To bed early, feeling depressed. Tomorrow the work begins in earnest. But what state will the soil be in?

Friday, 10 December

We start marking out and cutting beds with help from four African workers who belong to the house builders. Much nodding and a lot of serious looks. Not at all sure how much of my conversation they understand, but they work at a steady pace, and relentlessly, even if they do always seem to be in a tight group.

Word comes to me that we have committed a solecism by not greeting the tribal chief, Mrs Balizulu, on our arrival, as is the custom. Even NM must go and see her to pay his respects on his return. Ask what I can do. Am told: 'Nothing. She will come to see you.'

Mid-afternoon she arrives. She has a swathe of black linen wrapped around her head and a bright orange top. She greets me with an African hand shake – one normal handshake, a grasp of the thumb, and then another handshake. All a bit Masonic. She asks to plant something. I offer her a choice. She picks a New Zealand flax with spiky leaves, and with her bare feet pushing on my stainless steel spade, she digs a hole. She then talks volubly to the plant, makes a dish-like hollow in the soil around its crown, and splashes water on the ridge, like a priest sprinkling holy water. She speaks little English, except 'okay', but as she leaves she assures us, via Zet's interpreting, that 'You are welcome here. Now you will not be killed.' I feel very reassured.

By the end of the day – 6.30 p.m. – all the concrete footings for the slate-edged paths and beds are finished, and we have also planted up the beds of succulents, including two monsters eight feet and ten feet high – *Aloe ferox* – which cost £2.50 each. Oh that plants in British garden centres were so competitively priced! It later transpires that they were pulled up from some waste land. Good turf, however, costs £10 per square metre. We are making do with the existing rough stuff.

Everyone is in high spirits at supper, thanks to a sunny day and much more work done than we thought possible.

It also transpires that the tribal chief was seen earlier in the day wearing her normal clothes – a brown dress and a leather trilby. Clearly she had made an effort and I am very grateful.

Saturday, 11 December

Arrive at the garden at 8.30 a.m. on a baking hot morning. The slate tiling begins and Charlie and I plant more exotics. A real slog of a day. Things don't seem to be going so fast – perhaps we're tiring in this heat – but the local ladies (again in cotton finery) cook us a traditional lunch of corn cobs, chick pea gunge, chicken (seen running around only a couple of hours before we ate) and other local delicacies, hard to identify but tasty to eat. Tommy, whose idea of exotic and inedible food begins and ends with a curry, is not impressed and yearns for a Berni Inn. He searches among the exotica in vain for something resembling ham and eggs.

We plug away again in the afternoon, but in spite of the fact that we are still laying slate at 7.45 p.m., by the light of fluorescent lamps from NM's verandah, we do not finish the hard landscaping, which is a bit of a disappointment.

Carol Haslam, our executive producer, protested outside South

Africa House in London when she was a student, carrying her placard demanding, 'FREE NELSON MANDELA'. She and I are shown around the inside of the house in the afternoon. Very interior designerish and very splendid. I sit in NM's chair in his study to check the rill for alignment. Perfect. Heave a sigh of relief. The family millstone sits proudly at the end. I realise that I have sat in NM's chair even before he has, which is a bit of a cheek.

I ask if it would be possible for Mr Mandela to be brought back at 5 p.m. exactly tomorrow. The head of security smiles. They will do their best to get him back tomorrow, rather than the day after, but as he is returning from the United States and a meeting with President Clinton they can make no promises. My heart sinks.

We retire for a late meal and I ask for an early start the following day, at which no one seems to demur. (Though how I have the nerve to ask them to a) have an early night, b) not drink too much and c) leave the hotel at 7 a.m., I have no idea.) Slave driver.

Trouble getting to sleep. Mind whirring. Finally get off at half past one.

Sunday, 12 December

The Big Day. After a troubled night, waking hourly and imagining all the things that can go wrong today like NM not coming back, for assorted reasons including the death of his mother (she died years ago), and the possibility that if he does return I shall be shot by a security guard as I approach him.

The morning is fine and warm and our pace of work seems to increase. The gang of four are madly planting up everything I placed out the night before, and lobbing rubbish over the garden wall on to their lorry. The pool is finished and gets filled, in spite of the fact that for the last two days the house has had no water due to storage tank problems. (How very like the life of our own dear Queen.) The workers are trying to fit a new one which, yesterday, came tumbling down from its scaffolding platform with a deafening thud that convinced us that loss of life must have been the result. Happily it was not. But one of the men is now limping. We rig up two water butts outside the garden at the foot of a downpipe as our modest contribution to water storage.

We get word that it is likely NM will be back today. Still no confirmation of the time, though.

Charlie checks her water jets. They now operate by remote control. (Wish I could write that without it looking like a *double entendre.*)

By 3 p.m. it is clear we will finish. I have butterflies quite badly. Begin to feel slightly sick. By 4 p.m. it is all over bar the sweeping. I poke and prod at the gravel with my broom, and make sure that all looks good. Wish I were not so anally retentive.

We have several pots from the local potter (all in one piece) – painted posts and stones from a local artist who worked silently except for the occasional 'y-e-e-e-e-s' and 'n-o-o-o-o-o-o-o-o' in response to questions. When asked who he was he replied, 'Ahm a p-a-a-a-ynter.'

The rill and millstone look great. The turf looks awful, but now seems to blend into the background. I remind myself that this is the Transkei, not Teddington.

We change into jeans and clean T-shirts, just around the corner under NK's verandah, and Charlie puts on a sarong. We wait. Will he come? Will he like it?

At 4.59 p.m. precisely – and I am not joking – a convoy of Mercedes cars comes down the Qunu road. He is here. We pull ourselves close in to the wall – Charlie and Tommy and Willy and me. And then he is here.

He walks around to the back of the house. He is taller than I imagined, around six foot three inches, and smiling. He can have no idea who we are, and yet his words and manner are welcoming. He looks around, a little bewildered, but laughing. Clearly, with Ahmed Kathrada showing him the way, he knows that this is meant to be some sort of pleasant surprise. 'Well, hello.' He stretches out his hand. It is not old and wizened. It looks like the hand of a thirty year old. Odd, the things you notice. I introduce him to the rest of the team, and explain that we have made him a garden. He gasps, looks at the altered landscape for a moment and then says: 'Gee whizz!'

I walk him round and he keeps repeating 'Gee whizz', as burly security guards jostle us to make sure that nothing untoward is planted in the garden.

His pleasure is clearly apparent. 'Don't tread on my plants,' he warns his wife. And then, mock seriously: 'You said we would never have any secrets from each other!'

'Ah, but this is a nice secret,' she replies, beaming.

His grandchildren swarm over the garden, splashing in the water. I worry that Tommy's newly laid slate will not stand the weight of a particularly burly security man, but I am powerless to intervene now.

We sit down for a chat, and he tells me about the importance of a garden, reading out loud to me the part of his book that had struck such a chord.

He looks at Charlie in her sarong and tells her, 'You look like a Spice Girl.' Then he says, 'Yesterday I had a meeting with the President of the USA – a great honour.' I could not help but think that the honour was all the President's.

After having a good look round he ushered us to the back of the house, gave us tea and signed our books for us. In mine he inscribed, 'To Alan, best wishes to a competent and caring journalist, N. Mandela'. I muse on using it as a reference.

He told me about addressing his first public meeting on being released from prison. 'It was a church meeting,' he said. 'Outdoors. There were three million people ranged across the hills and down into the valleys, stretching far, far away.' He looked at me with a twinkle in his eye. 'It took them two weeks to count the collection.'

We talked, and drank tea, and I asked the question to which everyone wants to know the answer. 'After twenty-seven years in prison, why is there no bitterness?'

He shook his head and smiled. 'There is no time.'

He looked across at the garden and nodded in its direction. 'Thank you so much for my garden. It is wonderful. I will look after it for as long as I can.' He patted me on the shoulder and shook my hand again.

And then he took my cup and saucer from me and I went home.

The garden is still thriving. Someone known to the family sent me some pictures a few months ago. The beds and borders are fuller now, thanks to warm, wet weather. I hope it gives him pleasure when he sits in his study chair and looks along the narrow rill to his mother's millstone. He has touched many hearts during the course of his life. I hope we have touched his.

40

Telling Tales

'"And what of your daughter, Mrs Fitzherbert, should she not find a husband?"

"Oh, I shall suggest that she writes. It is a suitable accomplishment for a girl of poor aspect and overactive imagination".'

Mrs Maskell, *Dorchester Square*, 1893

People say, 'How do you discipline yourself? How do you make yourself get up and write? I'd just stay in bed.' Well, perhaps they would, if they didn't like their job. I write because I have to. I have to garden and I have to write. They are the two most fulfilling addictions I know, and I really do relish being among plants, or sitting down and crafting copy. Writing is a kind of exquisite agony. But it is far easier than getting up every morning and catching the 7.45.

By the mid 1990s I had written more than thirty gardening books and one about English rivers. But there was a niggle at the back of my mind. It was probably Miss Weatherall, correcting my grammar, reminding me not to use exclamation marks for dramatic effect, or simply refusing to believe the extent of my vocabulary. Poor Miss Weatherall. Maybe I really need to thank her. Clearly her red Biro remarks at the end of my essays dug deeper than even she intended.

The niggle was a simple one: why couldn't I write stories?

Probably because Miss Weatherall wrote 'Straight out of *Chick's Own*' whenever my imagination got the better of me. No. Stop it. That's enough about Miss Weatherall. But that is exactly why I wanted to write stories – to exercise that part of the imagination which most grown-ups have to keep locked away.

It is the supreme luxury – discovering characters, dreaming up a story. All authors are asked, 'Where do you get your ideas from?' My reply is always the same. I have no idea.

Neither have I any idea how I had the nerve to start. I mean, if you have one reasonably successful career, why rock the boat? Why risk public failure and the subsequent opprobrium just for the sake of having a go? Because you have to, that's why. Because it's fun taking risks. Both Jilly Cooper and Rosamunde Pilcher encouraged me: 'Get on with it, of course you can do it!' But I went about it in quite the wrong way.

I had this idea about a TV gardener. Very original. Well, you know what they say – write about what you know. Characters tend to come into my head before plot. The characters help evolve the plot. And when things get going they take complete charge of it.

Mr MacGregor I called my gardener, with a nod and a smile in the direction of Beatrix Potter, but with a different spelling. Peter Rabbit's *bête noire* is Mr McGregor. I wrote out a synopsis and two chapters and sent them off to three publishers.

Now if you send an unsolicited manuscript to a publisher it goes on to something called the slush pile. There it may fester for ever and a day. The proper thing to do is to find yourself a literary agent and get them to send it. Then the publisher is obliged to read your manuscript. (They can still return it but at least you know it's been skimmed.)

One publisher, Bantam, sent me back a rejection slip; another, Bloomsbury, asked to see more copy, and the third, Michael Joseph, invited me out to lunch. I went to lunch.

Luigi Bonomi is half English and half Italian. He is plump, jocular, sharp and extremely good company. He kisses you when you meet. Even though you're a chap. I'm used to it now. And I've always liked Italian holidays.

Over lunch at Clarke's restaurant he explained that his eagle-eyed reader Chris Beith (female) had spotted my manuscript on the pile, read it, liked it and put it in front of him. 'I don't know if this is THE Alan Titchmarsh,' she said, 'but it's quite good.'

Well, you know what it's like. Sometimes you just hit it off with somebody, and not just because they like what you do. I spent some time explaining that I wanted to write more, and that I did not want my book to be seen as a 'celebrity novel'. I was a writer, I insisted; I had been a writer for twenty years. I was not a Martin Amis or an A.S. Byatt – nothing so cerebral. I was happy to be a Dick Francis or a Mary Wesley. I want people to read my books because they want to disappear into a story. He nodded indulgently. I hope he believed me.

Shortly afterwards Luigi became a literary agent. He auctioned my book for a considerable sum. He is still my literary agent and I bless the day we met. Of course, there was one slight snag. I now had to write the thing. One synopsis and two chapters do not a book make.

Between the months of November and February my television work is only slight. *Gardeners' World* and *Ground Force* are not filmed then. It's the off-season and the garden, too, is a little quieter, though seeing the amount of work Bill and Sue put in at that time you wouldn't think so. That is the time of year when I can sit down and concentrate on book writing. A novel takes me around eight months, so we're well into the growing season – June – by the time I finish, and I am then fitting in the writing around my television work. I can write from about nine in the morning until two in the afternoon, after which time no good will come of it. I might as well go out and dabble with the dahlias.

I have a little pavilion at the top of my garden. It has heating but no telephone, only an intercom with the house for the 'Lunch is ready' call, or the 'How long will you be?' enquiry. It is quiet. It is filled with pictures of boats. It is white inside and pale blue outside. It has a verandah. It is my private paradise.

In the winter of 1997 and 1998 I sat and I wrote my first story. I discovered several amazing things:

1. When you write fiction you reveal as much if not more about yourself than when you write non-fiction. Under the disguise of a character you can often voice feelings that you would be too embarrassed to claim as your own. Does that make this volume less than honest? No. Just different! Characters are less concerned with how you feel about them, and how they will be interpreted; as a result they tend to speak more freely.

2. Characters are more important than plot. Get to know your characters well from the beginning and they will dictate (quite literally) the flow of the narrative. Not all writers work in this way, but I know that I cannot type a sentence of speech without knowing exactly how the character who is speaking is feeling, and how he or she relates to their interlocutor and to other characters in the story.

3. Characters will often say things you do not expect. This would appear to fly in the face of the previous point, but the reverse is true. Your subconscious knows far more about your characters than the conscious part of your mind. If someone had said this to me a few years ago I would have thought they were barking. Writing fiction makes you highly aware of the depth and complexity of the human subconscious. And I am still talking Dick Francis rather than Martin Amis.

4. Always go with the flow – don't fight it. Whenever I have tried to consciously manipulate the activities of my characters I have got into trouble. Now this is a perverse sort of feeling. You are, after all, inventing the entire novel, cover to cover, but there is a kind of subliminal inventiveness which will seem natural and on-going. Think of it as a car on a motorway. It needs only gentle nudges at the steering wheel to keep it going in the right direction, once you've pointed it in the right direction. Don't try to yank the steering wheel. It will end in disaster. What can be fun, though, is to get another character to put obstacles in the way, but only if that character has a reason for doing so.

5. If nothing is coming go out and potter in the garden.

6. I may not have a clue what I am talking about.

Once I started writing fiction I discovered the kind of book I write. This may sound odd. Aren't you supposed to plan the sort of book you write? Maybe you are. I wasn't at all sure. I just sat down and got on with it. I discovered that I write romantic fiction. Odd for a man. Men are meant to write adventure stories, thrillers, science fiction, horror – that sort of thing. It's women who write romantic fiction. That was a bit worrying.

I have a basic idea of the plot, which I try to arrive at when I'm mowing the grass or weeding in borders. It's a rough structure, a beginning. Sometimes I am unsure of the end. Rosamunde Pilcher describes it as a washing line, on which ideas and events can be hung. To me it's a bit like a train journey. I know where I'm starting from, and I know some of the stations on the way, but not necessarily the order in which I will arrive at them. And I am always ready for diversions and cancellations. (It pays to be a realist.)

I write stories about ordinary folk, sometimes in extraordinary circumstances. I didn't have a deeply disturbed childhood and my family is not terminally dysfunctional. I'm a relatively happy soul, but it is my misfortune as an author that misanthropy is frequently confused with intellectuality. Divine discontent strikes all of us from time to time, but I would derive no pleasure from earning a living out of it.

No. I reasoned that I had to be honest about it; romantic fiction was clearly my bag. And anyway, books written from the woman's point of view have had it their own way for too long. I wanted to write about a certain sort of man – fairly sensitive, occasionally misguided, human, good-humoured and, in the main, loving. A lot of men are. They are just fairly quiet about it.

It was a challenge, having a central character who was sensitive but manly rather than wet. It seemed to work. I hope I struck the right balance. I had the good fortune to find a wonderful editor in Clare Ledingham at Simon and Schuster who really took the book to her heart and helped me make it better. She doesn't write any of it, just nudges me in the right direction, rather like the director of a film.

Letting go of your characters is a wonderful feeling. When I hear someone else talking about them as though they were real people – which they are to me – it is a great thrill.

I have written four novels so far. There are more to come. One author I met said she had novel ideas in her head that were coming in to land every few weeks, like planes at an airport. I wish my mind were so fertile. When I finish one novel I have not the faintest idea what the next one will be. I probably need to clear out the cupboards to find room for it.

All four of them have made it into the best-seller lists. If I sound boastful I apologise, but I can hardly believe it. Oh, I'd like to be cool and detached, but I've never managed to achieve that. Success still genuinely surprises me. And where fiction is concerned, I still have the feeling that I've been allowed to play with the grown-ups.

Of course, there are the difficult bits. You have to cope with the flak. Like the Bad Sex Awards.

I had not really thought about putting love scenes in my books. They just sort of happened. Sometimes it is necessary to show how physically attracted to each other your characters are, and closing the bedroom door and leaving three dots on the page is not quite enough. But I knew I didn't want to be sordid, to go in for the naming of parts. As far as I can see there is nothing remotely romantic or even arousing about the word 'penis'. No. Not for me at all. But I did want my love scenes to be sensuous. So that's how I wrote them. Most people have no problem with them (I mean, most of us have been there) but a few had a go.

It all came to a head after *Mr MacGregor* when I was invited to the *Literary Review* Bad Sex Awards by Auberon Waugh. I should have had more sense than to go. 'How lovely of you to accept. Meet me at the *Literary Review* offices,' he suggested. 'We'll have a drink there first and then go on.'

Naïvely I imagined that all authors who had been invited to the bash at the In and Out Club would be going round to the office for drinks first. What a treat. Even if it was a bit of a dig. I mean what is 'Bad Sex'? I soon found out. From the Dickensian building where the *Literary Review*'s offices are housed we were taken to the In and Out Club in Piccadilly. In the front seat rode Stephen Fry. I sat in the back, sandwiched between Auberon Waugh and Naim Attallah. I did a lot of listening.

The bash was in full swing when we arrived – lots of literary types. Lots of black. Lots of smoking. Lots of noise. Eventually Auberon Waugh rose to his feet and made a courteous speech about this year's finalists, and invited certain selected guests to read out the half-dozen bonniest *mots* that had been considered the best contenders. My bit about 'liquid noises' was there among the work of a clutch of literary giants who had circumspectly declined to attend. I winced as my words were read out loud. I heaved a sigh when the winner was announced as Sebastian Faulks for a scene from *Charlotte Gray*. But Sebastian Faulks was not there. I was. They gave the award to me as runner-up. It is a model of a girl lifting her skirt, while a dog with a cigar blows smoke towards her nether regions. The competition was sponsored by Hamlet cigars.

It sits in the loo at home, a timely reminder that not all publicity is good publicity. Except that it did do wonders for sales.

There have been other winners of the *Literary Review* Bad Sex Award – Melvyn Bragg is one – but everyone has forgotten them. I seem to have become stuck with the thing, and with each successive novel I become more nervous of love scenes. People always call them 'sex scenes', anyway. Why not leave them out? Because they are a part of the story, and if you let gentle ribbing put you off your stroke (if you see what I mean) then you are not worth much.

I make no extravagant claims for my stories. They are not seminal. They are not mind-improving. They are just stories. I like to think they explore human relationships in a sensitive way without being too trite. They are written from the heart. Feel-good books, I suppose, but I don't think there's anything wrong with that.

41

Her Majesty's Pleasure

'Radical intellectuals have no time for the Monarchy. They see it as an anachronistic reminder of serfdom. They would do well to observe the effect that meeting the monarch can have on the afore-mentioned serfs. Lucky the President who can match that.'

Geoffrey Pleydell, *Constitutional Misconceptions*, 1953

I have a friend who teases me about my attitude to royalty. She is a left-winger. Lives in a big house in Hampstead. I don't argue with her. I just sit quietly when she gets a bit sneery. She'd be happy to have a President tomorrow. I think we're better off the way we are. Oh, I know that the monarchy is powerless in the legislative and directly governmental sense, but it has several attributes that no politician since Churchill has ever possessed. It is historic, it is still regarded as 'special' and, provided that certain members of the royal family can get their act together, it still has a magic and mystery that gives the man in the street a bit of a thrill.

You can argue that things are not what they were, that some members of the royal family have led 'the firm' into disrepute, but then Henry VIII and Edward VIII did their bit in that direction, too. It's happened before. It will happen again. It happens to Presidents, too.

I'm not a political animal. Like most voters I'd be happy with any government that could sort out the big three issues – health and education and transport – and any party which had some faint knowledge of how the countryside works. But I do wish someone would be pragmatic about the advantages of a royal family when it comes to imports and exports and international diplomacy. Tourists don't come to Britain to see the changing of the MPs after a General Election. They come to see the Changing of the Guard.

The royal yacht *Britannia* was not simply a floating palace. When it was not being used by the Queen, it became a floating trade centre. On these 'Sea Days' – dozens of them every year – important export deals were struck over the royal china. Millions of pounds were brought into Britain. But the yacht had to go because it wasn't 'the People's Yacht'. No. But it was 'the People's Money'.

On the diplomatic front, when a government leader fails to make an impression, a crowned head handing over a jewelled order can make one heck of a difference. It's not party political; it's practical.

Being impressed is what you are meant to be by royalty. It is its stock in trade. I rather like being impressed. I certainly was when I got the letter. And a bit surprised, too.

It came on 16 November 1999, from 10 Downing Street. 'The Prime Minister has it in mind,' it began, 'to recommend to Her Majesty the Queen that you be made a member of the Most Excellent Order of the British Empire.'

I checked the name and address on the envelope. No mistake there. I read on. There were instructions. I was not to tell anybody. Difficult. Well, I wouldn't tell my mum. Not yet. But I told Alison. She says she never repeats anything I tell her. It's the people she tells who repeat it.

It said I would hear nothing more until my name was gazetted

in the 2000 New Year's Honours List on 31 December. I looked
at the form. I had to tick a box to say 'yes', I accept, or 'no', I do
not accept. It was a bit like the pools. I ticked the 'yes' box and
waited.

It did occur to me that the Queen might not accept the Prime
Minister's recommendation. That she'd say, 'Oh, I don't think so,'
when he read my name out during his Tuesday evening audience. But I don't suppose it works like that.

Anyway, I was chuffed to bits when my name appeared in the
paper: 'Alan Fred Titchmarsh, for services to horticulture and to
broadcasting.' Funny, really. I'd never thought of it as 'services'.
It was just what I did. Nice to be rewarded for something you
do because you're passionate about it. And it was the MBE, which
another friend of mine tells me means My Bloody Effort, as
opposed to the OBE, which means Other Buggers' Efforts.

The really top honours – the ones connected with St Michael
and St George – CMG, KCMG and GCMG – are frightfully grand.
According to Sir Humphrey Appleby in *Yes Minister*, they stand
for Call Me God, Kindly Call Me God, and God Calls Me God.
I'll happily settle for My Bloody Effort.

I waited for the call to the palace, but it was ages coming. In
the meantime my agent had a request for me to speak at the
Annual General Meeting of a Women's Institute in Norfolk. In
January. I asked her to thank them and say that much as I would
love to say 'yes' I was busy writing my next novel and would have
to decline. My agent told me that the President and the President's
daughter would both be there. I said that it was very good of
them to turn out but that I still had the book to write.

She said, 'Alan, I don't think you understand. The WI is in
Sandringham. The President is the Queen Mother and her
daughter is . . .'

'What date do they want?'

Well, it would have been churlish to decline. Especially after the gong.

Alison and I drove to Norfolk on a January morning, and lunched in a local pub, turning up at the village hall on the Sandringham estate at the appointed time of 2 p.m. The Queen was due at a quarter to three (the Queen Mother having been confined to bed with a chill as her anxious staff cosseted her so that she could enjoy her hundredth year).

It was a modest sort of hall, just like any other village hall in the country, except that there was a carpet on the floor that had been woven for Queen Victoria's Golden Jubilee, and green velour director's chairs that had been placed along one side for the ten-yearly group photograph.

There were just twenty-eight members of Sandringham WI – all of whose husbands work on the estate – and the photographer, the church organist, Alison and me. We said hello and were made a fuss of. 'But you've got the Queen coming as well,' I offered. 'Oh, we see her all the time. It's you we're excited about.'

After a while a commotion outside heralded the royal arrival. The door at the end of the hall opened, and in came the Queen, in a kingfisher blue coat and hat, wearing gloves and carrying a handbag. Her lady-in-waiting melted into the group and the Queen stood there while we sang the National Anthem to her.

It is quite difficult knowing just how to sing 'God Save Our Gracious Queen' when you are standing only feet away from the royal presence. It is easier in the Royal Albert Hall where distance offers anonymity. Close up you are torn between a clearly enunciated and deferential offering sung in her direction, or a softly murmered rendition that avoids all eye contact. I hope we struck the right balance.

After we'd sung 'Jerusalem' the Queen smiled sweetly and was ushered to her seat for the photograph. She sat in her usual spot

– front row centre – with the other members of the WI grouped around her. Alison and I, and the organist who had played the anthem on a harmonium, were the only spectators.

'I shall take six photographs,' said the rather dour photographer.

'I don't know whether you are an optimist or a pessimist,' replied the Queen, before smiling once more for the camera.

Flash, flash, flash. 'That's three,' said the Queen. 'Halfway.'

He took the other three, dismantled his equipment without a word and left through the kitchen.

The chairs were moved now to the body of the tiny hall, and tables were arranged to accommodate the members of the committee and the President's daughter. The secretary read out the minutes of the last meeting from an exercise book and the Queen was asked to sign them as a true record of proceedings. They gave her a Biro, and I watched as she penned 'Elizabeth R' with a blue-topped Bic.

The Queen then read us a recipe which Queen Elizabeth the Queen Mother had sent especially. It was for curing a chill. It involved boiled cabbage leaves which were laid on the chest of the patient. The Queen read out the instructions and then gently raised her eyebrows. I had visions of her up at the Big House, standing over the Aga, stirring cabbage in a large saucepan and then ministering to her mother. It seems sad and strangely prophetic now, bearing in mind that just over two years later the Queen Mother died of a chill, but at the time it was related with a twinkle in the eye and a lightness of touch of which the older Queen would have approved.

And then it was time for me. I have a sort of one-man show. I perform it six or eight times each autumn to coincide with my book tour. 'An Evening with Alan Titchmarsh' it's somewhat unimaginatively called. I would give the Queen an abridged version, 'Half an Afternoon with Alan Titchmarsh'.

The committee and the Queen rose and moved to become the audience, and I went round to the other side of the table. As I stood up I saw the Queen's face right in front of me. It came as a bit of a shock. 'Oh! We're a bit close, aren't we?'

'Yes,' said the Queen. She took hold of the table. 'I'll push, you pull.'

I hoped like anything that she would smile at the funny bits. She did not. Instead, she threw back her head and laughed. She has the most wonderful laugh. I was cooking on gas now. The others laughed, too. I don't think they were being polite.

There were questions at the end. She didn't ask one, but she did come up and chat to Alison and me over tea, a relaxed, fun conversation, that was all the more special because it was natural and unforced. We talked about all sorts of things. I won't tell you what. Some confidences are best kept. They are one of life's most underestimated pleasures.

The Queen laughed her way through the WI entertainment – a sort of potted pantomime – she looked kindly at the exhibition of fans and Victoria sponge cakes, and then she left, turning at the door and saying cheerily, 'Well, goodbye.'

As we drove home Alison said, 'It's funny, isn't it?'

'What?'

'That dream you always have about taking tea with the Queen. We've just done it.'

It was June when I finally went to pick up my gong. We made a proper day of it – stayed at the Ritz the night before – well, you only do it once. We had a chauffeured Bentley to the palace. The girls had wonderful hats. I wore a morning suit and carried a top hat.

The policeman saluted us as we swept into the central quadrangle. We went up the red-carpeted steps, and Alison and the girls were directed to the ballroom where the band of the Coldstream Guards played songs from the shows. I made my way, as instructed, to the Long Gallery, lined with massive Rembrandts and Titians, where the MBEs, OBEs and CBEs gathered to be instructed on the intricacies of an investiture. There was no wine; only orange juice or water. Wise, probably.

After a while we were called to order by the Controller of the Lord Chamberlain's office, a very clean gentleman in a navy blue tunic with lots of gold. He wecomed us and suggested that we be as relaxed as possible. 'The more relaxed you are, the more you will enjoy it, and the more you enjoy it, the more you will remember.'

We nodded gratefully.

'Just one or two practical points. The Queen will be standing on a dais. Do not get on to the dais with her.'

General hilarity. Someone asked, 'If we have to talk to her, what do we call her?'

'There is no "if" about it. This is a conversation, not a royal monologue. Usually, on the first occasion when you address the Queen it is as "Your Majesty", and subsequently it is as "ma'am", to rhyme with jam, not marm to rhyme with –'

'Farm?' someone offered. More nervous laughter.

'And when the Queen shakes hands with you, that is an indication that your time is up. Do not try to engage her in further conversation.'

And then we were gently shepherded, ten at a time, towards our fate. We could see the goings-on in the ballroom on a television monitor. Being a 'T' and a lowly MBE, I was among the last of the one hundred and thirty to go.

I looked around at the gilt and the brocade, the Old Masters and the ormolu and breathed deeply. A time to savour the moment. A time to wonder what the Queen would say to me as she hung the medal on the hook they had fastened on all our suits.

And then I was being walked along the back of the ballroom and down the side to take my position in the final queue.

I heard my name and, at first, thought it must be someone else's. 'Dr Alan Titchmarsh,' announced the Lord Chamberlain. I have two honorary degrees, one from the University of Bradford and one from the University of Essex. I don't use the titles in everyday life, but I did put them down on the form for the palace. I moved jerkily forward for the regulation number of steps, bowed in what I thought was a courtly fashion (Alison said it was far too deep), walked forward another three steps and smiled.

I waited for the question. What *would* she say? And then she spoke. 'Are you busy?' she asked.

To be honest, it came as a bit of a disappointment. 'Yes,' I replied, and explained about *Gardeners' World* and *Ground Force* and the writing. She murmured one or two other pleasantries, and then she stretched out her hand to indicate that the audience was over. As she did so she smiled.

'Well,' she said, 'you give a lot of ladies a lot of pleasure.'

On the way home, I don't think my feet touched the ground.

42

Gnome or Mr Nice Guy

"'Have you been to one of his dos before?'"
"Aye. Once."
"What were it like?"
"It were all right. If yer like laffin.'"
Two gentlemen talking in the lavatory of the King's Hall, Ilkley,
before a performance of 'An Evening with Alan Titchmarsh'

It was that great humorous writer P. G. Wodehouse who said that he could die happy, now that he had received a knighthood and his likeness had been immortalised by Madame Tussaud's. On a more modest scale I know how he feels. The letter came in the summer of 2000. They had conducted a survey, they said, and people wanted to see me in Madame Tussaud's. (They probably wanted to see me stuffed, said a friend. I let it go.) There was no mention of the Chamber of Horrors.

And so, on the appointed day, I went along to Baker Street. The queue outside Madame Tussaud's stretched for a hundred yards or more. Almost all the people in it were Japanese. They wouldn't have a clue who I was. What a disappointment I would be to them. I could imagine their incredulous looks as they read the name plate. 'Who he?' I bowed my head and went in through a side door.

The Tussaud's people were very pleasant. They gave me sandwiches and asked me to sign the visitors' book. I signed, between Prince Andrew and Fidel Castro.

They stood me on a turntable, leaning on a hoe, and said a pleasant smile would be best, rather than a toothy grin. I know my teeth are not on a par with Julia Roberts', but at least they are all my own. Not that Julia's aren't. This sort of experience makes you think seriously about orthodontics.

They slowly revolved me on the turntable and took endless photographs, and video footage, then they began to measure me – everywhere – with pairs of callipers. They noted down their findings on an enormous chart, which looked rather like the plan of campaign for the Battle of Britain.

They paused for a while and began whispering to one another.

'What is it?' I asked.

They looked furtive. 'Well, you don't have to do it . . . but it really would help us.'

'Do what?'

'It's just that the clothes sit so much better if we can photograph and measure you . . . well . . . with no clothes on.'

They noticed the look on my face. Did they ask Prince Andrew to do this? Or Fidel Castro? Unlikely, I thought.

'Not totally naked. You can wear a pair of shorts.'

It was an olive branch I thought I had better take.

'They are in the kitchen. Over there.'

I walked in the direction of the pointing finger and found the kitchen, and a pair of Lycra shorts over the back of a chair.

'You can leave your shoes and socks on,' they shouted.

Picture me, then, on a warm summer's day, in a garret high above Baker Street, clad only in a pair of Lycra shorts, suede loafers and socks, leaning on a hoe and gently revolving while people took photographs of me.

Percy Thrower was the last gardener to be immortalised in

wax. Somehow, along with Fidel and Andy, I think he might have politely declined to remove his clothes.

As I went to put on my clothes once more, they told me that the previous person to wear the shorts had been Tim Henman. I hoped they'd rinsed them.

When I was once more respectably clad, there came a knock at the door and several ladies bustled in. They were very work-manlike and intense. One had paints and a palette and proceeded to match my facial and hand colouring in oils. Another whipped out a small pair of scissors and took a snippet of hair. The third had a large tray of glass eyes which she proceeded to match against my own. She looked like a waitress in an Albanian restaurant. Once she had found what she wanted – grey-green and slightly bloodshot, I think – she smiled triumphantly and left. I was just grateful that they had not arrived ten minutes earlier and caught me trying to hold in my stomach.

I mentioned this fact in a magazine column and had a kindly letter from a Belgian lady who said:

Dear Mr Titchmarsh,

Don't feel embarrassed about those extra inches around the waist, or what the French call an 'embonpoint'.

In Flemish we have this saying: 'Goed gerief moet onder een afdak hangen.' Meaning, 'Good tools should be kept under a shelter.'

And we don't mean garden tools.

Cordially,

Marie Louise Guns

Several months later I returned for a second sitting. My head was sculpted in clay now, and my sculptor, Louis Wiltshire, had to make any final adjustments – a tweak of the nose here, the elongation of a wrinkle there. Then he took me to a room where they poured a warm rubber solution over my hands to make a cast, and my two rings were measured to be copied.

Another sitting came a month or two later when the head was cast in wax, and a fourth and final check-up when the colourist went to work. It was every bit as thorough as an antenatal clinic. But then they were giving birth.

Eight months after that first embarrassing session I was called in to see the final likeness, dressed in my own clothes.

Seeing yourself in 3-D is a strange experience. I'm used to seeing myself on the box. I don't like it much. I watch my programmes occasionally; I don't make a point of being in for them. But I do know what I look like. And yet, to be able to walk around yourself, standing there, is almost like visiting yourself on earth. Like being an angel and stepping outside yourself. Weird, yet wonderful.

I thought I would discover that they had not got me quite right. I've seen a few of the likenesses in Madame Tussaud's that are not – well – spot on. But their techniques have improved. My waxwork *is* me.

At the grand unveiling in front of a row of paparazzi, Alison was asked which one she would rather take home. There was a brief moment when she mused on having a quieter life, but I think I won on the recount.

The kids have not seen it – me – him yet. But Camilla came in with a newspaper a few weeks ago. 'Have you seen this, Dad?'

'What?'

'They say you're the most groped waxwork in Madame Tussaud's.'

'Get away.'

'It's true. Apparently they have to clean the lipstick off you twice a week.'

'You're having me on.'

'I'm not. It says so here. I suppose they could be wrong. Who are you standing next to?'

'Do you really want to know?'

'Yes.'

'Brad Pitt.'

She thought for a moment, and then she shook her head and folded up the paper. 'Must be a case of mistaken identity.'

I blame it all on the survey. I don't know who started it. It wasn't me. They had this poll to find out who was the sexiest man on TV, and I came second to George Clooney. Well, I ask you. How can you believe stuff like that? It seems to me that every day I grow more like a gnome. But I go with the flow. I'm convinced that it's a national plot just to see if I'll really believe it, and then they'll all leap out of the bushes and say, 'Ha, ha, fooled you.' It wouldn't surprise me.

But then everything else does. I seem to have gone through life being surprised – partly at my luck, partly at my success. It embarrasses me to even call it that. To be allowed to do what you want to do, and to do it in the company of people you love is a wonderful thing. So if I keep being 'relentlessly cheerful' you'll forgive me. There's a very good reason for it.

One thing I do believe is that it's a good idea to quit while you're ahead, so after this year I will be bowing out of both *Ground Force* and *Gardeners' World*. It may be rash to leave two programmes in the same year, but the time seems right. There's nothing sinister about it. Having designed sixty-six *Ground Force* gardens I think I've taken the series as far as I can. And my jokes are getting noticeably feebler. Charlie and Tommy will continue to front the show without me but I've taught them all I know (except for a few bits that I've kept to myself).

I've presented *Gardeners' World* for seven years now, and although it's nowhere near as long as Geoff Hamilton's seventeen, it seems a good, round number. Seven year itch and all that. I do enjoy making the programme, and it took me long enough to get there, but it is a weighty responsibility, having to transform part of the garden on a weekly basis and be ready for a camera crew every Friday morning for ten months of the year. As Geoff rightly warned me – you can say goodbye to holidays.

Over the past couple of years, one or more of the other presenters has also turned up each week at Barleywood. They are a good bunch, but I would be less than truthful if I did not admit that I have found it difficult, watching someone else dig my soil, or put in a plant. With my right-hand woman Sue it's different. We've gardened together for fifteen years or more and become used to each other's little ways. No two gardeners do things the same way, you see. I guess it's like having two cooks in a kitchen. Maybe I'm becoming a grumpy old man, but a garden has always struck me as a very personal thing. Heigh-ho.

What I do hope is that the programme will continue to pass on gardening skills and garden craft, and employ presenters with sound practical experience. It would be a great sadness if it were to sacrifice knowledge for glamour.

There will be one more dramatic change to my life this year. We've decided to move house. It will be a huge wrench leaving Barleywood after twenty years, but I reckon I have one more garden in me, and I'd like to make it around an old house. We've found a Georgian farmhouse, just three miles away, surrounded by an old brick and flint wall. Well, it's every gardener's dream isn't it, a walled garden? Bill and Sue will continue to help; I wouldn't want to do it without them.

We'll keep the woodland and the meadows above Barleywood, so we'll be able to watch our trees grow, and although I'll try not to look over the fence when I'm mowing the rides in the wood, I hope someone will love the place as much as we have for the last twenty years.

I'll continue to write my stories for as long as people want to read them, and with any luck there'll be a little more time to dig my garden and sniff the roses. I won't be disappearing from the screen. There are other programme ideas in the pipeline, and another series of *How to be a Gardener*, which was a pleasing success. It was a chance to go solo, a programme for the raw beginner. I'd thought about it for several years before I got a chance to make it. There were comparisons with Delia Smith's *How to Cook*, and her controversial decision to spend a long time showing viewers how to boil an egg; I took my time explaining about soil, light and water. But the series went down well with those who were honest enough to admit to their lack of knowledge, and it was refreshing to be able to start from scratch, tell people why plants need what they need and, yes, to concentrate on things that grow rather than on decking and water features.

It was one of the happiest programmes to make. My producer, Kath Moore, had previously worked on a programme called *A Life of Grime*, about everything from slum clearance to sanitary inspectors. As far as she was concerned life had now, quite literally, become a bed of roses. She spent most days grinning from ear to ear, and when she wasn't, her furrowed brow would gradually melt and she'd say 'Oh, I see!!!' as another tricky operation was explained in words of one syllable.

You can get it in the neck for oversimplifying things, but I really did want to start from scratch and risk the consequences.

I read the reviews of the first series in fear and trepidation. A.A. Gill in the *Sunday Times* saw it as a covert plot to take over the world: 'You must resist the cosy charm. It hides a soul of fungi; he has neat DDT in his veins.' Jaci Stephen in the *Mail on*

Sunday reckoned that in real life I wore a yellow nylon vest (not guilty, your honour, when I do they're black cotton), but the *Daily Telegraph* reviewer made everything worth while. He said that it was the first television series in a long while that he would be keeping on video. He is thirty-something. Gotcha!

AFTERWORD

Is that it, then?

I think so. I've probably told them enough.

More than enough, I reckon. And are you still denying that it's an autobiography?

Yes. It's not comprehensive enough for that. It's more of a memoir.

More of a swank, they'd say up north.

Yes. I suppose you're right.

Did you enjoy it?

I'm not sure. I think I found out a lot. Realised things I didn't realise before.

Do you think they did?

Who knows.

Those quotes at the opening of each chapter will make you sound well read, anyway.

Oh dear.

Why 'Oh dear'?

I'm afraid I made them all up – apart from the Oscar Wilde one.

Showing off again?

Probably.

So what now?

I'd better go. I can hear my mother calling, 'Come away. That's enough. Nobody's looking at you.'

Wise woman, your mother.

PHOTOGRAPHIC ACKNOWLEDGEMENTS

All photographs from Alan Titchmarsh's private collection, with the exception of the following:

© BBC: 14 above, 15 below, 17 below, 18, 19 above right and below, and 32. © Susan Bell: 25 and 26. © Cole Studios, New Malden: 12 below. Bolton's catalogue cover courtesy Garden Answers: 17 above. © Mike Kelly / BBC: 19 above left. © Eddie Mulholland / Telegraph Group 2002: 20 below. © Kipper Williams / Sunday Times: 27 below right.

Every reasonable effort has been made to contact the copyright holders, but should there be any errors or omissions, Hodder & Stoughton would be pleased to insert the appropriate acknowledgement in any subsequent printing of this publication.

INDEX